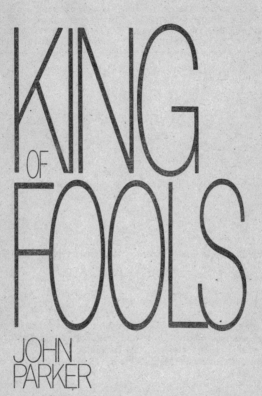

KING OF FOOLS

JOHN PARKER

ST. MARTIN'S PRESS/NEW YORK

First published in Great Britain by Macdonald Futura.

KING OF FOOLS

Copyright © 1988 by John Parker.

Library of Congress Catalog Card Number: 88-30618

ISBN: 0-312-92091-1   Can. ISBN: 0-312-92093-8

Printed in the United States of America

St. Martin's Press hardcover edition published 1988
First St. Martin's Press mass market edition/March 1990

10 9 8 7 6 5 4 3 2 1

CONTENTS

FOREWORD

My own connection with this story goes back to 1987, when I was contacted by John Parker and subsequently met him in the buffet bar of the perhaps appropriately named Kings Cross railway station in London. He informed me he had written a new book about the Duke and Duchess of Windsor and that in the course of his research had reached the conclusion that I might well be the by-blow of Edward VIII. As this statement implied both illegitimacy and royal blood, I asked if he had any evidence to support this slightly startling theory. I use the word *slightly* because frankly the idea was not entirely new to me.

During the twenties and early thirties the Prince of Wales (later to be King Edward VIII and then Duke of Windsor) had been on very friendly terms with my parents and indeed was best man at their wedding and was godfather to my sister Elizma. He favored the family house as a hunting box and here I think lies the key to this rumor. As stated in the book, John Parker had heard from three separate sources in the hunting shires where I myself have ridden to hounds for some twenty-five years that my facial resemblance to the late Duke of Windsor was more than just a curious coincidence. Despite their almost daily attempts to break their necks, these aristocratic hunting hard-riders often survive into ripe old age, with memories of those dizzy days of the twenties.

But to say more would be to poach on the preserves already well covered by John Parker's intriguing if disturbing account of the lesser-known aspects of what must rank as one of the great tragic love affairs of the century. After reading the book, I must confess I should be quite content with mere blood in my veins, for the royal blood of my alleged sire seemed to have soured somewhat. Here was a man who appeared set on giving lie to the belief that mankind is divided into fools and villains. For in John Parker's story, the Duke of Windsor contrived to be both.

TIMOTHY SEELY
JUNE 1988

PROLOGUE

If Winston Churchill knew, and believed, the contents of a highly secret report on Mrs. Wallis Simpson, which made astonishing allegations concerning her sexual activities in a Chinese brothel in 1925, then he disregarded them. If he knew, as he surely did, of the rumors that Edward, as Prince of Wales and heir to the throne, had fathered an illegitimate son in the early thirties, thus causing his parents considerable anguish, then he put it to the back of his mind.

Churchill, six years after the war had ended, had decided upon a mission of peace, to bring together the two estranged branches of the world's greatest monarchy and have the Duke and Duchess of Windsor returned to the fold. He had recently visited the duke and duchess in Paris and was truly moved by their plight. "We are," said the duke, "like stateless persons. We have nowhere to go, nowhere to live, no purpose in our lives." In a nutshell, he wanted to return to England, leave these foreign parts whose language he did not speak well, and return to his family and old friends, to resume, perhaps, some form of public duty.

He had been at a particularly low ebb recently, and to whomever had come to call in recent months, he would relate the same story over and over again, starting from the bitterness he felt over the abdication which had been (he said) forced upon him, to what he believed to be the incredibly harsh treatment of himself and his wife by the rest of the royal family and particularly by King George and Queen Elizabeth.

Yes, the duke was miserable; more so now in that year of 1951 because for the first time since his marriage to Wallis Simpson, he thought he might be losing her, to a particularly disreputable homosexual character with whom she was having an affair. The duke, even after twelve years of marriage and the recent pain of having Wallis indifferent, hurtful, and belittling to him in public, nonetheless still adored her.

He felt there was only one solution to the present crisis in his life: they should return permanently to England and his wife should be given full acceptance and recognition as a true member of the House of Windsor, on equal terms with other royal wives. After all, he was the second most senior member of the family, in age if not in rank.

Churchill listened to this familiar story, and after that brief visit resolved to make another attempt to do something for his former king, to whom his devotion had been restored, though never with the same vigor after the darkest hours of the war when Windsor's defeatist talk and treasonable acts had brought from the wartime prime minister the threat of court-martial. Only Windsor now spoke of that period with any degree of bitterness. For Churchill, it was over and done with, and he would not encourage any view that Windsor had ever swerved in his loyalty to king and country, though he must have known then the extent of documentation recovered after the war that suggested a very different story.

They both knew, but never spoke of it, that Hitler had offered Windsor fifty million Swiss francs to hold himself in readiness to return to the throne, once German forces had crossed the Channel and annexed the British Isles.

"Only the King must go," Hitler wrote in May 1943. "In his place . . . the Duke of Windsor. With him we will make a permanent treaty of friendship." The eyes of Wallis Simpson had lit up, it is said by witnesses in the room, when she heard of Hitler's offer. Churchill also recognized that any lesser royal personage than the duke would have been arrested, either during or after the war, and tried for treason and consorting with the enemy.

Churchill had consigned the whole matter to the past, and bore Windsor no grudge. Not so the duke's relations in London; they could neither forgive nor forget so quickly the disgrace and trauma visited upon them by his grave acts of irresponsibility. The royal family back in Britain had refused to acknowledge the existence of the former Mrs. Simpson, save for reluctantly granting her the title of duchess, though without a royal prefix.

King George's response to the duke's repeated requests for him to grant the duchess an audience and the right to be called Her Royal Highness was one of vehemently expressed opposition. On no account could she be granted that right. Churchill saw it as a total impasse, as he journeyed on to Marrakesh after visiting the duke and his wife, and he became determined to try to heal the rift. But how? The wounds were deep and hurtful on both sides. It seemed to him that perhaps only Queen Mary could persuade her son the king and his wife to come to terms with the Windsors.

Churchill invited Major Jack Coke (the Hon. Sir John Coke), Queen Mary's equerry, to his holiday villa in Marrakesh to talk out the whole situation. Coke listened intently to what Churchill had to say and agreed to act as an intermediary. Coke then went on to the South of France, to Antibes, where he stayed for a week with the Duke de Grantmesnil, who was one of Windsor's closest friends and advisors at the time. Grantmesnil, on behalf of the duke, made a similar plea to Coke, begging him to advise Queen Mary to agree to an HRH for the duchess. The Windsors wanted desperately to resume a place in English society, with a dignified and respected role as befitting a former king, a phrase which the duke himself used often when talking of his future, seemingly oblivious to the consternation he had brought upon his family in his selfish pursuit of his personal desires.

Coke agreed that he would at least try to form a bridge, and would set a new bid for friendship in motion; then it would be up to the family itself.

Coke told Grantmesnil that Churchill had made a similar suggestion; it was then that Coke mentioned the China Report.

"You are aware of this dossier?" Coke inquired. Grantmesnil said he was; he had heard it canvassed as long ago as 1936, but did not know the full details. Coke told him exactly what the report alleged and, as we shall see, if true it represented an undeniable and irreversible argument as to why the royals should never want to take the duchess into their midst.

The China Report was presented to King George V in 1935, after he had demanded to know "Who *is* this woman?" It had been prepared by British intelligence, whose clear brief had been to dig up as much dirt as possible on Mrs. Simpson. This they had obviously achieved. It was one of three top-secret reports prepared on Wallis Simpson prior to the abdication. All would be in Prime Minister Stanley Baldwin's hands as the crisis neared its conclusion.

The first, containing the allegations that she indulged in sexual activities of a most deviant nature in the open cities of China in the mid-twenties, was perhaps the most damaging. The other two referred specifically to the period of her romance with the Prince of Wales and contained names, dates, and places concerning her association with leading Nazis and Italian Fascists before and during Edward's short reign.

Grantmesnil insisted, on the Duke of Windsor's behalf, that Jack Coke should make his recommendations to Queen Mary. The duke, he said, sought a precise reply. Coke countered that if Churchill and Grantmesnil felt the China Report should be ignored, they should say no, now. Grantmesnil replied "If" (and he repeated *If*) "the dossier were genuine and true, I cannot recommend the rank of HRH for the Duchess."

Jack Coke sat back and pondered the situation for a moment; and then he spoke. He felt, in all honesty, that he could not approach Queen Mary. He was sure she would throw it straight back at him in the curt, cold manner he well knew she was capable of in moments of displeasure. It wasn't that Coke himself had been particularly shocked by the allegations against Mrs. Simpson. They had been more than matched by Edward's own relatives in a series of prewar scandals that had jolted the very foundations of the monarchy. Mrs. Simpson's alleged sexual misbehavior happened in Chinese brothels; those royals involved in dubious exploits had erred rather closer to home. From the Jazz Age of the twenties right up to the outbreak of war, some of the younger members of Britain's royal family followed the example of the heir to the throne in his quest to sample all the experiences that life had to offer.

The Mountbattens, original members of the prince's charmed circle, scandalized society with their various affairs. Edwina Mountbatten's liaisons ranged from her long absences in the company of a lesbian-inclined sister-in-law to her much publicized fascination with black men. Her husband sought the company of other women, and equally the solace of men friends, to the point where he was reprimanded by Queen Mary for his continued associations with men of a theatrical background.

Edward's youngest brother, Prince George, the Duke of Kent, was a bisexual whose conquests became the talk of court circles. His most famous lovers included Noel Coward, black singer Florence Mills, and a young man in Paris to whom he wrote love letters that had to be reclaimed by a courtier on the payment of a large sum. He also had an illegitimate son, who was adopted at birth.

Even the staid and dull Prince Henry, Duke of Gloucester, ran into trouble with a woman and was extricated from a delicate situation by his wife, who paid £15,000 hush money to the woman whom he had flaunted openly in hand on Society and whose child was born soon after their affair ended.

Edward's own indiscretions provided much gossip that culminated in his devotion to Mrs. Simpson. The rumors took many shapes; even after his affair with Wallis had begun, the upper strata of Leicestershire society could hardly contain to themselves the story that he had fathered a son by the wife of one of his best friends. The birth certificate does not, of course, name the Prince of Wales as the father, but the child in later years would himself boast of his incredible likeness to Edward.

Whatever the young royals were up to, British intelligence was never far behind, eager to record events that were diligently reported back to the king. The Prince of Wales and Mrs. Simpson would become the main attraction in these reports, as their increasingly dangerous links with officials of Nazi Germany and Fascist Italy became a matter of grave national, constitutional, and security importance.

Apart from the China dossier, Mrs. Simpson was held to be suspiciously close to Joachim von Ribbentrop, who had been given carte blanche by Hitler to entertain her and her friends on a lavish scale. She had also been befriended by other important Nazis and Italian Fascists, including Mussolini's son-in-law, Count Galeazzo Ciano, with whom she had an affair and who had granted her husband Ernest valuable cotton concessions in Abyssinia.

They and their associates and friends among the pro-Hitler British aristocracy were playing a dangerous game. Dangerous affairs; dangerous politics, which no apologist for the Windsors and their awful lifelong friend Sir Oswald Mosley, can ever excuse . . .

· ONE ·

PRINCE CHARMING

With a remarkable display of prophetic wisdom, Keir Hardie, the conscience of the House of Commons and a founder of the British Labour Party, rose to give his unswerving views on the birth of Prince Edward, the boy who would be king.

"When we are asked, as the House of Commons representing the nation, to join in these congratulations, I take leave to protest." Amid uproar from his fellow MPs, Hardie spoke first of the young prince's grandfather, the Prince of Wales, later to be Edward VII. "The fierce white light which we are told beats upon the throne reveals things . . . which are better to keep covered. Sometimes we get glimpses of the Prince at the gaming table [referring to a recent incident in which the prince and his friends had been accused of cheating at baccarat] and sometimes we see him at the race-course. His Royal Highness draws £60,000 a year from property which makes up some of our vilest slums . . ."

Then as the Commons storm grew, he addressed himself to the latest royal birth. "The assumption is," raged Hardie, "that the newly-born child will be called upon, some day, to reign over this Empire, but up to the present we certainly have no means of knowing his qualifications or fitness for this position. From childhood, this boy will be surrounded by sycophants and flatterers and will be taught to believe himself of superior creation. A line will be drawn between him and the people he might be called upon to rule. In due course, following the precedent that has already been set, he will be sent on a tour around the world, and probably rumours of a morganatic marriage will follow, and in the end it will be that country called upon to pay the bill.''

As a prophet of royal destiny, as the Duke of Windsor recognized in his autobiography, Hardie's words were, as the duke put it, uncannily clairvoyant. The young prince, born on the evening of June 23, 1894, would indeed complete his tours of the world; for his entire life he would be surrounded by sycophants and flatterers; he certainly believed he was a superior creation; he would embark on an irresponsible romantic escapade that would produce attempts at a morganatic marriage; and the country was finally left to pay the bill, both emotionally and monetarily.

It was as if Keir Hardie had plotted a course which the boy, first as prince, then as king, and finally as a duke, became intent on pursuing with foolhardy, masochistic, and selfish determination—characteristics for which he was first loved and then despised by those closest to him.

History would show that the birth of Edward Albert Christian George Andrew Patrick David was the beginning of a new dawn for the British and European monarchies over which his great-grandmother, Queen Victoria, then ruled supreme. But it was a dawn which would finally see the end of royal influence over governments and politics, and the survivors of this great line would come to receive the adulation shared by movie stars rather than the subservient worship their predecessors had known.

In the year of the birth of Prince Edward—David to his family—Queen Victoria ruled over more than half the world's surface. It was her favorite illusion that by joining the monarchies of Europe by marriage, she would end all future threats of war. She herself sat as queen/empress over the vast British Empire; her eldest daughter Victoria was Dowager Empress of Germany; her grandson was Kaiser Wilhelm II; and the Czar of Russia, Nicholas II, was her grandson-in-law. The King and Queen of Denmark and the Queen of the Hellenes were related by marriage, as were other European monarchs, who regarded her with some awe, even during her long period of reclusive widowhood when her dementia was spoken of, *sotto voce*, by only the most courageous.

Though her awesome influence remained, as her austere and formal reign moved into its final stages, the activities of her relatives indicated that they did not share the same attitudes as the great queen. Abroad, there were already rumblings of revolution over the excesses of the Russian court and in Germany Kaiser Wilhelm was becoming increasingly bombastic, while at home her own son, soon to be King Edward VII, was involved in scandalous affairs that made her government shudder.

All this troubled her immensely, given that her concentration was somewhat limited on any topic other than mourning for her beloved Albert, the late Prince Consort. There was joy, however, at the young Edward's birth, the firstborn of her grandchildren, the Duke and Duchess of York. Victoria was then seventy-five and in her fifty-seventh year of sovereignty.

Her heir, the Prince of Wales, was fifty-two and still openly consorting with mistresses who, like Lillie Langtry and Alice Keppel, became famous because of his attentions. His wife, Princess Alexandra, perhaps one of the most beautiful of English queens, kept up her charade as the contented royal spouse with an outwardly radiant personality that shrouded the immense unhappiness and humiliation she suffered because of her husband's adulterous behavior.

Edward and Alexandra's eldest son, Albert Victor, Duke

of Clarence, was next in line to the throne, but in 1892, he was stricken suddenly with pneumonia and died, shortly before he was to marry Princess Mary Victoria of Teck. His younger brother George, then twenty-six, was following a career in the Navy and at that time had no thought of marriage. He had never expected to find himself in the direct line to the throne and pursued his chosen life with enthusiasm. He had achieved his own command and was a promising officer, but Victoria now had other plans for him. She called him to her side and instructed him that, after a suitable period of mourning, he should visit Princess Mary and "speak up for himself."

The death of Clarence would not be allowed to thwart her plans to make the princess into a future Queen of England. George must marry Mary, she decreed, and he must end his Navy career to begin his apprenticeship to be king, a job that would not be long in coming to him.

Here, then, was a union of two young people of royal birth, created by Victoria, based not on courtship and desire but on obedience to a queen and in expectation of a crown. Love, perhaps, would come later. In this case, it did not. They were married in July 1883 and were provided with a home at York House in St. James's Palace, which was as dour and colorless as George himself. The disciplines of the Navy had left him with attitudes more in tune with the strictness of his grandmother than with the devil-may-care antics of his father.

A country home was earmarked for them on the Royal Sandringham estate in Norfolk, and it was here that the young family would spend most of their early years. It was named York Cottage, and it became apparent from the outset of their family life that George and Mary both held the same view, that children should be seen occasionally and certainly not heard. Indeed the young prince, and his brothers and sister, did not see a great deal of their parents in their formative years. Their firstborn would recall that he remembered "tantalizingly little" of his early association with his parents, and those recollections he could make were usually associated with some miserable memory of chastisement, an aspect which clearly stayed imprinted on the young man's mind well into adulthood.

He wrote: "My parents first materialize on the threshold of my memory as two Olympian figures who would enter the nursery briefly to note with gravely hopeful interest the progress of their first-born. The mere circumstances of my father's position interposed an incalculable barrier that inhibited the closer continuing of conventional family life."

The young prince soon began to blame himself for the lack of parental attention he received and became obsessed by a constant fear that he was making a poor impression, which was turning his father from him and weakening his mother's affection. He blamed those in charge of his upbringing and recalled that one nurse would always pinch his arm before entering the room where his parents were waiting to view their children, so that he always seemed to arrive sobbing or bawling his eyes out. He would talk and write constantly of this aspect of his early life, and in the end came to the view that even if his parents did not care for him greatly, their lack of displayed affection had probably more to do with their extremely busy schedule.

Although the children grew, their parents' attention to them did not. Bertie (King George VI) was born in 1895, Mary in 1897, Harry 1900, and John 1905. Edward, Bertie, and Mary, who spent most of their early lives in their nursery rooms at York Cottage, slept in one room with their nurse and would sit and watch life at Sandringham from their window overlooking the duck ponds.

Trips to London, to the main family home or to see "Gangan," Queen Victoria, were infrequent. Sandringham was a hundred and twenty miles from London by horse and carriage or railway, but the journeys became highlights in those young lives, particularly when there was a grand family reunion. It was a daunting sight whenever Victoria's family forgathered. Together on grand occasions could be a vast array of the crowned heads of Europe, over whom Victoria watched like a mother hen.

Her death on January 22, 1901, was the beginning of the end for a monarchical structure which within a few years would be disfigured by war, revolution, murder, or coup, leaving it shorn of much influence in twentieth-century society. Now the mantle passed to her son and heir, Edward VII, who had matured into a kindly old gentleman, well versed in affairs of state after so long in the wings, although one whose liking for the company of attractive women had not waned.

Prince George became Prince of Wales and immediately began the obligatory tour of the British Empire, which took him and Mary away for almost nine months. Their children, left in the care of the king and queen, had love and affection poured upon them as they had never experienced before. Queen Alexandra, after the years of suffering her wayward husband, had much to give. She encouraged the children in their games, allowed them to miss lessons, and let them mix freely in a downstairs life they had seldom seen. The youngsters ran wild.

On their return to Britain in the autumn, George and Mary were horrified at the change in their offspring, particularly in the two eldest, David and Bertie, and immediately decided to reinforce discipline in the cottage nursery. Their elderly tutor, Helen Bricka, who had been in the family's service since she was employed as a governess to Mary, was replaced by two men. Frederick Finch, a nursery footman, who until now had been performing duties such as fetching and carrying, was placed in charge of the nursery. He was, David recalled, "a handsome and stalwart man of thirty," who would remain in the prince's service for many years, first as valet and later as butler. He was a respectful servant but had their father's permission to bare the boys' bottoms and spank them if they misbehaved, a task he performed with some relish. He was joined by Henry Hansell, who was to be the children's tutor, and between them the two men virtually brought up the children during their remaining nursery years.

Apart from the sight of the maids, and tea-time visits to see their parents whenever they were at York Cottage, their day-to-day life was conducted without the influence of women; there was, David would recall, never a shoulder to cry on, no cuddles or soft words, no sign of the affection that growing boys would receive in conventional family life. Here, perhaps, began the problems that haunted David for the rest of his life, first with his continual desire for male company which developed as he grew older, and later in his search for a mother figure who would lavish love and affection upon him and hold his head to her breast in times of adversity. The young prince was an attractive boy with the fairest of looks, but one whose eyes often displayed an empty sadness.

When their parents were not traveling, and were at home, their mother would have them taken to her bedroom around six in the evening before she took a nap. She would be resting on the sofa in her negligee. She would chat to the children about their day or ask them about their lessons. Sometimes she would read to them or teach them needlework. David, anxious as ever to please his mother and earn her praise, took up crocheting and became quite proficient with the crochet hook.

The children's relations with their father, however, were quite formal. David would be summoned to the library by a footman with the command, "His Royal Highness wishes to see you," but such summonses quite often meant an admonishment for misbehavior or a lecture, and it was here and now that the theme of David's future life, his duty and his service to his nation, would begin to emerge in what the boy felt to be a most foreboding way. It was drummed into him at every opportunity so that the young man began to dread the thought of what life had in store for him—a dread that would materialize later in his most deliberate disregard for everything that was expected of a future monarch.

These disciplines to which he had already become subjected became even more formal when the family moved to a permanent home in London. Since the king and queen had taken Buckingham Palace as their main residence the Prince and Princess of Wales and their family moved into their former home, Marlborough House, which had been for forty years the pinnacle of social activity and the society events that revolved around the former Prince of Wales in his heyday. The children were established in a nursery suite on the third floor overlooking Green Park and Buckingham Palace. One of the traditions maintained at Marlborough House was the sound of bagpipes. Every morning, the king had for many years been roused by a piper playing outside his bedroom door, and now the new Prince of Wales employed two kilted retainers who would march up and down at breakfast time to call a start to the day.

David was enormously impressed, and subsequently himself learned to play the bagpipes. It became his party piece for years ahead to play at social events or at dinner parties, until his future wife, Wallis, eventually tired of the sound of them and banned him from playing outside of his own room.

The haphazard education of the young princes continued under the tutorship of Hansell, though their abilities remained a constant disappointment to their father, who knew that if they were to follow the Navy career he wished for both of them, their academic achievements would have to improve substantially. Whereas Hansell reckoned the children would benefit from normal schoolroom competition, the prince dismissed the prospect totally, and apart from bringing in a special math tutor for extra lessons, he continued the children's education in the Marlborough nursery right to the time when David, then approaching thirteen, was ready to move to the first stage of the career his father had planned for him, by becoming a naval cadet at Osborne Naval College.

First he had to sit an entrance examination, which he did with trepidation, lest he should fail. Not surprisingly, the examination committee judged him to be the "best boy they had examined" and so the day dawned when David would be taken from the only life he had ever known, a cloistered protected environment, and placed in a school of boisterous young men where violence and homosexuality were commonplace. In his first letter home, he wrote: "Some older boys have forced my best friend to do some swinish things." He recalled that first day later: "The seclusion of my previous existence rolled up like a curtain and I was not a little afraid." He was regarded as something of a freak by the boys of Osborne, particularly by the seniors, and he was subjected to a number of pranks: his hair was dyed with red ink; he was trapped under a partly open window in a mock beheading ceremony; and he had to face for the first time harsh physical correction bestowed on boys by college tutors. Tears were plentiful and frequent. In his last term at Osborne he was joined by his brother Bertie, but their reunion was brief. David was about to be transferred to the Royal Naval College at Dartmouth for a further two years before he moved into the service proper.

That year, 1909, was the last time the young princes saw their Uncle Nicky, Czar Nicholas II of Russia. He had arrived in Britain with his entire family for a visit, but because of assassination fears the Russian government would not allow their supreme ruler to go to London and Buckingham Palace. Instead, the king and queen and their immediate family met the czar at Cowes. It was a memorable family reunion, with the Russians showing great affection for their British relatives. (David would see none of them again, since the entire family was massacred in the Russian revolution a little over seven years later.)

Further troubles lay ahead however. In the spring of the following year, soon after the king had returned from his annual pilgrimage to Biarritz, he was confined to bed with bronchitis, and died shortly before midnight on May 6, 1910.

Edward's funeral brought together for the very last time the great family of royalty, who had been linked together by Victoria's scheming. The czar was not allowed out of Russia for fear of assassination, but there were nine ruling monarchs in the funeral procession, led by the now King George V, followed by Kaiser Wilhelm II on a huge white stallion and the kings of Spain, Portugal, Denmark, Greece, Norway, Belgium, Czar Ferdinand of Bulgaria, the Archduke Franz Ferdinand of Austria, and the Grand Duke Michael of Russia. Few of them would survive the great uprisings that would shortly engulf their countries.

The death of the king after nine years on the throne meant for David the beginning in earnest of his preparation for the monarchy. He was now heir apparent, Edward, Prince of Wales, and there was a lot to be done to complete his education and preliminary training. His life would change completely, and as he approached his seventeenth birthday, David was withdrawn from his naval career before his formal graduation and launched headlong into the intensity of his heritage.

He recalled a warning given to him at that point by his father: "All eyes will be upon you. Remember to conduct yourself at all times with dignity and set a good example. You must be obedient and respectful and kind." The prince was immediately consumed with a feeling of sadness, the realization that he was embarking on a most restrictive existence that perhaps he did not want.

He was first invested with the Order of the Garter, to take his place in precedence over the peers of the realm at his father's coronation. Then he accompanied his mother and father on state tours to Scotland, Ireland, and Wales, and finally he was coached by David Lloyd George for his own investiture as the Prince of Wales at Caernarvon Castle. When Winston Churchill, who was then home secretary, called out his title, the small, frail youth nervously recited in parrot fashion the words that Lloyd George had taught him. Even then, the rebellious attitude he would eventually adopt in more acute ways was showing through. The night before the investiture he protested at the prospect of wearing a costume of white satin along with a coat of purple edged with ermine. What would his friends think? He had to be coaxed into it by his mother. "Your friends will realize that as a Prince you are obliged to do certain things that may seem a little silly," she told him. But if there was one thing he wanted at that stage of his life, it was not to be out of the ordinary. He had what he termed a "desperate desire to be treated like any other boy of my age." That would never be; nor could he expect it.

At eighteen a young man's thoughts may be turned toward the opposite sex, but as in his childhood, David's teenage years had continued without the influence of a woman's voice. They had been dominated by men. When in trouble, or feeling low, he could only seek the solace of his colleagues at the naval academy, or his valet Finch, or to a lesser degree his tutors. No female presence, apart from his grandmother, seemed to have impressed him, nor was there any change in sight.

First, he was given the rank of midshipman, and although he had not graduated, was allowed to serve for three months aboard the battleship *Hindustan*. On his return he was sent straight away to Magdalen College, Oxford, for what would be a rather unsuccessful attempt to instill into the prince the learning that had been so badly lacking thus far.

He arrived at the college diffident, lonely, and somewhat nervous about the mixed environment he faced for the first time. Because of his lack of a formal education, his suitability for university life was gravely lacking. As one tutor put it, he was like a lost lamb, and although he tried desperately to make up for his deficiencies there was never a way he could catch up with his colleagues. He spent eight "desultory terms" at Oxford, got drunk, and joined the officers' corps before finally he was whisked away without any academic achievement whatsoever to his name.

During holiday times, his father arranged a series of overseas excursions to improve his knowledge, first to France and later to Germany. He stayed at the palace of his Uncle Will, King Wilhelm and Queen Charlotte of Württemberg, met Count Zeppelin, and saw the latest airship that soon would be used to bomb London. He also stayed with Charles, the Duke of Coburg, ruler of the German duchy whose title was once held by the Prince Consort, Albert, before his marriage to Victoria.

Charles was no German by birth. He was British and destined to be Duke of Albany. But in 1900, when the Coburg dukedom fell vacant without a direct heir, Queen Victoria had promptly dispatched Charles, then only sixteen, to take up her beloved husband's domain so that the title would not die out. Coburg would always remain close friends with the Prince and would figure later in his life when he appeared back in London as Hitler's personal emissary just prior to the Second World War. Coburg would meet Edward on a regular basis and subsequently describe him treacherously as an ardent Nazi.

The prince at that impressionable age was overwhelmed by Germany and by the attention lavished upon him, particularly by Wilhelm. "Much of what I saw in Germany," he recalled later "impressed me and I admired the industry, the perseverance, the discipline, the thoroughness and the love of the Fatherland. . . . I ended up liking Germany so much that I planned another trip, little knowing that it would be five years before I sojourned there again."

The dark clouds of war were looming and Kaiser Bill was banging the drum. David resumed his training, switching now from Oxford to the Life Guard and was introduced for the first time to the London season: the coming-out of debutantes and the social whirl of parties and dances that he came to enjoy so much.

The first one he attended was recorded with some measure of dismay: "I had to dance, a thing I hate . . . danced with Miss B and was frightfully nervous. I was glad when it was all over." He was just beginning to get into the swing of this gay new life with newfound friends when it all ended as quickly as it had begun.

On August 4 Uncle Will and George V were parted by war. When the family that Victoria had hoped would end all future conflict between European nations was split down the middle, those who felt it most were the Battenburgs, now permanently resident in Great Britain.

Prince Louis and his wife Princess Victoria of Hesse were German by birth. Their son Lord Louis, known to the family as Dickie, and later Earl Mountbatten of Burma, was himself a cadet at Osborne where he was branded a German spy. His father, hounded out of the Admiralty where he was first lord, was forced to resign. Dickie, however, overcame the jibes and followed David's path to Dartmouth. Edward himself, like most young men in the services, was moved by the excitement of war. He was granted an immediate commission in the Grenadier Guards at Warley Barracks in Brentwood, and when they were put on forty-eight-hour standby, the prince thought the time had come when he and his fellow officers would see action in France.

It was, he said, the biggest disappointment of his life when he was called to his father's office and told he would not be allowed to join his unit in France. Lord Kitchener, he was told, would not permit a future king of England to face enemy action, nor the threat of his being taken prisoner, although as far as the latter was concerned Kitchener had perhaps overlooked the fact that the kaiser was unlikely to harm his favorite nephew.

In the end, however, the king relented and allowed his son to go to the Army Corps with the proviso that he should be kept well away from the fighting; but once when his divisional commander did allow him to accompany him on an excursion to the front, while he and the prince set off on foot to a vantage point where they could view the bloody mess of a recent German attack, the driver left behind in their car to await their return was killed by flying shrapnel.

On that day, David noted in his diary: "Then commenced probably the four most interesting hours of my life . . . we were able to see exactly what the assaulting parties of the Division had to undertake . . . they had to charge after the gas had been turned on . . . the dead lie out unburied and in postures and on the spot where they fell and one got some idea of the horror and ghastliness of it all. . . . I have seen and learnt a lot about war today."

He stayed in France through the winter of 1915–16 and although he remained, on his father's orders, away from the front, the squalor, the mud, the death were ever present. For a boy who so far had seen little of life from his protected and privileged position, it was a profound experience. "I have widened my education," he wrote, "not through book or theory but through experience of living under all kinds of conditions with all kinds of men"—a claim that to the millions of families who lost loved ones in the Great War must have sounded quite arrogant and patronizing.

Whatever the effects of the "experience," he returned from the war showing signs of bitterness, restlessness, and unease. Indeed, there was a nervousness surrounding the whole royal family, still shaken, not just by the war and the kaiser, but by the massacre of Czar Nicholas and his family, which King George believed could have been avoided. He had asked the British government to send a cruiser to rescue his Russian relatives before they were attacked, but the government had refused.

In Britain David Lloyd George was strutting around making profound statements which meant little and were promptly slung back in his face by a discontented public mourning the millions who had died, a public tired out and dispirited. They had won, but the effort had been supreme. The land fit for heroes was sick and disillusioned. It was Lloyd George who, far from continuing his republican ramblings, realized that the royal family had a major role to play in the revitalization and resurgence of Britain, and in the dominions which had contributed so much. It was Lloyd George's idea that while the king and queen should tour Britain and be seen by the people, the Prince of Wales should embark on a series of worldwide excursions, visiting every country in the empire with a message of thanks from the people of Britain and from their king.

Prince Edward had developed into a most good-looking young man, though slight and unforceful. The war, according to his father, had put some metal in him. He was a romantic figure, too, and though the stories of his conquests with women were rife it was largely a case of what might have been.

True, he enjoyed parties and the new night life that was now reemerging in London. But there were actually few women in his life. For three years during the war he had been seeing, at spasmodic intervals, Viscountess Coke, daughter-in-law of the Earl of Leicester and fifteen years his senior. He first met her in March 1915 during leave from active service and had poured out his heart on the frustration of being at such a time of life, heir to the throne, which he found so restrictive and to a degree boring. Marion Coke gave birth to a son at the end of that year and the Prince of Wales agreed to be a sponsor at the christening of the boy, whom she named David after him.

His puppy-love attachment to Marion Coke was still just as strong two years later, when he wrote to her from Buckingham Palace: "It is too nice of you to suggest a little dancing for me tomorrow night. It will be my only chance of getting out at all in the evening from this the most depressing of palaces." A couple of months later, he wrote again: "You have been too angelically kind to me for words and have absolutely changed my life."

Although there was never any question of Marion Coke leaving her husband and deserting a happy marriage for the dubious and infantile affections of the young prince, by July of that year he had found a new love, one who might, he thought, be a suitable candidate to join the Prince of Wales in matrimony. The girl was Lady Rosemary Leverson-Gower, youngest daughter of the Duke of Sutherland, and he became dazzled by her after seeing her in an Army hospital in France in December 1916, where she was working as a Red Cross nurse. He found her sitting at the bedside of a desperately injured soldier whom she had nursed nonstop for many hours.

By early 1918, the prince and Rosemary were meeting regularly and he wrote to a friend: "I have been seeing a lot of R who is charming. I expect you find as I do that when you come home it is nice to be with a nice-looking girl." There was great speculation over a royal romance, fueled by both of them in their apparent love for one another, as was recorded by the Dowager Lady Hardinge of Penshurst whose husband was then assistant private secretary to George V and subsequently private secretary to Edward VIII. She wrote that Edward wished to marry Rosemary, but there was opposition to the match. "One can only forever wonder how the history of our Monarchy in the twentieth century might have turned out if the Prince of Wales had had his way."

Edward went on to propose marriage to Rosemary, but made the mistake of not getting his father's opinion first. There and then any further speculation was halted. The king, while having no objection to the girl herself, whom he found delightful, felt that her mother's recent actions were hardly fitting to be associated with the crown. Millicent, Duchess of Sutherland, the woman who would have been Edward's mother-in-law, had been widowed upon the death of the fourth Duke of Sutherland five years earlier. Although a year later she had been married again, to Brigadier General Percy Desmond, she divorced quite rapidly and married a third time, at the age of fifty-two, Lieutenant Colonel George Hawes, who himself had been involved in homosexual scandal.

That wasn't all, however.

Millicent's brother, the fifth Earl of Rosslyn, was the infamous Harry Rosslyn, who had inspired the song "The Man Who Broke the Bank at Monte Carlo." When he inherited an income from his father's estate, of £17,000 a year, he became a professional gambler. By 1920, he had been bankrupt twice and on his third bankruptcy hearing six years later, it was estimated he had gambled away a quarter of a million pounds. He also was twice divorced and on his third marriage. Quite impossible, the king declared, to have such a relative so close to the monarchy. Rosemary would be a future queen if she married Edward. A bankrupt thrice-married uncle would never do. The king called Edward to his study at Buckingham Palace and informed him that after due consideration he had decided that such a marriage could not be permitted, and that was that. Queen Mary concurred with her husband's view, was perhaps even stronger in her opposition. (Doubtless, seventeen years later, when Wallis Simpson had taken a hold on her son's life, she must have regretted that opposition a thousand times!)

Edward, quite untruthfully, told Rosemary that his father wanted him to marry a European princess to keep up the royal line, but she soon discovered the truth. As Michael Thornton tells us from his original research for his book *Royal Feud*, Lady Victor Paget, one of her then closest friends related: "From that moment on, she always gave the impression that she had never intended to marry the Prince of Wales. I don't think it was in any sense a question of saving her own face but she minded very much that her family, one of the oldest in history, should not be thought good enough. As for the Prince, he was bitter and furious. I don't think he ever forgave his father. I also felt from that time on he would never make what might be called a suitable marriage to please his family." How right she was.

Rosemary dashed away from Edward, though without any animosity, but she was pleased that now she knew the truth of it, rather than the excuse he had given her. Within a year she had married the prince's best friend and heir to the Earl of Dudley, Eric, Viscount Ednam. The Prince of Wales attended the wedding at St. Margaret's, Westminster, and gave Rosemary a diamond and sapphire brooch as a wedding present.

They never lost touch. Indeed Eric remained the prince's friend for the rest of his life, and when Rosemary's first son was born ten months later, the Prince of Wales stood sponsor at the christening. She had two more sons, the eldest of whom, Jeremy, was killed after being struck by a lorry at the age of seven.

Rosemary herself died tragically, in a plane crash while returning from Northern Ireland in 1930. Edward was deeply affected by the news: the woman who might have been queen, and thus saved the nation and the prince's family from the anguish of Wallis Simpson, lay dead in an orchard in Kent, identifiable only by the pearls she was wearing.

·TWO·

ONLY MARRIED WOMEN ...

While still involved with Lady Rosemary, Edward had met and become immediately attracted to Freda Dudley Ward, a most beautiful, delicate creature who, like the Viscountess Coke, was married. Her husband was William Dudley Ward, the Liberal MP for Southampton and vice chamberlain of the royal household. A strange twist of fate had brought them together toward the end of the war. He was at a party at the home of Maud Kerr-Smiley, sister of Ernest Simpson who had not yet met Wallis, while Freda, daughter of a wealthy Nottingham lace manufacturer, was walking across Belgrave Square when an air-raid warning sounded. She ran into Maud's house to take shelter and was invited to join the party guests in the basement.

Freda, like the prince, was smallish and poured charm upon those around her. As a newcomer, she was immediately singled out for conversation by the Prince of Wales and was asked to join him.

There began a relationship that was to last for a dozen years. She became his prop, his shoulder to cry on, his confidante and comforter. But she knew in her heart of hearts that there could never be a future in it. She, a married woman who would soon be divorced, could never be accepted in the royal household. She did discuss the prospect over and over again with friends. They all told her the same. It was a situation without a future that would in the end bring her only grief.

The prince put all these thoughts to the back of his mind, disregarded the advice of his closest friends, and once more ran the gauntlet of disapproval from his father. He continued to visit Freda. She was "his friend." Long conversations with her became the norm. "I am fed up with this princing," he would say, "I must have a life of my own." Even then, as the Roaring Twenties were beginning, the thought of resigning his commission as heir apparent had crossed his mind, but what stopped him more than anything was the thought of confronting his father.

There were rows enough—over his attitude, his partying, his dress—and, during one interview, the king was heard to bellow, "You act like a cad. You dress like a cad. You are a cad. Get out of my sight." The king would also taunt him over Freda "the lacemaker's daughter." Not long afterward, the prince asked to be allowed to take up his own apartment, away from the direct glare of his father. At first the king refused, but later he relented and arranged for his son to move into York House at St. James's Palace, which had been used during the war by Lord Kitchener. The house was in an appalling state, old-fashioned and musty, but in the remaining few weeks before Edward was due to begin his empire tours, he and Finch began the task of making a home suitable for a young man-about-town.

The move from Buckingham Palace failed to slow the prince's growing detachment from George's gray rule. Outwardly, the charm for which he was well known continued to flow but inwardly, and among his closest friends, he was tormented by the lectures . . . "remember who you are" . . . and the goldfish-bowl existence.

Sir Frederick Ponsonby, keeper of the Privy Purse and courtier since Queen Victoria, took him to one side and reinforced the view of the king. "You are, sir," he told him, "making yourself too accessible. The Monarchy must always retain an element of mystery . . . remain on a pedestal." The prince disagreed. It was time, he said, to modernize, be more outgoing to the people. Sir Frederick replied quite angrily: "Sir, you are mistaken."

The king called Edward back for further guidance. "The war made it possible for you to mix with all manner of people . . . but don't think that means now you can act like other people." The pressure was relentless, but Freda Dudley Ward took the brunt of his torment, as was demonstrated in a letter written by his friend and cousin Dickie Mountbatten: "He has only one 'Mother' though he'd be the last person to admit it, and that is great friend Freda who is so nice and about whom you've probably heard—oh such wicked lies. She's absolutely been a mother to him, comforted and advised him, and all along he has been blind in his love to what the world is saying."

The motherly love that Edward had always yearned for but never had was being found in substitute fashion in his association with Freda. As Mountbatten said, she was sensible enough to realize that there were no strenuous sexual demands in their relationship.

Similarly, he could shower love and affection on his closest male friend of the moment, Dickie Mountbatten, as he was now known; the family name had been anglicized by the king after the Battenbergs' experiences in the war and they were now totally accepted into British society. Dickie had been up to Cambridge after Dartmouth and then had continued his Navy career. During leave, he had joined the London party scene and by doing so had renewed his friendship with his cousin Prince Edward, who was six years his senior.

Edward, clearly taken by Dickie's youthful zest, told Mountbatten's mother: "He is such a dear boy and is so marvellously sympathetic and understanding that I may say we are quite devoted to each other. He is a very exceptional boy, although a very advanced one and I have had to sit on him once or twice but only in the spirit of being his best friend."

The enthusiasm with which the prince told of their devotion to each other would have alerted suspicious minds, particularly in view of Mountbatten's own associations while at Cambridge. There he met and became closely attached to Peter Murphy, a homosexual left-wing socialite who was to remain Mountbatten's closest friend and confidant for the rest of his life, and indeed later moved into the Mountbatten home. Because of his relationship with Mountbatten, Murphy would in the fifties be investigated by security services and was branded in some quarters a Communist agent, a charge which both he and Mountbatten vehemently denied. If Mountbatten showed any homosexual tendencies at that point in his life Murphy would have encouraged them, although at the same time Dickie's attention to the opposite sex was not restricted.

Mountbatten brought Murphy into the prince's circle, as he did several other of his homosexual acquaintances in later years, including Noel Coward with whom they all became enchanted. With such friendships surrounding the pair, it was not difficult for onlookers to speculate over the prince's own involvement in homosexual liaisons; speculations that would become more open in the coming months, when Mountbatten would join the prince on his Empire tours.

Such was the aura of rumor around the prince that when it was combined with his continued modernistic attitude to the monarchy, King George considered abandoning the tours to keep Edward at home, to fill the gap in his education and to try to quell some of the hardening attitudes within him that the king didn't at all like the look of.

The dictatorial Lloyd George would not consider such a prospect and was more keen than ever that Edward would start his journeys as planned. He wanted a worldwide pageant in which the prince would play a "gay, many-sided natural role."

This was the background against which the prince set out on August 5, 1919, on HMS *Renown*, and his first public-relations mission, heading for Canada and then the United States. He was, perhaps naturally, consumed with nerves and dreaded the very thought of public speaking, but he was met with a reception of such enthusiasm and crowds that would not be matched in terms of a royal visit until much later in the century, when his eventual successor to the title, Prince Charles and his bride Princess Diana, would follow his route.

He was mobbed and surrounded and handshaken everywhere. Lloyd George was right. This was just what the country and its allies of the war needed right now. So much so that Edward was forced to switch from his right hand to his left when greeting admirers, since his right hand became so swollen doctors warned him it could be damaged permanently. His mother was not at all pleased. She wrote to him: "I feel angry at the amount of handshaking and autograph-writing you are compelled to face. This does not sound dignified, though no doubt these people mean well. You must tell them . . ." The prince wrote back: "I quite understand what you say about the handshaking and allowing myself to be mobbed and I can assure you that it isn't my fault as you imagine."

During the tour through August, September, and October he was so taken with Canada, its rugged beauty, wide-open spaces, and people, that he decided to buy some land there: but not just any plot of land. He chose on the spur of the moment a 4,000-acre ranch in Highwood River near Calgary; a most beautiful spot but hardly practicable. He knew nothing about ranching, although it was fully operational and left under management, and it was so far away as to be hardly a retreat to which one could go occasionally. So why had he bought it?

The purchase got him into deep trouble with his father who just could not understand his son's motives. A ranch?

In Canada? Why? "Now the Australians will expect you to buy a sheep station in the outback," the king growled in his rage. Edward could not give a satisfactory answer and didn't seem to know himself. Unless in the heat of the moment he considered that if indeed he ever did quit this life as a prince, which he knew could happen at any time, the ranch would be the ideal place to come and get away from the world.

In the event, although he visited the place quite frequently throughout his life, it was the only property he ever bought, apart from a small country retreat near Paris. And in the end, it all went sour when Edward lost a fortune drilling for oil on the ranch.

Back in England there was a brief respite from the demands of the dominions and, upon his return on December 2, Edward launched himself into the Christmas party whirl, knowing that in three months he would be setting sail again, this time for Australia. He called up Freda Dudley Ward, and the manner in which they renewed their acquaintance was hardly discreet, much to the disdain of King George.

Edward also sought out his young friend, Dickie Mountbatten. They were at a dance at Lady Ribblesdale's London home and that night a dream came true for Dickie. The one thing that he wanted most in his life at that time came to fruition . . . "The Prince of Wales came over and asked if I would like to accompany him on the Australian tour," Dickie recalled. "Of course I nearly jumped out of my skin for joy."

Dickie's role was to be a flag lieutenant to the commander of the royal tour, Admiral Halsey. In truth, it was always intended by Edward that his cousin would be ADC and friend to the Prince, and the Admiralty was in no doubt about that.

On April 7, 1920, the *Renown* called at San Diego en route to Australia and it was while in America that Edward had his first glimpse of the woman he would eventually marry, although she didn't register with him at the time. Brigadier Albert "Critch" Critchley, who had been a military tutor during the war and had met both Edward and Bertie, was at the time working for the U.S. government. The prince was due at the reception aboard the U.S. flagship *New Mexico*, and "Critch," who became close friends of the couple when they were Duke and Duchess of Windsor, recalls the meeting in his memoirs.

Critch had been introduced to a young American naval officer. Lieutenant Earl Winfield Spencer, Jr., and his wife Wallis, who had met and married him five years earlier, when she was nineteen. "They were at a cocktail party just prior to the arrival of the Prince of Wales and I had to leave early to attend a dinner given for the Royal visitor on HMS *Renown*. I had known the Prince during the war and we had a long talk about those days." wrote Critchley. "It was strange that in that evening I met them both, the future Duke and Duchess of Windsor."

On that journey to the antipodes, the Prince of Wales needed a friend, as he faced the rigors of such an arduous tour and the massive round of official duties that had been arranged for him; another sea of faces, thousands more outstretched hands. The very thought of it all sent Edward into a deep gloom.

It had been impressed upon Edward before he left that he must put up a good show. The politics of the area were still volatile. Freda Dudley Ward knew very well that the British government was asking too much of her young prince. And she noted before he set off: "Everyone knew. Everyone else knew but HRH. He'd gone from nursery to naval college and from there to war. He was innocent . . . he bloomed late and never quite blossomed; he stayed a little naive, a little childish to the end."

In these young hands were grave responsibilities as he represented his father in a task of great importance to his nation. It could not be treated with frivolity or lightly. But even as he set out, his reservations over the life he was leading had become apparent. Outwardly, Prince

Edward was charming, well mannered, and caring. Those close to him knew also of his deep moods of gloom, his short flashes of temper, his ability to demolish those unable to defend themselves with cutting sarcasm. And it was just as well that he had his cousin, sublieutenant Lord Louis Mountbatten, along with him as his aide, confidant, and special friend. Mountbatten's gushing infatuation with the prince knew no bounds, and he alone could perhaps put up with the moods. Mountbatten wrote: "You have no idea what good friends we are. . . . I wish he were not prince of Wales, then we could see so much more of each other." The feeling was apparently mutual. For days, Edward would lock himself in his cabin and would see only Mountbatten. "His staff can't go near him," Mountbatten wrote, "and I remain the only one who dare intrude." As they neared Australia after first visiting New Zealand, Mountbatten would have to call upon all of his coaxing skill to get Edward in the mood for another round of engagements following tumultuous receptions so far. It was no easy task, he admitted, to keep the prince on the rails. Edward spoke almost daily of his love for Freda Dudley Ward and missed her desperately. He was already homesick and was hating the trip, and as they sailed toward the welcoming Australia, another few thousand outstretched hands awaited them. News had preceded him of the offense he had caused in New Zealand when he failed to attend a banquet for returned soldiers and, two days later, refused to open club because of his overloaded schedule. Keith Murdoch was on his trail now and branded him the "unpunctual prince" for consistently turning up late for functions. At Gilgandra he suffered the indignity of being counted out, an Australian way of showing discontent, after he refused to get out of bed to wave to the crowd as the royal train passed through. Edward himself admitted: "Again and again on arriving in another city, I would be whisked off to clubs or even private houses . . . or whirled to a banquet or ball . . . midnight often found me with wearied brain and dragging feet and the orchestra blaring out by now hackneyed tunes . . ."

But there were the lighter sides to the rigors of the official duties. There were girls, sometimes five or six, in every proverbial port and they were pushed forward from middle-class families to be available to entertain and dance with the prince and members of his entourage. Some of the antics, and efforts to let off steam, brought behavior hardly expected of a royal crowd, and Mountbatten himself was making copious notes in an unofficial diary of events. His records were hardly discreet and often irresponsibly revealing, although they did appear to have been written on occasion with tongue in cheek. However, they were of a sufficiently sensitive nature to have made scandalous reading at the time if they had fallen into the hands of newspapers. Which is why Scotland Yard was called in when Mountbatten discovered to his absolute horror that his diaries had been stolen.

The loss of the diaries coincided with the disappearance of a photographer who was subsequently found trying to sell them to a newspaper for £5,000. The reason for Mountbatten's concern was easy to see, although when they were edited and published almost sixty years later by his biographer Philip Ziegler there was little cause for offense. Various entries spoke of meetings with girls, and then there was a detailed reference to "HRH and the admiral [starting] a fight . . . everybody joined in and were generally doing the maddest things . . . the dominating character was the admiral who could be seen laying out about six ladies in one go . . . and with tears in her eyes [the host] implored us to spare her carpets. After about half an hour peace was restored and the party collected their gear, including HRH's jazz set which had been brought, and took their departure."

Mountbatten's entry for the last day of the Australian tour indicated that some local girls were smuggled aboard *Renown*. He wrote "The Flag Lieutenant went on to Man-O-War Steps and there picked up a party consisting of Margaret Allen, Mollee Little, Aileen and Dolly Bell, Peggy McArthur, the captain's "bit" and Miss Dangar. Bert Bell was the only male. They arrived on board about half past eleven just before HRH returned with the Weigalls [a local couple]. The 'pieces' were put under cover while the ship proceeded out . . . after lunch everybody moved up to the reception deck and danced. About half past three it was discovered that the band which had played without a murmur had not had dinner, so the party broke up and retired to various rooms for the afternoon, reassembling for tea in the after cabin. One thing which worried the admiral rather was the fact that the Weigalls had to leave at a quarter to three leaving the young ladies on board unchaperoned but the respectability of HRH and the admiral was considered to be as effective as that of one lady chaperone. The party was eventually taken off at 5 P.M." and the prince sailed onward and eventually home to London. London, London. How he had missed it and the parties and Freda Dudley Ward into whose arms he fell. He was more experienced, more worldly wise, but Freda wasn't at all sure he was any more resilient to the pressures of being royal. At times, she said, he would actually burst into tears when discussing the way he thought his parents humiliated him with their criticism. "I tried to put some stuffing into him," said Freda, "and once he just said 'I want no more of this princing.' "

And after the trials and tribulations at Buckingham Palace, Edward more and more sought the escape of the now Roaring Twenties. There were parties every night. If it wasn't Mayfair, it was Chelsea, and if they didn't go to a private party it would be a nightclub; the fashionable ones were the Embassy, Ciro's, Quaglino's, and the Kit Kat. It was always the same crowd, Edward with Freda Dudley Ward, whose marriage had now become scarcely a shell of respectability; and among one of their closest friends was Sheila Chisholm who was related by marriage to one of the girls who had come aboard HMS

Renown for the party on the day it sailed from Australia for London.

Sheila was related to Roy Chisholm who married Mollee Little, one of the seven unchaperoned young ladies in Mountbatten's diary entry. Sheila Chisholm had been in the prince's circle for some time. She was Australian herself. Her father, Harry, brought her up in Sydney and in 1915 she married Lord Loughborough.

Coincidentally, she was related by marriage to Lady Rosemary Leverson-Gower, the first real love in Prince Edward's life. Sheila Chisholm's royal friendships would extend well into the twenties and early thirties. She and Lord Loughborough were divorced in 1926 and she then became Lady Milbanke, wife of baronet Sir John. She too would be around for the arrival of Mrs. Wallis Simpson into the prince's circle and it was to Sheila that the prince's friend, MP, and diarist Chips Channon, credited the enigmatic remark: "When Royalty comes in, friendship flies out of the window." How right she was, Channon postscripted.

(What exactly Sheila Chisholm meant by that remark may well have had some connection with a later development in this story: after the publication of the English edition of this book, a vicar wrote to the *Daily Express* indicating that Mollee Little left HMS *Renown* after a party onboard that last day carrying more than just memories of a royal friendship. According to writer Neil Mackwood, who was sent from England to Australia in April 1988 to investigate the vicar's claim, it is likely that Miss Little was left pregnant by the prince and was hurriedly married to the nephew of the prince's friend Roy Chisholm. Mollee was subsequently delivered of a son, who also grew to adulthood with a striking similarity to Edward and whose possible royal father was not entirely unknown locally. At Alice Springs, where he farmed, the young Mr. Chisholm was nicknamed "the duke.")

What had also become clear to Mountbatten and those closest to the prince was that he just didn't like the life he was leading. Even after the most successful engagements, he would often slump into a deep depression or the blackest of moods. He displayed his feelings at the time, when he wrote of the "great mental and physical strains" and the "lonely drives through tumultuous crowds and the feeling of terror of the smallest misunderstanding and being half killed by kindness." He hated the life. It was as simple as that.

This crisis in his mind, his discontentment with his lot, showed no signs of improvement. It was getting worse. At the end of the Australian tour and after a few months' recuperation, he was ready for the next empire visit planned by Lloyd George: India, last visited by his father in 1911, when King George was crowned Emperor of All India in a spectacular Coronation Durbar in Delhi.

India was still, his father impressed upon him, a great jewel in the empire's crown. The king told him before he left: "Whilst I do not approve of all that you do. I must concede you have done very well. But India is different. What went down well with white people will not go down at all in India. You must do exactly what they tell you."

As the *Renown* set sail again, there was grave concern in London as to how the prince would be received, particularly by Mahatma Gandhi and his radical supporters. The prince thought Gandhi a sinister and somewhat ludicrous figure. Will he spoil my show? Gandhi had already called a protest strike and instructed his supporters to stay away from the welcoming ceremonies for the prince. They were to hang black flags from buildings and stay inside as a protest against British rule.

There was nonetheless a great welcome, with all the pageantry that could only ever be seen in India, as the *Renown* steamed into Bombay harbor—although the rest of the tour was conducted in an atmosphere of nervous apprehension. Gandhi continued his campaign to boycott the prince. The government tried to overcome it by handing out free food; Gandhi countered by insisting that the food was poisoned and that the visit would be used to dispose by that means of a large number of India's starving population.

It was all too much for a people that loves pageantry, and there were fine attendances at Edward's parades. It was only as the entourage entered the constituencies of Pandit Nehru that the whole thing turned sour. The night before Edward was due to arrive, Nehru was thrown into jail. The result was that the entire native city of Allahabad went into hibernation; only troops lined the otherwise deserted streets.

Edward was so moved and upset by the experience that he wrote home: "I am depressed about my work here and I don't feel I am doing a scrap of good . . ." The king tried to reassure him in his response and said he quite understood why he should be feeling depressed by "the way that the natives have boycotted you in places where they have been intimidated by Gandhi . . . your visit is giving great pleasure to the natives if they were allowed to show it." Such was British misunderstanding of the grave problems they were to face in the subcontinent in its fight to control its own destiny.

Edward, though concerned about the appalling poverty that confronted him everywhere, and though he disapproved of the severe police tactics, had little time for Gandhi or what he stood for. He described him as an ominous shadow and accused him of bribery and intimidation in his efforts to wreck the tour.

But amid all this depression, the prince found a new friend. One of the officers co-opted to his staff in India was, to use his own words, "a gay handsome Irishman, Captain Edward Dudley Metcalfe"—known as Fruity to his friends.

At the prince's instigation, Fruity left India as a member of Edward's permanent staff, appointed to the post of equerry, and he remained after that a constant companion for years to come, right to the point of Edward's marriage to Mrs. Simpson, at which he would be best man.

As it happened, Edward needed a new friend. Dickie, having had what his cousin described as a "brainstorm," had gone and got himself engaged. Just three months earlier, in August 1921, Dickie had met Edwina Ashley, granddaughter of Sir Ernest Cassel, the son of a Jewish moneylender in Cologne who had subsequently made a huge fortune in banking. He was an adviser to Edward VII and became undoubtedly one of the richest men in Europe.

Edwina had been well taken care of in her grandfather's will, since upon Cassel's death she received almost £2 million. Mountbatten, whose own family fortunes were never plentiful and who had no wealth of his own other than a Navy salary of £350 a year, was clearly impressed both by her dowry and her beauty.

From that brief meeting there began a courtship by correspondence which became increasingly heated to the point when Mountbatten decided the time had come to take the plunge. He wrote to his mother: "I have made up my mind that each person knows within himself when he is old enough to marry. I am now. I have never really sown any wild oats and as I never intend to, I haven't got to get over that stage which some men have to . . ."

Edwina, captivated by his poetic love letters and no doubt by the thought of the title and royal association such a marriage would bring her, decided to join Mountbatten in India immediately. The prince arranged accommodation for her at the home of the viceroy, Lord Reading, which coincidentally they would occupy years later as man and wife. Mountbatten quickly sought the king's consent for the marriage, which was necessary as a member of the royal family, and their engagement was announced.

To say that it was entirely inspired by love would be an overstatement. It was to all intents and purposes an arranged marriage, the only difference being that Mountbatten had arranged it himself. It would be one based on her money and his position, which was hardly a sound basis for matrimony between two such extrovert personalities. As they would both admit in later life, they were constantly hopping in and out of other people's beds.

For the moment, though, it was champagne all round, with Edward, looking on wistfully at his best friend's newfound delight, agreeing to be his best man.

Dickie and Edwina would both, of course, return to India in 1947 to oversee its transition to independence, and Nehru's son, Jawaharlal Nehru, would become their great friend, particularly Edwina's, whose friendship developed into a warm relationship. On that first visit, however, Mountbatten appears not to have taken the slightest interest in the plight of the vast and impoverished nation. The prince wrote of his contribution: "Dickie's interest in the manifold problems of India was confined to that part of the country bounded by the white-boards of the polo field."

Edwina returned to England to prepare for the wedding, while the prince's caravan moved on to the Far East for another great round of engagements. By now the prince was so tense after so long on his travels that the slightest untoward incident would send him into transports of rage.

Dickie Mountbatten talked of nothing but his forthcoming wedding, which took place within a month of their arrival back in England, although he and Edwina barely knew each other. Fifteen hundred guests were at the ceremony at St. Margaret's, Westminster, where Edward oversaw the proceedings and gave the couple a silver globe with the tracks of the two royal tours Dickie had been on engraved upon it. Then the Mountbattens swept away for an equally glittering honeymoon, first to Germany and then to America and Hollywood. There they began the first of many encounters with the film stars and entertainers who would become such a part of their life.

In Los Angeles they stayed with Douglas Fairbanks and Mary Pickford and in New York they were welcomed

by Broadway; but always before long the question would
be asked: "When is your cousin going to be married?"
Edward was not even thinking about it, however, and
once confided to Dickie: "You see I'm getting quite an
old bachelor and am becoming a more confirmed one
each year. I suppose I'll have to take the fatal plunge
one of these days, though I'll put it off as long as I can
in case it'll destroy me."

Edward, visibly depressed after the Mountbatten wedding, as usual sought solace with Freda Dudley Ward,
who was ready to smooth away his problems. He loved
her in his own peculiar way but she knew, even as she
herself was heading for divorce, that there would never
be anything more than this between them. In any event,
it was not so much a sexual thing as one of sheer friendship. She said years later: "Yes, I could have dominated
him. He made himself a slave to whomever he loved."
But what kind of love was it? She was fully aware of the
massive problems that would be caused by taking it the
full course. Marrying a divorcée or even a commoner was
out of the question. He knew it. She knew it. In his
deep depressions he talked to her constantly about quit-
ting his life as heir to the throne but he had neither the
will nor the courage to confront his parents. Anyway, he
wasn't sure whether he wanted to marry Freda, even if
it were possible. She never pressed the subject, although
they were often indiscreet about their relationship, turning up together at the long round of parties and social
events to which they were both invited as stars of the
show.

King George heard about his son's every move and
was never backward in indicating his disapproval. The
storms and arguments between father and son continued,
verbally and by correspondence.

Freda's own marriage was kept alive only for the sake
of her two daughters, and soon the socialites were talking.
Lady Cynthia Asquith recorded: ". . . saw the Prince of

Wales dancing around with Mrs. Dudley Ward, a pretty little fluff with whom he is said to be rather in love."

King George would make constant and disparaging remarks about the prince's "little fluff," although he would admit after the arrival of Wallis that "at least Mrs. Dudley Ward came from a much better class and had an established position."

It was toward the end of the year of the Mountbatten's wedding that the rumors began: the Prince of Wales had found himself a bride. He would, said the reports, shortly be announcing his engagement to Lady Elizabeth Bowes-Lyon, a most attractive Scots lass from Glamis. The previous year, Edward's sister, Princess Mary, had struck up a firm friendship with Elizabeth while staying in Scotland. Mary had also introduced her to her brother Prince Albert (Bertie), who would shortly be created Duke of York, and it soon became apparent to his mother that he was deeply in love with her. "He is always talking about her," said Queen Mary. "She seems a charming girl, but I do not know her that well."

Not many months passed before Prince Albert announced to his parents that he intended to propose marriage to Lady Elizabeth; as his mother correctly perceived he was hopelessly devoted to her, but though Elizabeth was kind to him, there was no sign that she returned his love in any way. Prince Albert, who stuttered badly, was nervous in company, lacked confidence in speech, and had been a sickly youth, presented no great attraction to the young Scots lady who rejected his proposal of marriage with hardly a second thought.

Prince Albert persisted, and decided with his mother's encouragement that he would not give up his quest for her hand, though he learned with some disquiet that the Lady Elizabeth had received no less than five other proposals of marriage and there seemed no sign of his courtship ending in success.

By January 1923, the rumors had become quite public

that Lady Elizabeth had been selected as a royal bride and reports insisted that the king and queen had chosen her, not for Prince Albert, but instead for the Prince of Wales. Newspapers recalled that Queen Mary had even been to Scotland to look over the family, and so it was that on January 5, the headlines on most of that day's front pages proclaimed that Edward would have a Scottish bride, although the following day Buckingham Palace issued a prompt rebuttal. The report had no foundation.

The week after the press denials, Prince Albert arranged to meet Elizabeth at St. Paul's, Waldenbury, where she had played as a child. As they walked through the woods, he again proposed, and this time she accepted. They were married three months later and the king observed in a letter to Bertie: "The better I know and the more I see of your dear wife, the more charming I think she is. Everyone falls in love with her here."

Edward, however, still saw no bride in sight, though his parties and social life were taking on a new flamboyant style; and after the London season, there was the hunting season, which he had discovered could be equally entertaining socially, and a great deal more exciting. He would be whisked away by rail from St. Pancras station in London to Melton Mowbray in Leicestershire, often changing en route in his private carriage laid on specially for the purpose of his hunting trip. When he emerged at the other end of the journey, he would be wearing his hunting gear ready for the chase over some of Britain's most beautiful countryside, where social climbers gathered to join the most glamorous hunt in the country. At Melton, a car would be standing by to take him direct to a waiting horse. By 1923, he had so taken to the hunting scene and all the ancillary events around it that he took a suite at Craven Lodge Club, close to the station and the stables and, with the ever-present Fruity Metcalfe by his side, built up a string of hunters and steeplechase horses for use with the Quorn and Belvoir.

Melton was then a main center for the wealthy London

socialites, where they were joined by rich Americans over specially for the season, while famous cavalry men gathered there for off-duty sport. The richest kept suites at the Craven Lodge Club where, according to local records, "many a high-spirited frolic occurred." It was here, too, that the celebrated midnight steeplechase devised by Lady Augusta Fane took place.

Edward was given no privileges among the huntsmen while in the chase, though out of the saddle he was bowed to and pampered. He would be regularly rebuked for his style, galloping far ahead of the rest of the hunt and showing foolhardy bravado at a jump or fence which other young riders would attempt to emulate. The result was often a heavy fall by one or more of the front pack.

They were remarkable scenes, as hunt historian Frank Barratt described:

> I heard a terrific crashing of thorns and pounding of hooves and the Prince and Major Metcalfe came thundering down on the grass verge to the road; two strides and they were away again over the hedges as the hounds settled to run hard.
>
> This was desperate riding of the highest order and I doubt very much if the others would have tackled it if the Prince had not been in front. I saw looks of utter disbelief on the faces of regular followers as they filed one by one through the hunt gates after he had careered ahead over the most dangerous of fences. The thorn hedge the Prince had jumped was the type known as the bull-finch with a big drop on the blind side, formidable and nerve-racking.

On Quorn Monday, Barratt recalled, after the hunt had ended, someone suggested a race back home with fresh horses beneath them. The prince gave a whoop and it was on. "No hounds, no huntsmen, just eight miles of turf at a breathtaking gallop," Barratt recalls. "The cares of state would be truly blown away."

Was it the cares of state that had driven the prince to levels of sporting endeavor that he had never before tackled? Here in Melton, a new side of the Prince of Wales emerged; a devil-may-care rider who looked each and every time as if he was on some sort of proving mission, or earnestly intent on being the best on the field. No one could explain it; no one tried. Meanwhile, out of the saddle he went back to his normal pastimes.

Naturally cameramen always seemed to be on hand whenever the prince took a bad tumble, and his dangerous exploits soon brought rebuke from other quarters. After one particularly bad fall, which knocked out the prince for three hours, Prime Minister Ramsay Mac-Donald wrote to the prince: "Sir, would you please not consider it an excess of either my duty or of my interest if I begged you to refrain from taking chances that no doubt offer you exhilarating temptation," while the king wrote formally: "Dear David, I must ask you to give up riding steeple chase and point-to-point races." For the time being the prince was calmed, though he remained a devoted huntsman.

However, at Melton he was now attracted not merely by the chase. He called it his second home and joined in the local socializing with some gusto, though the night life was rather less demanding than on the London club circuit. All Melton had to offer, apart from the glittering house parties, was the Embassy Dance Club, where the prince's patronage was followed by many distinguished visitors, including his brothers, Harry, Duke of Gloucester; George, Duke of Kent; the Earl of Sefton; Lord Tennyson; and the Duchess of Westminster.

Melton was his hideaway, where he felt safe from the prying eyes of London. There were many secrets he wanted kept, and Melton gossip tended not to stray too far. But for Edward and the charmed circle, scandal was never far away.

·THREE·

NEW YORK, NEW YORK

⸻◆⸻

It was a cause of constant concern to the king that his son was constantly trying to get to America, where the Jazz Age was in full swing. This was Edward's kind of life now, and he wanted more of it. He was there in the autumn of 1924, after initially persuading his father that he needed to cross the Atlantic for public duties and to check on his ranch in Canada, while in fact all he really wanted to do was to get into the New York night life just as soon as possible. He had arranged to sail over with the Mountbattens, and as soon as it was learned that they had booked their passage, the prince's social set clamored to get a berth on the *Berengaria*.

Indeed it was a fine party that included Dickie Mountbatten's brother George and his wife Nada Milford Haven, the Earl and Countess of Airlie, the Duchess of Westminster, Fruity Metcalfe, and Lady Diana Cooper, who was traveling to New York to appear in *The Miracle*, on Broadway.

The night before embarkation, the prince stayed at Broadlands with the Mountbattens and the Ashleys, while the following day there was a great dockside party as his entourage of fun-seekers began arriving for the journey. The *Berengaria* had once been the *Imperator*, the German flagship on the trans-Atlantic route, and the superb royal suite had originally been reserved for the kaiser's exclusive use. Now his cousin Prince Edward was shown to these magnificent quarters for his full and private use on the voyage. He and his entourage played shipboard games and joined the organized fun. At the traditional fancy-dress ball, the prince turned up as a Limehouse Apache, danced till 4 A.M. to the ship's jazz band, and applauded the singing of the resident vocalist, Sophie Tucker.

He was to be the guest on Long Island of Mr. and Mrs. James Burden, and it was clear from the start that the prince was in a party mood and ready for a totally self-indulgent time. The New York press made the most of it as they followed the prince's party to the races, polo meetings, motor-boat racing, private and public dinner parties, or lavish house parties for several hundred guests. *The New York Times* noted his activities, "streaking up and down Long Island in the fastest motorboat or dashing off in a borrowed car for a late night dip in the Sound."

There were one or two public engagements of a suitably serious nature to make the trip take on a more down-to-earth tone; visits to schools, museums and art galleries were followed by the prince's frequently delayed trip to Canada. The king frowned on it all and resolved that autumn, as the reports of his eldest son's wanton behavior came flooding back, that none of his sons would again visit New York during his lifetime.

For the Mountbattens, the New York trip had proved to have a particularly unsettling influence on an already severe marital problem; their constant rows had become extremely public and seemed to erupt whenever they were together. The Navy had been taking up more and more of Dickie's time and Edwina was not one to sink into seclusion while he was away. Peter Murphy had taken on the role of peacemaker, and according to both their diaries he had become a virtually permanent resident in the Mountbatten household, a situation which would continue for many, many years. (Indeed, their children would come to regard him as a member of the family.) But whenever he wasn't there, Dickie and Edwina went for each other's throats. Murphy wasn't in New York that autumn, and when trouble blew up, the lack of Murphy's calming influence allowed the situation to get out of hand.

Edward was already on his way to Canada, but when the time came for the party to head back for England, Edwina calmly announced that she would be staying on in New York with Nada Milford Haven. It was the choice of companion as well as the sheer disobedience of his wife that angered Dickie. Nada was well known to have lesbian tendencies, and of course there'd been a great deal of gossip because she and Edwina were often going off alone. Two wealthy young women whose husbands shared a devotion to their careers in the Navy, they shared a lively interest in the great wide world: people, travel, adventure, and all matters sexual or entertaining.

Dickie burst into tears when Edwina told him she was staying on, and promptly set sail without her. It was to be the first of many temporary separations that their marriage would endure. At the time, however, it looked serious, and a permanent division seemed in the cards and was certainly rumored back in London, where news of the New York encounters had already filtered back into the social whirlpool, ahead of their return.

On board the *Berengaria* during the voyage back to England, Noel Coward, who had been playing on Broadway, checked himself into a first-class cabin adjacent to Dickie Mountbatten, and there began a long and lasting friendship between the two men that was taken up again immediately upon their return to London.

There, Prince Edward at once intervened in the rift between Dickie and Edwina. Calling Dickie to see him at St. James's Palace he asked about the "queer gossip surrounding Edwina," and warned his cousin there should not be any fuss. The king was already extremely angry over his own exploits in New York. Any public discussion about the Mountbattens' marriage would certainly encourage the wrath of the staid monarch.

Dickie agreed: there would be no fuss. Edwina was implored to return to England and they were soon back in public view together, sitting in the front row as Noel Coward's guests at the opening night in November of *The Vortex*. However, the apparent happiness of these two most famous socialites was a cover for the real state of their marriage and they would for the time being lead separate lives, he working and playing polo, she remaining in their London home and returning to the country only on weekends for house parties. Things settled down again, but not for long.

For Noel Coward, the encounter with Dickie Mountbatten and the subsequent friendship that he had so skillfully engineered meant that he had secured a connection to a second member of the royal family. He had met Mountbatten's cousin—and Edward's brother—Prince George, Duke of Kent, in 1923 when Coward was twenty-three and the prince twenty. Coward himself admitted years later that his relationship with the prince had become a sexual one, and in later life, when his homosexuality had become well known, would boast of the affair with Prince George, of which he seemed rather proud.

The Duke of Kent was by no means consistent in his approach to sex, except that he did enjoy the excitement of being in the company of entertainers and show-business people. In 1926, he was captivated by the minute but dynamic black singer, Florence Mills, who came to London in a C. B. Cochran revue, and his taste for black women apparently continued well after his marriage to Prince Marina.

The Prince of Wales, meanwhile, spent the winter preparing for another grand tour, this time to Africa. Lloyd George had been ousted from power, but the empire tours would be continued under the new regime, and Edward left in March 1926 aboard HMS *Repulse*, first for southern Africa and then on to South America, with Fruity Metcalfe at his side.

At the end of it all, he had, during these great tours, visited forty-five countries and traveled 150,000 miles, which in terms of modern travel seems somewhat insignificant but at that time was a vast and onerous undertaking. He returned thirty-one years old and very tired. Whatever his faults, in the previous ten years he had given his all, and Lloyd George had pushed him far beyond the call of duty.

On his return, it was back into the social whirlpool, but the gaiety of the Roaring Twenties that was being so enjoyed by the socialites took what Edward described as a slight "skip in the rhythm." The masses faced scandalous poverty, unemployment, and degradation. The General Strike was called and the nation came to a standstill. Exactly what good the return of the Prince of Wales should do was hardly imaginable, particularly in view of his attitude to the uprising.

He sided with the upper classes, and though the government wanted to use him and the royal family as a stabilizing force, the truth was that he lent his support to putting down the strikers.

Although warned by his palace advisers to keep out of politics, Edward reckoned that it was "like asking a man in a burning building to retire to his room while firemen coped with the blaze." What actually came out of his dash back to England was the sight of the prince in a new light. He had been called the "people's prince," all for the common man. Now he was emerging with a new attitude that would materialize ten years later when he encouraged the suggestion of a "King's Party" being formed around him.

Politics, he now claimed, were his concern, and the general strike was perhaps the point at which his political sympathies began to get the better of him and reveal another aspect of his insensitivity. The strike, he felt, was unique because of the reaction to it of the upper

classes. He believed they regarded it as a strike against
the constitution, and their response was to "leave their
businesses, their suburban houses, their landed estates,
their clubs and their leisure, determined to restore the
essential services of the nation."

His friends thought the same way as he, that they were
putting down something that was terribly wrong and "they
put on a first-class show." This new kind of pomposity
the prince would show with greater frequency: the confidence drawn from his tours gave him the will to believe
that he could now, at last, do and say anything he damn
well pleased.

Edward's friends in the strike-breaking activities included Edwina Mountbatten. She had been on a shopping excursion to Paris when the strike began, and spent
several thousands of pounds on new attire and other
luxuries that could have helped keep many impoverished
British families in rations for a year. On her return, she
discovered that Lord Beaverbrook, who at various times
counted himself a close friend of the Mountbattens but
just as regularly criticized their extravagant and extreme
life-style, was appealing for volunteers to help run his
strike-bound Fleet Street offices. Edwina joined in quickly
and thought it would be quite amusing to man the office
switchboard while Lady Diana Cooper was acting as a
free-lance journalist, telephoning the office with news
stories and being connected on the telephone by Edwina.
Such fun, they recalled.

The strike passed, and the prince's set returned to a
normal life. Edwina was busily preparing to take over a
new London house in Park Lane and buying another
home, a villa in Malta, in readiness for Dickie's appointment to the flagship of the Mediterranean fleet. His brother
George had also been posted to the Med and he and
Nada took an apartment close to Dickie's villa. Edwina
found it not unpleasant to contemplate an occasional
sojourn in Malta while her husband was at sea, though

she would never stay there for too long, away from the London scene that she loved.

Although she and Dickie were still together, at this time they saw little of each other. He had built up an expensive and extensive stable of polo ponies and with the help of Peter Murphy was writing a book on polo. He would think nothing of flying back to London from the Mediterranean for a polo match, or traveling to Paris for a weekend's leave, more often than not without Edwina.

It was on one of these weekends in Paris that he teamed up with his cousin Prince Edward; they had arranged to meet in the French capital and planned to stay for several days. Discretion was never a major attribute of either of them, and news of their bachelor-style exploits and the company they were in, male and theatrical, reached Buckingham Palace, as it always did. Queen Mary was furious at both of them and ordered Edward's immediate return to London.

It was during this period that Edwina's name was being romantically linked with not just one but several famous names, and there was considerable speculation over Edwina's intentions regarding her marriage. The most persistent gossip was over her affair with a wealthy polo-playing American, Laddie Sandford, whom she would later say "caused me more unhappiness than I have ever known."

Dickie also looked elsewhere, quite apart from his bachelorlike excursions, and became intimately friendly with the only other woman who would become part of his life and remain so until death separated them.

Yola Letellier was the beautiful wife of a French newspaper proprietor and a mayor of Deauville. She became Dickie's lover and, more important to him, a close friend to whom he could pour out his troubles. Only Edward was closer to him then than Yola. It was a loving friendship that would last thirty-five years. Eventually, Edwina got to learn of Yola's presence in Mountbatten's life but adopted a strangely tolerant view; although, given her own excesses in love, romance, and sexual appetite, there was little she could really do.

Although from time to time they reexamined the state of their marriage, for the most part, as the months of 1927 rolled past, they continued to lead separate lives. Mountbatten tried again for a reconciliation and wrote her a long love letter from his ship HMS *Warspite*, and at the end of 1927 their rift was temporarily healed, only to be tested again a short time later when troublesome news arrived from America. It appeared that Edwina was about to be cited as the corespondent in a divorce hearing, so the repercussions for the royal family would have been, to say the least, difficult. But after Beaverbrook, the newspaper tycoon, was enlisted to find out all he could and try to stop the action "with whatever money resources or social influence was required," nothing more was heard of it.

By now Edward was back in darkest Africa. After several weeks of official duties, he went on a private safari into Tanganyika. His party were all kitted out in bush gear, khaki shorts and shirts, and slept under canvas. They made their way south in a convoy of trucks in what the prince described as an "idyllic excursion." It was not to last long, however. When the party reached Dodona, among the messages for him was one from the palace, and another from the prime minister, requesting his immediate return to London.

During his absence the king had been taken seriously ill, and there were fears that he would not last long. Edward was required straight away to take over the king's duties in the affairs of state. Although by the time he reached England the crisis was over, Stanley Baldwin warned Edward that he must now expect to have to take over more of the palace work and his father's official duties. (The date was December 11, 1928—eight years exactly to the day when he would abandon the throne and his royal responsibilities forever.)

Ironically, also, his brother Bertie had written him a note in which he said, "There is a story going around the East End that the reason you are rushing home is that in the event of anything happening to Papa, I am going to bag the throne in your absence."

The drama of the king's illness saw the beginning of the rift between Edward and the Church of England, or more particularly, its head, the Archbishop of Canterbury, Dr. Cosmo Lang, which reached such a bitter and vitriolic division during and after the abdication. Edward recalled the incident that led to a major showdown with Lang: "My father was clearly still very ill; he could hardly be moved and endured a great deal of pain. There was also a wound in his back from an operation for streptococcus infection which was exceedingly slow to heal." Yet Lang, Edward said, insisted on going through with the organization of a national thanksgiving day to celebrate the king's survival of his recent illness. "It was so hypocritical," said Edward. "My father was still a very sick man, yet we all had to go through the charade that he had fully recovered, although we knew very well that he could have a relapse at any moment."

A few days before the thanksgiving service in Westminster Abbey, the king received, at Buckingham Palace, J. A. Thomas, a humorous Welsh minister, whose wealth of stories the king enjoyed. One made the king laugh uproariously but suddenly he stopped and put a hand to his back; an abcess that had grown on the wound of his operation had burst with his laughter and a great volume of pus emerged.

Even in the knowledge of that gaping wound, Lang pressed ahead with his service for the king, who himself felt obliged to attend. "What the crowds who cheered and waved to him did not know," said Edward, "was that still more pus from the abcess was seeping through his jacket." Following that, relations between Edward and the church were never the same again. Already he viewed Lang as a hypocrite, and in the end it would be the church that brought his coming scandal into public view.

Through the winter of 1928–1929, Edward took over more and more the mantle of the monarchy and soon had his first political clash with Prime Minister Stanley Baldwin. He'd accepted an invitation from a group of businessmen to make a tour of the North Country to put "some heart back into the miners" after their traumatic and bitter struggle with the pit managements. He made the mistake of not consulting Baldwin, but before he was due to leave, the prime minister summoned him to the House of Commons. "Sir, I have just heard of your proposed trip," he said, "and I should like to know under whose auspices you are going."

The prince was astonished that he should be challenged on the issue of his tour. "But why, Mr Baldwin? It has never been my understanding that I am expected to notify the government of my movements."

"No, sir," said Baldwin. "But your visit might have political repercussions."

"You know that I stand outside of politics," Edward replied sharply. "My only reason for going is to see for myself what the shutting down of so many mines has done to people who depend on them."

Although Baldwin warned him that a general election was not far away and that the prince must not allow himself to be used, the tour went ahead; and Baldwin lost the election. Edward returned to a gay social life, and the plight of the miners remained totally unaffected by any of these events.

That summer a new love came into Edward's life; in fact he had become more adventurous in his relations with the opposite sex. He saw her at the Leicester Fair, where he had just made a speech thanking local farmers for allowing the use of their land for a hunt, and added some strange advice: "Keep your eyes open for anything that is new, and do not reject it without a fair trial."

Suddenly his own attention was focused on Viscountess Thelma Furness, a beautifully slender American of twenty-five, who was one of the twin daughters of American Consul Harry Hayes Morgan, known as the Magnificent Morgans. Thelma had been headstrong as a teenager, and her approach to life had altered little since. She had eloped at the age of sixteen with James Van Converse, whose grandfather had founded the Bell telephone company and who was twice her age. Her sister Gloria also eloped; marrying Reginald Claypole Vanderbilt, heir to the railroad millions, she was widowed at the age of twenty-one and began quite a riotous existence.

Thelma's elopement had led to a not entirely satisfactory marriage and after her divorce she had met and was attracted to another man who was very much older than she. He was the wealthy and widowed Viscount Furness, head of the Furness Shipping Line.

At Leicester Fair, fourteen miles from the Furness hunting lodge at Melton Mowbray, the Prince of Wales asked: "Who is the beautiful American girl" after catching her accent during conversation. To him, all things American still held a peculiar fascination. Within a week she was dining alone with him in his apartment at York House.

Six months later, Thelma, whose second marriage would also end in the divorce courts, had joined Edward on an African safari to Nairobi where, under canvas, she found heaven. "This was our Eden," she wrote, "and we were alone in it. His arms about me were the only reality . . . his words of love the only bridge to my life. Each night I felt more completely possessed by our love, carried ever more swiftly into uncharted seas, and, I felt content to let the Prince chart the course, heedless of where the voyage would end."

Romantic stuff, but it would all end in tears. Edward's

quick-start love affair with Thelma did not inspire in him the same devotion as she herself was offering. Thelma could not even command the exclusive attention of her Prince Charming, who continued to see just as much of Freda Dudley Ward as he did of her. They were the two mainstays of his life, and they shared his social life equally, though never together. There were others, too, who could capture, perhaps only briefly, the prince's love and affection. It was as if he had suddenly discovered the sheer delight of the female body.

There had been in his early adulthood various speculations about his latent homosexuality, bisexuality or, as some said, sheer shyness because of a rather small endowment. His closeness to Mountbatten and his lack of success in producing a bride who would become a future queen led to stories, which contained more rumor than fact, about his occasional preference for male company. As the era of the twenties moved to a close, however, he had entered a phase in which women had become important to him; his charm and politeness in their presence were noted, as was the occasional secret liaison outside his quite open associations with Freda and Thelma.

And then there was Mrs. Wallis Simpson, arriving quietly and coolly at first but whipping up a considerable tornado as she went . . .

FOUR

FRIENDS AND INFLUENCES

Her arrival caused not a ripple of interest in the village-like community of socialite London, but within the space of five years, the old king would be demanding to know, "Who is this woman my son and heir is associating with?" He would not be pleased with what he discovered.

The file that would be prepared for him at the highest level in British intelligence would show a woman whose emotional and marital background had been, to put it mildly, most unsuitable; whose early life had been punctuated by traumatic times; a woman hardened by the cruel and sexual demands of men which she had first seen confronting her mother and which she would soon herself face.

In London, where breeding and social standing mattered, they would say she came from the wrong side of the tracks in Baltimore. Wallis would be angered by such an inference. Even today others support the view that she came from the stock of two fine old American families whose background was amply suited to association with British royalty. Indeed, in her family there was distinguished ancestry that could be traced back to the British ruling family, but that in itself could not begin to obliterate the disgrace of her immediate past, nor present her in any way as a suitable bride for a future king.

Wallis Simpson had masses of blue English blood. Genealogists traced her descent from Edward III and from Isle of Man royalty. There was even in her family tree the dukedom of Manchester, to which, coincidentally, her friend Sir Oswald Mosley could be linked. There was another strange coincidence. One hundred fifty years before Wallis and Elizabeth Bowes-Lyon, Duchess of York and the future queen, became sisters-in-law, the latter's most famous ancestor, George Washington, was saved on the battlefield in the War of Independence by a soldier who took in his chest the thrust of a British saber which had been aimed at the future president of the United States. That heroic soldier was a Montague, from whom there is a direct line of descent to Wallis Simpson.

Genealogists, anxious to establish Wallis's fine old family background, were keen to show her most prestigious ancestry; but by the time the Montague line had reached the birth of the child who would be called Bessiewallis, the Montagues were a penniless Virginian family. Her mother, Alice Montague, married into a wealthy family when she became Mrs. Teackle Wallis-Warfield. His family, bankers from Baltimore, were strongly opposed to the match; they thought Alice was a fortune hunter, and had no real interest in the tubercular and least successful of the Warfield children.

His brother, Solomon, tried his damnedest to separate them, but it would appear that Alice was already expecting a child, who would not be long in arriving after she and T. Wallis were married in November 1895.

In her autobiography, Wallis would say that her parents married in June, but she was mistaken, or merely trying to hide the truth. It has even been suggested that Wallis was born out of wedlock, probably two years earlier. (Since her mother does not appear to have officially registered the arrival of her daughter upon this earth, the truth will never be known.) Wallis always gave her birth-date as June 19, 1896, which would have meant that she was born seven months after her parents were married, but even she appeared unsure. "Out of curiosity I once asked my mother . . . she answered impatiently that she had been far too busy to consult the calendar, let alone the clock."

Queen Mary's own investigations into the personal background of Wallis put the birthplace considerably earlier, though no evidence to support that theory has been produced, or at least not publicly.

Whatever her age, in 1896 Bessiewallis lost the man she believed to be her father. T. Wallis died from tuberculosis at the age of twenty-six and Alice was forced to accept the hospitality of her brother-in-law, Sol, who took mother and child to the family home in Baltimore where Alice's formidable mother-in-law was still very much in charge.

There they remained for five years. In fact until Alice and her child were banished from the house and out into the world by Wallis's grandmother, who suspected that Sol had fallen in love with his sister-in-law—which, in such a fine family, would never do. Alice got a job making children's clothes and took rooms at a cheap hotel. For a short time, when finances became desperately depleted, she lodged with Aunt Bessie Merryman but somehow or other, she managed to raise enough money to rent a three-story house in East Biddle Street, Baltimore, where she took in paying guests.

In later life, Wallis always resented the suggestion that her mother ran a boarding house. But the Duke de Grant-mesnil suggested to me that the way in which Wallis's mother reestablished herself and her finances was by running a house of ill-repute.

Certainly, Alice had been attending to the needs of one John Freeman Rasin, the bawdy son of a none too reputable local politician. He was a hard-drinking laya-bout whose conduct and whose association with Alice were much discussed in the parlors of Baltimore's upper-crust homes.

Uncle Sol, seeing the life to which his niece was being subjected, tried to get Bessiewallis away from her mother and back into the family home, but was thwarted when Alice married Rasin in 1908. Wallis was then twelve, and though Uncle Sol continued to provide for her education, she remained in the care of her mother and stepfather until 1916. Sol obviously did not rate his niece's chances in life too highly, for when he died he left most of his $5 million to a local home for retired gentlewomen, with the provision that there should be a room permanently available for his niece whenever she required it.

In the spring of that year, Wallis went to stay with friends in Florida, where she met a handsome naval pilot, Lt. Earl Winfield Spencer; he was twenty-seven, and eight years her senior, but his family had money. She was attracted to him, and to his heirdom to a Chicago stock exchange fortune. They married six months later. At first, Wallis wrote in her autobiography, she was blissfully happy, though even before the honeymoon had ended it began to dawn on her that she had married a drunk who was, in her words, soon on a downward spiral, stumbling from one bottle to another.

His excessive drinking became the talk of all who knew them. Stories abounded of his all-night binges; the rows; his frequent outbreaks of violence when he would break up the household furniture. Once, in a fit of rage, he locked Wallis in the bathroom for several hours.

For months, Wallis endured the stormy marriage, until Win himself departed the marital home and announced he was moving in with a former girl friend. Wallis neither heard nor saw anything of him for almost four months, until, early in 1921, she heard he had been transferred to Washington, grounded from flying, and attached to the Navy Department. Win pleaded with Wallis to join him and to try again at a reconciliation; also her mother was now living in Washington and working as a hostess at the Chevy Chase Club. Wallis agreed, but she would regret it.

He had changed not one bit, and his drinking, his affairs, and his violence were just as bad as ever. This time it was Wallis who left, vowing to get a divorce, though knowing she would get no sanction or support in such a move from her Episcopalian family. Soon she was living the life of a single woman and attractive enough to be the center of attention in the smart set of Washington, which she entered with ease. First, there was an affair with Mussolini's ambassador, Prince Caetani, and through him she met the man who would become the first real love of her life, the sleek and charming Argentinian attaché Don Felipe Espil. He was thirty-five, rich, and had the aura of a classical South American lover.

Although she did not name him, Wallis even admitted in her autobiography, "He was the most fascinating man I ever met. He was both my teacher and my model in life." She unashamedly set herself at him; she wanted him and did everything she could to make him want her. With her great skill of manipulating men she succeeded in luring him into an affair that became the scandal of Washington.

It was a thrilling social whirl in which she found herself, and one which, strangely, was being noted by Naval intelligence in a special file they had started on her, as an officer's wife.

It would end in tears. Wallis discovered that Felipe had not been faithful to her and they parted bitterly. Coincidentally, Win was back in touch with her, pleading once again for them to get back together. He just had been given a new posting. His bosses in the Navy Department, fed up with his drinking, sent him to take command of the *Pampamga*, a scruffy 1,200-ton gunboat in the South China patrol and in the thick of war. It was indeed the worst place in the world any naval officer could find himself, trying to provide semiofficial protection to American interests caught between revolutionary factions.

He arrived to take his new command in March 1923, but the activities of Wallis in the ensuing few months, and indeed for the coming two years, are shrouded in mystery. Her own account of this period of her life is scant in detail, but from official naval records it can be established that in January 1924, long after Win's departure to the South China patrol, she was to be found in Paris, apparently under the watchful eyes of naval intelligence.

Her activities in the coming months would prove to be of great interest to British intelligence when they were asked in 1934 to provide a complete dossier on Wallis for the private and confidential attention of King George V. Wallis had traveled to Paris with her friend Corinne Mustin. Both saw it as a cheering-up trip; Corinne had recently been widowed and Wallis herself was still suffering from the misery of her breakup with Felipe.

Five gay and exciting months in the French capital would solve all that. They sailed aboard the *President Garfield* and in Paris they were soon in the company of naval staff equally enthusiastic at having two unattached young women in their midst. Again, Wallis's encounters became the subject for tasty local gossip. It was also a matter of intense speculation as to how she was managing to live on a meager allowance from her husband, whose own naval income was hardly handsome. By July she was back in America, and at a loss as to what to do with her life. She had contemplated pursuing divorce proceedings against Win, but his pleadings for another try at their marriage and the prospect of a new adventure in the Orient intrigued her sufficiently to agree to join Spencer in Hong Kong.

She was given clearance to travel to Hong Kong, a long and arduous journey, first aboard the troopship *Chaumont* which called at Honolulu and Guam and finally linked up with the *Empress of Canada* at Manila Bay, to which she transferred for the onward voyage to China. Spencer's own ship was already moored at Hong Kong for repairs when Wallis arrived, and there was a tearful yet somewhat strained reunion on the dockside as she stepped ashore to embark on what she herself would describe as one of the most exciting times of her life.

She arrived on September 8. In that very week the civil war in China became a full-blown conflict, and in little more than a month after her arrival Win Spencer would be ordered to proceed to Canton, and into the thick of the murderous war in which thousands of innocents were being massacred and where the skies were filled with the smoke of fires and guns, pounding day and night.

There are many gaps in Wallis's own accounts of her months in Hong Kong and China, but naval logs indicate Win's erratic movements. What is also clear is that the newly reunited couple did not stay together for long, a fact noted in the China Report to King George V. According to that report, during his leave Win took Wallis to what were known as the Singing Houses of Hong Kong, which were in reality high-class brothels, widely used and popular with senior naval personnel and travelers who could afford the rates. Girls were recruited at almost the age of puberty to be trained in the most sensual and erotic aspects of lovemaking, to provide wealthy clients with their every sexual whim or desire. They were called Singing Houses because of their respectable air of entertainment, in which the sylphlike Chinese beauties danced and sang soft, enticing songs.

The houses were superbly and elegantly furnished; restful and sumptuous for weary naval officers fresh from the rigors of the Chinese conflict. Customers would be entertained and then shown to rooms where the prostitutes awaited them. The China Report stated that Wallis was captivated by the young women and in one of the most famous and elegant of these houses, she took part

in regular and various sexual practices, including sophisticated threesome activities. Wallis is said to have
been eager to learn the ancient skills of lovemaking taught
to the prostitutes. They were known as the Fang Yung
dispensers, adept in techniques in which the woman
induced her male partner into deep relaxation through
massage over every part of the body, using the tips of
the fingers. By this method, prolonged sexual arouse-
ment of the male could be achieved. Wallis learned the
total art and would use it to her full advantage in the
future.

These initial diversions in Hong Kong soon ended.
The arrival at Win's door of a naval ensign would finally
wreck their marriage for good. He told Win that on the
journey to Hong Kong he had met and fallen deeply in
love with Wallis and wished to marry her. Whether Wallis
herself was a party to this prospect, she never revealed,
but Win took it seriously enough to kick her out, there
and then.

Wallis had heard there was an American court in
Shanghai and decided to go there and try to get a divorce
from Win, whom she would see only once more in her
life. She knew not how she would live and eat, but
anyone who was familiar with China in that age would
also know that it would be difficult to manage on the
$225 a month she was alloted from her estranged hus-
band's perhaps somewhat spasmodic naval pay. And so
by the end of November she had arrived in the wild open
city of Shanghai, wild but also sophisticated and cosmopolitan. Almost every major nation of the world was
represented there, either diplomatically or by trade or
business. It was a city of intrigue, spies, sex, gambling,
and every other kind of vice. Opulence rubbed shoulders
with the abject poverty and degradation of the bottom
strata of Chinese native life. Missionaries condemned it
as a modern-day Gomorrah as they surveyed this vast
playground with its elegant houses of prostitution, its
dancing academies, its bars, clubs, and merchant houses,

and, of course, the Bund, the most infamous thorough-
fare in the eastern world.

There was also an underworld that would have made
Chicago and Al Capone look like a Sunday school, and
it was largely under the control of three powerful gangs
that collaborated to keep the right-wing rulers in power.
They were dealers in opium, controllers of prostitution,
protectors of brothels and gaming houses. In fact, brothels were very much part of the Shanghai scene and they
carried exclusive-sounding names. In the "front" of these
houses, there would be drinking and entertainment,
games, or even areas for business meetings; at the rear
and upstairs there would be discreet sexual parlors.

Wallis headed straight for the Bund, which she found
lived up to its reputation of bustle and excitement. She
checked in at the famous Palace Hotel and from there
met a fellow American who went under the name of
Robbie and who knew everyone worth knowing in
Shanghai. Her own description of that meeting was quite
vivid: "He came towards me, young and handsome,
beautifully dressed. We had a drink together, very pleasant. Then he suggested dinner, and it proved to be even
more pleasant. This was the simple beginning of a delightful friendship." Robbie and a business partner owned
a large house where they entertained the more amusing
members of the foreign colony, then predominantly British. From knowing no one, Wallis admitted she was drawn
into a totally different kind of world of garden parties,
race meetings, dinner parties, gambling, and so on. At
dinner with Robbie and others in the Majestic Hotel on
Bubbling Well Road, she danced in a sunken courtyard
by the light of colored lanterns. "It was here in the
company of Robbie that I first heard Vincent Youman's
"Tea for Two" and the combination of that melody, the
moonlight, the perfume of jasmine, not to mention the
Shangri-La illusion of the courtyard, made me feel that
I had entered the Celestial Kingdom. No doubt about
it, life in Shanghai in 1924 was good, very good and in

fact almost too good for a woman under a dangerous illusion of quasi-independence," she said.

Wallis became a paid hostess at the house owned by her new boyfriend's partner. It was on the edge of the Fourth and Fifth Maloos of the International Settlement close to some of the most exclusive brothels in Shanghai. Here, roads such as the infamous Meeting Together Happy Lane and Park Lane contained handsome, luxurious double-front and three-story houses, with ropes and poles strung across the street to hang the red lanterns. Off Park Lane, there was an archway into a cul de sac of houses patronized only by wealthy foreigners. No Chinese were allowed. Here, in this brothel heart of Shanghai, the investigators for King George would center their report on Wallis Simpson, and among those who would be asked to supply information was Roger (later Sir) Hollis, who would join the swarm of international intelligence men in the settlement. Hollis, who later became head of MI5, did not go to Shanghai until 1926, when he worked for the British American Tobacco Company. Also in Shanghai at the time was Richard Sorge, the Comintern agent and spy who was executed by the Japanese. According to Chapman Pincher in his book *Their Trade Is Treachery* it was Sorge who recruited Hollis to the Russian cause. Wallis would be in the thick of the international intrigue and this had not escaped the notice of American naval intelligence, which kept a permanent watch on the better end of Shanghai society, to log who was meeting whom. Wallis would be particularly noticeable; she was living like a queen, to coin a phrase. And in the naval reports on her, there would be an entry that she was suspected of spying for an unnamed Russian who had been escorting her and, if the contemporary security reports on her are to be believed, for whom she would do anything for money. Noel Coward was also there, though he never met Wallis at that time. It was during four days of a bout of influenza while staying at the Cathay Hotel three years later that he wrote *Private Lives*. In the brothels of Shanghai, the girls practiced the erotic Tao of Loving in which lovemaking was regarded as necessary to the physical and mental health of both men and woman, and it was in this art that Wallis would also take a particular interest. Explicit books were available in the city for the Taoist to learn the 2,000-year-old art in which great emphasis was placed upon the skills of sexual prowess. Indeed, ordinary women, not just prostitutes, would discover from the literature how to make their men enjoy frequent and prolonged sexual activity without premature ejaculation.

Wallis would find this knowledge very useful in later life when she met the Prince of Wales who, according to Thelma Furness, was a poor lover when she knew him and achieved sexual satisfaction so rapidly that his partner would be left entirely frustrated. For some reason, Wallis found it necessary to leave Shanghai in a hurry. She claimed in her autobiography that it was to go on a shopping expedition to Peking, but since that entailed a hazardous journey of almost a thousand miles, there seemed some doubt as to the real reason. She traveled the dangerous and uncomfortable trek first by taking a coastal steamer, a rusty and leaky tub, to Tientsin and transferring there to a train that would take her into a war zone. American consul officials at Shanghai, who were still keeping tabs on her, warned that if she became involved in an international incident, the Navy would be informed she had traveled against their advice. The train was indeed stopped on a number of occasions during the journey, and she faced local Chinese who came aboard in shabby uniforms and armed with rifles, searched the carriages, and then let the train continue on its way.

In Peking, Wallis checked into the Grand Hotel de Pekin and was soon pleased to discover a friendly face. Gerry Green, a serviceman she had had a brief fling with on her trip to Paris with Corrine Mustin, was now attached to the U.S. Legation Guard in Peking. And as Gerry whisked her onto the dance floor at the Grand just a few nights after her arrival, she came face to face with another friend from the past, Katherine Moore Bigelow, a young widow she had known four years before who was now married to a wealthy American, Herman Rogers. They took Wallis back to their house and invited her to stay. The Rogers were on their second world tour, on the proceeds of Herman's family business from which he had retired at a youthful thirty-five to become a writer and traveler—and part-time supplier of intelligence to the American legation. They would become Wallis's devoted friends.

The Rogerses' home was in the Tartar City near the Hatamen Gate and from there, Wallis would venture into the night life of Peking and a world beyond her dreams. Through Herman's dinner parties and her association with Gerry Green, she plunged into a new social whirlpool where, in her own words, "every woman could be a Cinderella and midnight never struck." Peking was a city of all pleasures which were enjoyed particularly by the 2,000 foreign traders and diplomats. Lavish parties were an almost nightly event, and Wallis discovered to her delight that there were ten men to every unattached woman and few, she admitted, had honorable intentions. Among the diplomats she met was Count Galeazzo Ciano, who would become Italy's consul general and Mussolini's son-in-law, with whom she was captivated and he her. Ciano's exploits with women in various parts of the world, including Hitler's Germany after the outbreak of war, would become legendary, and his 1920s liaison with Wallis was discussed in Italian diplomatic circles in London before and after the abdication of Edward VIII (a fact confirmed to the author by Mrs. Joan Cecchine, a woman with extensive, firsthand knowledge of contemporary politics in Italy and Britain and with a wealth of private detail about the Windsors. She was born into a British diplomatic family, became sister-in-law [through the marriage of her sisters] to two senior Mussolini diplomats, and through her own marriage became sister-in-law to

Eisenhower's wartime aide, General Murdoch, later to become head of NATO in Italy. Further, she became a close friend of Edward's aide, Fruity Metcalfe, in Britain during the war, when she was working in the intelligence community. Her recollections have enabled the author, at various stages of this book, to include much previously unpublished material.)

Wallis, in that period in China, discovered a new skill, gambling, and became particularly adept at poker. She played for high stakes, on chips bought by wealthy men escorting her, another aspect of her life which investigators for King George would note. It provided another source of income needed to supplement a monthly allowance that barely covered her spending on clothes and jade in a single week. Jade became a passion; and she bought lots of it. Her wardrobe was extensive and needed to be for her extravagant social life. Only the patronization of escorts could ensure she could keep up with the life-style. She had planned to stay in Peking only two weeks but was there for almost a year. Once again, her departure was hurried though Katherine Rogers was not at all upset by that, since Wallis, not satisfied with the attentions of countless other men, had also become too close for comfort to Herman. In fact, Wallis's abrupt departure was caused by an "illness." She was taken to the hospital with problems of a gynecological nature. Word spread that she had become pregnant by an Italian diplomat, and Count Ciano was among the favorite candidates as the possible father. Further, the gossip was she had had an abortion from which she had contracted an infection. Wallis herself described it as "an obscure internal ailment"; but it was sufficiently bad for her to be quite ill on the journey home to America. When the ship docked she was admitted to a hospital in Seattle where she had a further operation. Wallis returned to Washington, D.C., in 1926 and discovered that her mother had been divorced, had married for a third time, and was now Mrs. Charles Gordon Allen. Her own divorce pro-

ceedings against Win Spencer were commenced at about
the time she met Ernest Aldrich Simpson, the son of an
American mother and an English father who ran a ship-
broker's business in New York, for which Ernest worked.

He was a quiet, reserved man, of whom Wallis wrote:
"He had a quiet wit . . . he was a good dancer, fond of
the theatre . . . and an unusually well-balanced man. I
had acquired a taste for cosmopolitan minds and Ernest
obviously had one."

A year younger than Wallis, Simpson had been to Har-
vard and then went to London where he served in the
Coldstream Guards. In 1923, he married Dorothea De-
chert and they had one child, a daughter they named
Audrey. In 1927, he also would be divorced—and Dorothea would accuse Wallis of stealing her husband.

She had what it takes to steal a man, said Dorothea.
"Simpson walked out on me while I was ill in a Paris
hospital . . . she [Wallis] moved in and helped herself
to my house, my clothes, everything." Dorothea didn't
like her from the moment she saw her, and it was with
great alacrity that she would tell all and sundry what a
nasty piece of work Wallis Spencer was. After the Simpsons were divorced, early in 1928, Ernest moved almost
immediately to his London office. In May, Wallis arrived
and they married in July.

It was all down to one of those strange fatalistic co-
incidences of life that events began to take their course.
Simpson's sister was Maud Kerr-Smiley, in whose house
Edward had met Freda Dudley Ward. Now she was helping Wallis to get established.

She found the couple a furnished house to rent in
Upper Berkeley Street and later they moved into a more
permanent home at 5 Bryanston Square. New friends
were found for them, and being American, Maud arranged for the Simpsons to meet Connie and Ben Thaw.
Ben was first secretary at the American embassy. Connie
took to Wallis straight away, and through her the twice-
married American lady, now thirty-four years old and

with some horrendous experiences of life behind her, entered the charmed circle. Indeed it was at a cocktail party at the London home of Connie's sister, Thelma Furness, that she saw for the second time in her life the prince she would marry.

Edward had also recently moved into new quarters after quietly uprooting himself from Melton which he now seldom visited. He had persuaded his father to let him have a home of his own and chosen Fort Belvedere, a rambling eighteenth-century house owned by the Crown, at Sunningdale, close to Great Windsor Park. "What could you possibly want that queer old place for?" asked the king. "Those damn weekends, I suppose."

The house had stood empty for almost a year and was in a terrible mess. Nothing had been done to it in the way of repairs or modernization for years, but Edward couldn't wait to get it. He took possession officially in April 1930 and with great enthusiasm began the massive task of refurbishment. "I loved it, the whole prospect of that house," he recalled, "and I began to begrudge every hour that darkness prohibited our work. I found a new contentment here. Soon I came to love The Fort as I have loved no other material thing. More and more it became for me a peaceful enchanted anchorage where I found refuge from the cares and turmoil of my life."

He ripped out the innards and added all the creature comforts that were lacking in the house: bathrooms were installed en suite with every bedroom where possible; the walls were stripped and repaneled. In turn, Thelma and Freda helped with interior decor, and with his own hands Edward began clearing the overgrown shrubberies and gardens, planting new trees and bushes so that the whole became a fine, elegant, and attractive residence.

Lady Diana Cooper, a frequent visitor after the Fort was completed, summed it up in her recollections: "It became a warm, relaxing home in which the comfort could not have been greater than the desire on his part for his guests to be happy, free and unembarrassed."

Thelma frequently was Edward's hostess at dinner parties at the Fort, and the house became what he had been seeking for a long time, a home away from the palace where he could entertain his friends as he wished, such as by playing the bagpipes till four in the morning.

The novelty soon wore off, however. In the winter of 1930, Edward was back at Melton Mowbray for a house party at Thelma's. The Simpsons had also been asked at the last minute when Connie and Ben Thaw had dropped out, and for the first time since they were together briefly in 1921, when she was Mrs. Earl Spencer, Wallis came face to face with Edward. He didn't pay much attention to the Simpsons at the time, although he recalled later that as a prince he had felt obliged to speak to the newcomers to their social circle, particularly since Wallis was an American.

Thelma, after that, showed Wallis a number of kindnesses and got her an invitation to a garden party at Buckingham Palace, at which Ernest and Wallis were to be presented to the king and queen. Edward saw them again, for the first time since Melton Mowbray. "I saw her approaching slowly in a line of women with feathers and trains," he wrote. "When her turn came to curtsey before my mother and father I was struck by the grace of her carriage and the natural dignity of her movements." Later, Thelma asked Ernest and Wallis back to supper at her London home. They accepted and so did Edward. And there it all began.

Politics, as well as Mrs. Simpson, would become something of a diversion to the prince as Britain entered the disastrous decade of the thirties, and Edward could not help but be drawn into the discussions. Since many of his closest friends had pro-Fascist leanings, there could be no doubt that the development of his political thinking would edge ever closer to their view. Edwina Mountbatten's father, Wilfred Ashley, was a great supporter of the Germans and he and the prince had many long conversations. The famous Mitford family, whose senior members were friends of the royals, had various members similarly attracted to the uprising Nazis. Edward's friend Sir Oswald Mosley was adopting a Fascist stance and there would be many others ready to bring influence to bear upon the prince as he began his final preparations to assume the monarchy.

Mosley—Tom, as he now wished to be known—was a particularly intriguing character to all those who knew him. A great orator and an even better heckler, he'd first attracted attention by his outrageous attacks on ministers in the early twenties, particularly on Winston Churchill and Lord Curzon, although the latter reluctantly had accepted Mosley into his family. When Mosley married the foreign secretary's daughter, Lady Cynthia Curzon, his wedding, attended by two reigning monarchs and two queens, was one of the social highlights of the year.

Mosley was once a shining hope in the Conservative party, and now both he and his wife became fervent battlers in the Labour party. He was a key man in Ramsay MacDonald's government, and by 1929 had been appointed to the influential duchy of Lancaster and was being tipped as a future prime minister.

But MacDonald rued the day that he placed his trust and faith in the man. Mosley wanted power quickly and power his way. Within a year of his appointment, he was sniping at MacDonald's cabinet. They were out of touch with opinion, he said, and when they rejected his widely acclaimed plan designed to relieve unemployment and the growing financial mess of the nation he quit the Labour party and went out on his own to form what he called the New party.

He was convinced the country would back him as he launched his New party with a great fanfare of publicity. Edward, who had been acquainted with Mosley for years, asked to be kept informed of his progress, and several giants of the political world showed an interest. Even Churchill and Lloyd George accepted invitations to his meetings. Aneurin Bevan, John Strachey, Harold Nicolson, and Harold Macmillan all came and looked. Others stood on the sidelines to see how Mosley fared.

However, all quickly went out the back door when they saw the extent of public reaction. The New party was a disaster. In the 1931 general election, it fielded twenty-four candidates. All were soundly defeated, so when MacDonald came back to head a national government Mosley was out in the cold. Those who were close to him knew that his politics were edging toward Fascism. He was fascinated by Mussolini's Italy and watched closely the developments in Germany, all of which inspired him to form the British Union of Fascists.

The fascination for Fascist regimes was shared by the prince and a number of those friends whose social circles overlapped those of Mosley, who was of course a member of the aristocracy. Although he had for the moment disclaimed his baronetcy, he had retained his claim to his family's landed estates in the north of England. His sister-in-law, Lady Alexandra Curzon, known to her friends as Ba-ba, had married Edward's friend and equerry Fruity Metcalfe, and as Mosley's Fascist army got under way, she earned the unkind nickname of Ba-ba Blackshirt—not entirely without cause, for both she and Metcalfe had already begun to show an unhealthy interest in Nazism.

As the bandwagon of Mosley's movement began to roll, it was clear that he had plugged into an ugly side of Britain, as the nation plunged deeper into the economic crisis that had affected Germany and the rest of Europe; there were more than two million people out of work in Britain, and what was happening in the Fascist countries had its appeal to many observers, particularly in the upper classes. Consequently, Mosley and his BUF were attracting a great deal of interest, both overt and clandestine.

Edward fell into the latter category. He could not help becoming aware of it all, bearing in mind the friends who were now encircling him, and this was one aspect of his political interests which would soon be brought to the notice of the British security agencies.

Mosley's theories were based on exactly the same kind of doctrines that had brought Mussolini and Hitler to power, though of course at this stage the full horror of Nazism and Hitler's intent were neither known nor appreciated. He set up his headquarters in London in early 1932, but soon had to move to larger premises as recruits queued to join and dress up in the black-shirted uniforms that had become Mosley's trademark in his emerging bid for power. The BUF's new headquarters, which could hold 5,000 inmates at any one time, would soon be filled with students wanting to learn everything about this new, exciting crusade; its club rooms rang with the laughter and song of men who felt that the advent of Fascism had made life worth living again. Tom Mosley was the supreme leader: his chief of staff was the son of an Admiral, Ian Dundas, and one of his lieutenants was William Joyce—later to become the infamous Lord Haw Haw, and hanged for treason. All members were given a badge with an emblem, identical to that of the Italian Fascists; it was compulsory to wear black shirts when on duty and they all received a membership card extoling the virtues of British Fascism.

In the middle of this rise of British Fascism, there was more than a whiff of scandal surrounding Mosley's personal life. He had been for some time now having an affair with Lady Diana (Mitford) Guinness who quite suddenly left her husband Bryan, a member of the brewing family, and set up home in Eaton Square, purely to make herself available to Mosley whenever he wished to call. She was then twenty-two years old, extremely attractive, and a mother of two children, whom she brought with her to the new house. Cynthia Mosley—Cimmie to her friends—had become aware of her husband's infidelity, but apart from the occasional outburst, had done nothing to try to make him end it. For quite some time, Mosley had, in effect, two wives, although he always insisted he would never leave Cimmie for Diana.

They had a house in the country, a flat in London, and now Diana's house in Eaton Square which Mosley visited often, tapping on the window with his walking stick to signal his arrival. Diana seemed to be under no illusions about her place, and remained apparently content as the "other woman."

In the event, the triangle was resolved tragically. Cimmie died in the spring of the following year from appendicitis. Despite his love for Diana, Mosley's grief at the death of his wife was apparent to all who knew him and for months afterward he threw himself into his work with renewed vigor.

Also Diana's divorce had yet to be finalized, and since her husband had chivalrously agreed to be the guilty party they had to tread warily. She and Mosley continued seeing each other, of course, in spite of a certain hostility from Cimmie's friends, but during that summer, Diana and Unity Mitford got out of the way by traveling to Germany for the first great Nazi rally in Nuremberg, where they began their long and infatuated relationship with Hitler. Although Unity, in particular, was overwhelmed by the little man, Diana was harder, more sensible and political. They came back full of stories of the greatness of the Nazi movement, fully converted to the Nazi concept, as were other members of the family.

When Mosley, in the meantime, took Ba-ba Metcalfe away on a motoring holiday in France, Fruity Metcalfe was not at all happy about his wife's show of affection for her brother-in-law. Indeed, other women in the Mosley family appeared to be steering him toward Ba-ba and away from Diana. Fruity, who was on virtual twenty-four-hour call for the Prince of Wales, naturally became insanely jealous, particularly after he found Mosley walking around the garden with his arm around Ba-ba, rehearsing a forthcoming speech.

At the same time, Ba-ba herself had become the subject of some speculation over her association with Count Dino Grandi, the Italian ambassador to London who was seeking her attentions for more reasons than one. Apart from the obvious connection with Mosley and the tie-up with Mussolini's Fascists, Grandi saw her as a route into the Prince of Wales's circle, which he was quite desperate to join.

The Ba-ba relationship with the count was also important to Mosley. Grandi arranged a personal meeting with Mosley and Mussolini, as a result of which Il Duce sent a £20,000 donation to the BUF in a single payment, one of many, to help fund the British movement. Upon receipt of the money, Grandi wrote to Mussolini in the following terms: "Mosley has entrusted me with expressing his gratitude to you for sending the large sum which I have today arranged to have paid to him. As soon as he got back from Rome, he came to see me; I have never seen him so sure of himself and so confident."

On the romance front, however, Diana Guinness won the day, as she secured Mosley's permanent affections and joined him often at the country house. Ba-ba meantime went off to Nuremberg to another Nazi rally and sent Tom Mosley a picture postcard of Hitler's house.

Ba-ba's good friend Edwina Mountbatten also had an attack of wanderlust and spent many months traveling to all parts of the globe. The birth of the Mountbatten's second daughter Pamela (the first, Patricia, was born in 1924) had done nothing to curb her enthusiasm for travel, or the quest for life and all its experiences.

Nor had the arrival into the Mountbatten household, in the form of occasional visits, of the young Prince Philip of Greece. Philip, later to marry England's future queen, had experienced a traumatic childhood. His parents, Prince Andrew and Princess Alice (Mountbatten's sister), had been rescued from probable execution after being thrown into jail when accused of treason during the Greek revolution. King George V answered the pleas of their family and persuaded his government to send a warship to evacuate the entire Greek royal family to exile in France. As Princess Alice became increasingly eccentric in her habits her husband became increasingly fond of the gay life in Monaco, to which he had absconded. They had very little money and although Alice opened a shop in Paris she gave all the profits away to the Greek refugees who would call upon her, leaving herself and her family just as poor. Finally, Mountbatten, his Uncle Dickie, brought Prince Philip to Britain, where he was shunted from relative to relative, but remained particularly under Mountbatten's wing.

Edwina cared for all her family, but still the children were left in the care of nannies or governesses just as Dickie Mountbatten was left to his own devices, in the Navy or playing polo. Their paths did not often cross. Edwina's adventures at this time took her for long stays in America, then to Mexico, Guatemala, Honduras, and the West Indies, forever searching for pleasure and new and different things to do.

In early 1932, she and Nada went to Germany and then on to a long trip to the Middle East, into Arabia, traveling overland across rough country to Baghdad. They were confronted by hostile nomads and faced arduous and dangerous journeys through mountains and desert. What had driven her to embark on such a vast and perilous journey?

A possible explanation is that she wanted to get away from the attendant publicity to a new and sensational story breaking in Britain about her scandalous life. In May, *The People* newspaper ran a story under the headline "Society Shaken by Terrible Scandal," which went on to say that a "woman highly connected and immensely rich has become involved with a coloured man." The allegation was that they had been "caught in compromising circumstances." Although neither was named in the article, the inference was clear: the man was singer Paul Robeson and the woman, Edwina Mountbatten.

The newspaper went on to say that the woman had been "given the hint to clear out of England for a couple of years to let the affair blow over and the hint comes from a quarter which cannot be ignored." In other words, Buckingham Palace had instructed Edwina to leave the country.

In fact, the Palace had advised the Mountbattens to sue *The People*, even though it would mean they would both have to go to court and stand before judge and jury.

This they did, and so for the first time since the previous Prince of Wales, Edward VII, had given evidence over allegations of cheating at baccarat, royal personages were in a court of law.

Edwina vehemently denied that she had ever met Robeson and she won her case, at a cost to *The People* of £25,000. The truth was that Edwina had long been fascinated by the singer, with his deep bass voice and magnificent physique. Their friendship was widely known in society and many people remember him at Edwina's parties. The figure who suffered most seriously in this trial was not Edwina but Robeson. He was deeply hurt that Edwina could stand up in court and declare that she had never met him, when their relationship had been so close and when he had been invited to her house so frequently. He never got over it.

Mountbatten himself had long since become used to his wife's affairs; in any event his own record of late was not without blemish. For the past two years, he had often been in the company of Noel Coward, and Buckingham Palace viewed with dismay his theatrical friendships. All in all, they were most concerned about the public image of this pair, as indeed they were about most of the Prince of Wales's closest friends, although Mountbatten himself seemed more concerned about the damage the court case might do to his promotion hopes.

Mud sticks; once more the Mountbattens and their marriage were under great strain and subject of more and greater gossip. Edward, knowing their feelings of despair, came to the rescue as best he could, and mustered from the entire royal family a show of public support for his old chum. The Mountbattens were invited to dine at Buckingham Palace the day after *The People* court hearing and Edward threw a dazzling official party for them at York House a couple of days later.

Ernest and Wallis were there, indeed were everywhere the prince went, and the phrase "just the three of us" came into common usage when they were discussed, which was often. Their meetings had been regular since the prince invited the Simpsons to a weekend at the Fort earlier in the year, and ever since he had made a practice of dropping in to Bryanston Court for tea or cocktails and conversations with such modern people as were frequenting the flat. "The talk was witty and crackled with new ideas that were bubbling up furiously in the world of Hitler, Mussolini, Stalin, and the New Deal. Wallis was extraordinarily well informed, her conversation deft and amusing," Edward recalled.

Dickie Mountbatten got wind of what was going on from Freda Dudley Ward. She still saw a fair bit of Edward, but since increasingly he was rejecting her invitations she telephoned Dickie to express her concern. Mountbatten went to see his cousin and took with him a list he had prepared in advance of eighteen eligible European princesses whose ages ranged from fifteen to thirty-two.

"Why don't you get married?" Mountbatten doubtless had in mind the sort of arrangement which had worked for Edward's grandfather. He had mistresses all his life and Queen Alexandra never interfered with his social life; surely the same could work for the present Prince of Wales? At least it was a solution to the growing crisis of having an unmarried heir apparent who was showing absolutely no sign of choosing a wife, or a suitable companion to be his queen, or of starting a family to continue the direct line of descent.

Such an arrangement, as a last resort, must be considered: this way the prince would have his cake and eat it. He could have affairs, on the quiet, with Thelma, Freda, Wallis, or whomever he liked, provided he had a wife sitting beside him who would become queen. Edward, however, dismissed the scheme and the princesses out of hand.

So there it rested. The Mountbatten plan, which could have saved Britain from its greatest constitutional crisis of the century, was shelved forever, never to be mentioned again.

From there on, the liaison between Edward and Mrs. Simpson gathered pace. Everyone could see what was going on: a courtship under the very nose of her existing husband. Before long, Wallis had eliminated all other contenders for the prince's affections, including his male chums. Thelma and Freda were ditched quite dramatically. Chips Channon wrote in his journal, "It is a war to the knife between the past and the present."

Thelma went first. She had been away on a trip to America and news of her activities there had reached Edward's ears before she returned to London. Upon her arrival back he came straight out with it. "I hear you've been seeing the Aly Khan." He accused her of having an affair, which she denied. All that had happened, she maintained, was that they dined once or twice together in New York, and she was surprised to discover that he was booked on the same cruise home across the Atlantic. A couple of nights later, she was invited to a dinner at the Fort for the coup de grâce. The Simpsons were there and Edward seated Wallis next to himself. Thelma recalled, "Wallis looked me in the eye and a defiant cold glance told me the whole story." The next morning Thelma packed her bags and left.

Freda's good-bye was just as cruel, but Edward couldn't face her to tell her himself. She had been in London at the bedside of a sick daughter and when the child recovered she rang York House, as she had done countless times before, to speak to him. The servant who answered the phone could merely tell her, most apologetically, that he had orders not to put her through. So soft, gentle Freda, whose friendship with Edward went back to 1918 and those rough times at the end of the war, was no longer needed to smooth the selfish brat's brow.

Word soon got around. Thelma is out. Freda is out. The socialites who surrounded the prince were quick to respond to his new love: invitations came thick and fast. Chips Channon recorded some of the encounters as the London season of 1934 began. "Emerald Cunard had a dinner party last night for Diana Cooper . . . and at 11.30 the doorbell rang and there was the Prince of Wales with Mr. and Mrs. Simpson. It was an impromptu visit, the Prince was as charming as only he can be sometimes, and now is so rarely. He took them all out to the Embassy for supper." And in May, he wrote, "We went to the opera and were joined in Emerald's box by the Prince of Wales and Menage Simpson. I was most interested to see what an extraordinary hold she has over the Prince. At the interval she told him to hurry . . . and she made him take a cigar out of his breast pocket."

Wallis herself could hardly believe that at that point she was any more than a brief encounter for the prince, a passing phase in his life, or another toy that the spoilt child wanted. But as the weeks of early 1934 came and went she began to realize that there could be something more. She grasped firmly at the opportunity, regardless of Ernest. As far as she was concerned, he was there to fall back on if nothing came of her blossoming romance with the prince. Was it at all conceivable that she could take a more permanent role in his life? Was it possible that she could even become queen?

She would have known from her gentle probing among her friends for information that the guilty party in a divorce was still not permitted at court, and that the Royal Marriages Act prevented the prince from marrying whom he pleased, unless he gave up his title to succession. Undeterred, however, Wallis began to become more and more part of his life, which was, after all, what he wanted. Socially she was always around, usually with Ernest somewhere close, and by the middle of the year she had virtually taken over the running of the Fort, where she and Ernest were spending most weekends. The staff didn't care for her at all. Whereas Thelma had been kind and smiling and brought them presents, Wallis was cold and piercing, while if she passed any of them in the corridor or hall she would stare ahead unflinchingly without any acknowledgement of their presence. She also encouraged the prince in his increasingly grumpy attitude toward them, which arose from the suddenly acquired notion that they were all spying on him, since so much gossip about the happenings at the Fort was filtering back to Buckingham Palace.

After Wallis had also installed her own wardrobe at the Fort, Lady Diana Cooper reported back to the gang, after spending a weekend there, that as well as having become the mistress of the house, she was glittering and more stunning than she had ever seen her, with lots of new clothes and simply dripping with new jewels, which she assumed could not possibly have been bought by Ernest, who was by now almost penniless.

During the summer, the blossoming romance moved a stage further, when Edward invited the Simpsons to join him on holiday in France. Ernest said he could not go because of business appointments; Wallis said she would not dream of missing it and asked her Aunt Bessie to supply some respectability to such an obviously precarious situation by acting as chaperone. The party went first to Biarritz, then on to the South of France by sea, in an aging steamer which the prince had chartered. In Cannes, after rough seas on the way down, it became a truly romantic holiday; balmy days and moonlit nights. Aunt Bessie grew increasingly worried that the prince's attention to her niece was more than just a platonic, pleasant friendship.

But even amid the growing fascination with Mrs. Simp-

son, the Prince of Wales had not ruled out the occasional
dalliance with other women, it seems. Indeed, if anything his interest had been aroused by his association
with Wallis, and he once spoke vaguely of a spot of bother
involving a Swedish woman around this time but would
not be pressed on the "bother." In September 1934, he
left Wallis and his friends to return at their leisure from
France. He flew back to attend the launching of the *Queen
Mary* and other public engagements. It was toward the
end of the month, and with Wallis out of the way, it is
said, that he had a brief encounter with a past friend.
According to one story told to the author, he went looking
for his old flame Freda Dudley Ward but she would not
see him. Instead, he met her sister Vera Seely whom he
had known almost as long and who was once herself
extremely fond of him. After their reunion, the story
goes, she would be left carrying his child. Nine months
later her son Timothy Ward Seely would be born.

There always have been many claimants to the illegitimate fatherhood of the Prince of Wales over the years,
and when he heard this story, the author treated it with
similar scepticism to the rest. I had been told it on the
gossipy hunting fields of Leicestershire and Nottinghamshire. One woman even wrote to me offering to deposit the name of the person she "knew" to be Edward's
son with a local solicitor. Her information also produced
the name of Tim Seely, and certainly when I first saw
him myself I was stunned by the likeness to the Prince
of Wales. His family's royal connections, I would soon
discover, had extended over many years. Apart from the
prince's friendship with Freda Dudley Ward, Edward
was also best man at the wedding of her sister Vera to
Frank James "Jimmy" Wriothesley Seely at St. Mary's,
Nottingham, on February 5, 1925. He would also become
godfather to the Seely's second child, a daughter named
Elzima (now dead).

Jimmy Seely and the prince had become good friends
on the hunting field, and their daring exploits at the head

of the pack became the talk of the Quorn and Belvoir. The young prince would also become a frequent guest at the Seely's home, Brick House, in Radcliffe on Trent, Nottinghamshire, and their eldest son, Michael, would recall coming home to find both the Prince of Wales and the Duke of York (later King George VI) in their parlor, two future kings under their roof at the same time. The Seelys were then a moderately wealthy family, having owned a lace-making factory and then, more productively, eight coal pits. Jimmy Seely thought he would become a millionaire from the mining profits and spent his gains accordingly; but he failed to account for nationalization, which would take away his coal and his land without proper compensation. He bought a 1,500-acre estate at Arnold, Nottinghamshire, where the eldest son still lives.

Vera Seely was very fond of Edward in her youth. Indeed, it is not uncommon for younger sisters to fall in love with their elder sisters' boyfriends, and at some point prior to her marriage Vera may have felt she was more entitled to Edward's affections, since Freda was already married.

At any rate, with this information, it did not seem beyond the bounds of possibility that Edward, with new sexual confidence as his involvement with Wallis developed, returned that September day in 1934 for a passing affair with Vera Seely.

Eventually, there would be rumor on the hunting fields that Vera had indeed given birth to the prince's child, and that rumor would be fueled in years to come by Tim Seely's likeness to him. I had to put it to the family, finally, and was surprised by the somewhat relaxed response to the question: Is the Prince of Wales Tim Seely's father? The eldest son, Michael, replied, "Of course we have heard the rumour but it was never confirmed to me by my mother. She was a very beautiful and romantic person and dearly loved His Royal Highness in her youth."

Tim Seely himself is an enigmatic character who broke the mold of the family's landed traditions. After leaving

Eton, he went to the Royal Academy of Dramatic Art to train as an actor. He retained however his passion for horses and hunting and to this day rides regularly in Nottinghamshire and Yorkshire. He has also ridden frequently with the present Prince of Wales, Prince Charles. I spoke to Tim about his origins, which according to his birth certificate show he is the son of Vera and Jimmy Seely. But he admitted: "This rumour of my likeness to the Prince of Wales is something I have lived with all of my life. I have no evidence of him being my father and frankly I just do not know."

It is for everyone who sees him, however, an intriguing and fascinating first few minutes, peering into a face with such an obvious likeness and with so many similar characteristics.

But Wallis would soon secure the position as the only woman in the prince's life. When she returned from France there was no stopping her, and Ernest knew the time had come to think of other things. In November Wallis was presented at court again, having been invited with her husband by the prince to a reception prior to the wedding of Edward's brother George, the Duke of Kent, to Princess Marina of Greece.

Edward took the opportunity of presenting Wallis to his mother. "This is a great friend of mine," he said, bowing toward Mrs. Simpson. The queen touched her hand and in a clear gesture of dismissal moved immediately to speak to another guest, but over the winter months Edward introduced her to his brothers, and it became clear to anyone who knew that Wallis was assuming a dangerous importance in Edward's life.

He had secretly taken her out to the Mediterranean on at least two occasions, and she was there introduced to Dickie Mountbatten whose ship, HMS *Wishart*, had become something of an entertainment center on special occasions, not to mention the best-performing naval unit in the Med. As he pushed his career forward with considerable vigor, men responded to his strict discipline and emulated his own great effort to succeed. When they did well, he rewarded them and there was plenty of fun for all. Noel Coward, who loved to be among sailors, was a regular visitor, and once after a grueling regatta which the *Wishart* had won, the men returned to the ship to find the captain's guest had prepared an abundance of dry martinis, while the ship's band, trained by Peter Murphy, was on hand to accompany the entertainer and lead the singsongs. Those with particularly sore bottoms after the race found the captain had prepared a special soothing grease that could be applied to tender places.

When Mountbatten first encountered Wallis on a Mediterranean visit, the two eyed each other cautiously. Here together were the two people the prince had been closest to in his entire life, and Mountbatten was slightly nervous about how they would get on. Like many others in the charmed circle, he would muse over what hold Mrs. Simpson had over his cousin; what was it that she had in her makeup that made her stand out, in the eyes of the prince, above all others. A friend and confidant of both, one who knew them for many years, described her to the author as a woman who had a unique ability, almost as if trained in the art, to make men feel at ease and to attend to them in a way that was unpatronizing yet extremely caring. "When the Prince moved to the Fort, his greatest love and passion became his garden," their friend said.

> He knew the names of every tree, every shrub and every seedling he planted. Wallis took the trouble to learn about it too, and would spend hours with him in that most beautiful of gardens.
>
> More than that, she was a great manager of people, the ideal hostess, the best party organiser, the most proficient and imaginative cook, the best planner of the seating arrangements at dinner and placing the right people next to each other.
>
> She observed closely the Prince's likes and dislikes. She noticed what annoyed him, or saw when people were

getting on his nerves and had that ability to shut them up. If the conversation flagged, she could instantly revive it; if it was leading in a direction she knew would displease him, she could expertly turn it.

She knew that for his entire life his every need had been looked after; whenever he travelled, his valet would go on ahead to place his own sheets, his own photographs, his own towels and toiletries in a hotel or house in which he might be staying. Wallis, as she began to involve herself in more and more of his life, arranged everything. He idolised her for it, and in the end, could not do without her.

She was not a particularly sexual woman, outwardly, but there is no question that Mrs. Simpson led the prince into sexual experiences he had never before encountered. Their friend again:

I was at a house party at the Fort that night which I believe was the first time they slept together [although the prince subsequently sued an author who suggested that they had made love before they were married and before Mrs. Simpson's divorce from Ernest]. It was a very lively evening, with a great deal of conversation and jollity at dinner and then, as usual afterwards, the carpet was rolled back and the gramophone turned on. Ernest was feeling unwell. He had a large boil on the back of his neck. Since it was giving him a great deal of pain and discomfort he decided to go to bed. The party went on until around 2 A.M. I suppose, and those who were travelling left, and as a house guest I retired to my bedroom. I do know that that night, David went to Wallis's room, which was separate from Ernest's, and spent the rest of the night there. Believe me, it was the talk of the servants' quarters the following morning, and David came down beaming like the proverbial cat that had got the cream.

Those of us who knew him well enough could see

that he, and all of us, were heading for trouble. The man whom I admired so much and who I regarded as my King until the day of Queen Elizabeth's coronation, was going to destroy his great heritage. We could see it happening before our eyes, and those of us who attempted to offer words of caution were, I am afraid, brushed aside. He was blinded and astounded by her, and nothing could move him from the path he was taking. He believed, in his distorted thoughts, that he could make everything work out in a way that would suit everyone; that he could take Mrs Simpson as his wife and she would sit beside him when he became King.

That was how the infatuation with her had taken over his thoughts. I think sometimes he did allow himself to consider the worst, that he would be prevented from marrying her. And I think that in those moments he had decided, long before the abdication, that he would quit his Royal life for her. Sad, but true.

·FIVE·

THE NAZI CABAL

Freda Dudley Ward, though holding no rancor toward Wallis Simpson, would say later she thought Wallis had got Edward by witchcraft. In words that were remarkably similar to those of Dorothea Simpson when Wallis went off with Ernest, Freda said, "I blame him for nothing. He was a doomed character." In his own recollection of the period, Edward himself wrote, "I was in my fortieth year, the outermost limits of my youth . . . I had sown my wild oats, a fairly meagre planting, and my hope was to put down roots . . . but something was still lacking . . . a partner to share my life. Presently, I began to cherish a hope that this might be taken care of too." He seemed at that point to have settled on Mrs. Simpson, come what may.

That autumn in 1934 the king announced the engagement of Edward's youngest brother, Prince George, who would be given the title Duke of Kent before his marriage to Princess Marina of Greece.

George had also sowed his wild oats aplenty, and marriage would not stop him. His associations with Noel Coward and other entertainers in the twenties had given way to friendships with less celebrated youngsters in society. "George loved to be loved," said a former palace equerry. "He had more brains than any of his brothers and more taste . . . but he was a scamp. He was always in trouble with girls. Scotland Yard chased so many of them out of the country that the palace stopped counting."

An American girl with whom he had had an affair two years earlier had introduced him to drugs for the first time, and as his engagement to Marina was being announced, he was still addicted. He had been encouraged in this addiction by a young man from South America, whom the Prince of Wales sent for and personally dispatched from the shores of Britain to Paris with a suitable payment.

Since the youngest prince's wedding was set for November, the king and queen required names from their offspring for the guest list for a reception two days before the wedding. Edward had put down the Simpsons, whom the king promptly crossed off. Edward protested to his parents: "The Simpsons are remarkably nice and if I cannot be allowed to invite my friends, then I will not come either." The king relented and Wallis on that night made a sparkling entrance to a gala of European royalty, diplomats, and influential government figures, in addition to the social cream of London. On her wrist, she wore a stunning bracelet the prince had given her, and Princess Marina's brother, Prince Paul of Greece, told her "You are wearing the most striking gown."

Ernest Simpson looked on with apparent embarrassment, knowing full well that his wife stood there glowing in a gown and accessories paid for by Edward, who was taking compensation by booking almost every dance, leaving Ernest to stand alone for long periods.

For the first time in her life, Wallis was seeing royalty in full flow; she also came face to face with the woman who would become her greatest adversary, Elizabeth, Duchess of York. Dowager Lady Hardinge of Penshurst recalled the meeting: "Mrs. Simpson went down badly with the duchess from the word go. It may have been that ostentatious dress she was wearing, or the fact that she had allowed the Prince of Wales to push her forward in the most undignified manner. The duchess was never discourteous, but you could always tell when she did not care for someone and it was very apparent to me she did not care for Mrs. Simpson at all."

After Prince George's marriage, Mountbatten was the only member of Edward's family who remained a regular visitor at the Fort. Dickie Mountbatten may well have found himself in a difficult position in regard to giving advice over his cousin's obvious attentions to Mrs. Simpson. It would have been a case of the pot calling the kettle black. Edwina's continuing adventures were the talk of the Mediterranean fleet. She rarely stayed at the Malta villa long. She would suddenly rush off to Paris or Rome or Cannes, and there were long periods of absence when she would take off, quite without warning, to America, leaving the children in the care of the nannies, and Dickie to continue his career.

There were new rumors about her associations, and one name mentioned was the Prince of Wales's friend, Hugh, Earl of Sefton. They were seen dining often, and at times they were joined by her husband's cousin, Prince George, and his current lady friend. Her public humiliation of Dickie had not diminished. Edwina, having entered what her friends called her "black period," spent a great deal of time in Harlem, New York, which she said had become her "spiritual home." There was lots of gossip about her, and whenever she was in the company of Mountbatten, the difficult atmosphere between them was now hard to conceal from their friends.

She would turn up for official engagements and be at his side for the Navy parties; then she would be off again like a bee in search of honey. What a lot of talk the prince's little gang provided for the dining tables of aristocracy throughout the country, in the nightclubs, and at the parties! Yes, the elite of British society were chattering away.

Though Mountbatten retained an apprehensive regard for Mrs. Simpson, there always remained a gulf between them that he could never cross. He recalled: "I made friends with the lady to help influence him in the right direction." What that meant might have seemed obscure to those outside a close court circle. Influence? Right direction?

Edward, his head turned by Mrs. Simpson, was beginning to talk and act in public with some kind of new vision and a confidence never seen before. He had shown a particular interest in the developments in Germany during the past year as Hitler had come to power, enforced a one-party state, and disbanded all trade unions. Edward had corresponded at length with Tom Mosley about Fascism, among other things, and they continued a steady correspondence up to and after abdication.

In the prince's circle there was much talk of the Mosley phenomenon. Where, for instance, was the money coming from to finance the extravagances of the Blackshirt organization? The banners, the meeting halls, the pomp of the parades were not cheap to stage, and the remnants of the New Party Fund to which people like Lord Nuffield and Lord Rothermere and many others had contributed were long exhausted.

Although Mosley would deny that he was receiving funds from abroad, the true facts were that money was coming in almost weekly. While some was channeled through Swiss bank accounts, other finance was being channeled into a secret BUF bank account in Paris, not just from Mussolini, but also from prominent people in England who wished their donations to remain anonymous. Further, Count Grandi was also handing direct to Mosley bundles of cash in small denominations of various currencies which were delivered in "most secret and personal" packets for the Fascist leader. These payments had long been suspected by Ba-ba Metcalfe, who more than anyone in London society was a confidante of Count Grandi, and it is therefore inconceivable that discussion in this incestuous circle of Mosley's Italian connection should be kept from the Prince of Wales. And if even a hint of it were known to him, his intervention in any discussion of Italian relations at government level must be highly suspect. But, as we will see, intervention came swiftly once he had ascended the throne.

Other highly placed associates were giving support to Mosley at this time. Lord Rothermere had thrown the weight of his entire newspaper operation behind him and was making high-flown statements about the BUF, which he saw as a pointer to the way that Conservative policies in Britain should be heading. His national newspapers carried headlines like "Support the Blackshirts," and "The Blackshirts Will Stop War." They were, said Rothermere, the only force in Britain working for national discipline.

All the time, the Blackshirts were becoming more and more like their Nazi counterparts in Germany; in towns and cities where they held their rallies, the flamboyant banner parades attracted wide attention and had considerable appeal to the downtrodden masses. They shouted "Hail, Mosley," like "*Heil*, Hitler," and held out their arms in the same salute. William Joyce had introduced anti-Semitic Jew-baiting into his speeches which Mosley made no attempt to stop—and indeed would subsequently copy. These two were the key BUF speakers, and they whipped up fervor wherever they went.

Edward found himself strangely in tune with what they were saying. From the basis of a caring, socialist ideal that would end poverty for all time emerged the violent fascist doctrine and the rantings of hooligans who wanted to dominate the world. The sinister tones of racism and anti-Semitism, and the outright thuggery meted out by the Blackshirts, were things now appearing in Britain in a slavish copying of what was happening in Germany. Joyce in particular had become outrageously anti-Jewish and the turning point for Mosley to throw the BUF wholeheartedly behind these policies seems to have come at the time when he hired London's Olympia in June 1934 for the biggest Fascist rally ever staged in London.

Here Mosley and the British Fascists were shown in their true light, if what had gone before had not been enough. Interrupters at this meeting were pounced upon by the Blackshirts and beaten to the floor; violence reigned and the overwhelming strength of the Blackshirts won the day. Mosley faced a torrent of criticism and abuse, but it did not daunt him one bit. He blamed the Jews and Communists for trying to wreck his meetings and claimed they deserved all they got. If anything, this rally stirred him to greater ambitions. He fervently believed that power would eventually come to him, whether achieved by democratic means or, if necessary, by force. Force, he had shown that day, could win.

It was at this point that Lord Rothermere came to his senses and began to tone down his newspapers' support of Mosley, though he did not withdraw it completely. Yet in spite of what was happening, there were many influential people close to royalty and government leaders who believed that Britain should strive for a peaceful coexistence with Germany, even if that meant Hitler's being allowed to break out of the confines of the armament and boundary treaties negotiated after the Great War.

There were also various influences closing in around the Prince of Wales in an orchestrated effort to foster his personal friendship with the regimes of Germany and Italy, which Lord Rothermere still believed were a model for the rebuilding of Britain. Winston Churchill, in his wilderness years, was almost a lone voice in Parliament who warned of the need for Britain to rearm and to take the German menace seriously. But the Prince of Wales, though a great friend of Churchill, was siding with the pro-Germans, while among those who were influencing him in that direction was Wallis Simpson herself. Her recent association with Joachim von Ribbentrop, a rising star of the Third Reich, had already been noted by MI5.

Ribbentrop, typically arrogant, with an exceedingly dull wife and posing as a champagne salesman, had already made inroads into London society and in particular into the prince's circle. That had always been his aim. Hitler had sent him to London specifically to promote Anglo-German relations, and he was darting back and forth with extreme regularity. In Berlin, he was intriguing for power alongside Hess, Bormann, Goebbels, Ley, Himmler, and Göring, while in London, he jostled for position close to the Prince of Wales. Emerald Cunard introduced him to many of Edward's friends and he became a regular at cocktail parties, dinners, and country-house gatherings.

There were many other suspicions harbored about the extent of Mrs. Simpson's links with the Nazis. Prime Minister Stanley Baldwin had been given a security report which is said to have shown that Wallis had for some time been in contact with German Monarchist circles, who had contacted her quite independently of Ribbentrop. Through these Monarchist connections, she is said to have been invited to the German embassy, and on a number of occasions had even stayed the night there. The Germans were extremely anxious to court her and please her—and, ultimately, the prince, and they had made contact with her almost from the beginning of her relationship with the prince.

The Monarchist circles referred to could well have meant Wallis's friendship with the Bismarcks—Prince Otto von Bismarck and his beautiful wife, Princess Ann-Marie. He was attached to the German embassy in London and they had befriended Wallis, whom both thought was charming and amusing. Wallis and the princess would remain firm friends throughout their lives. Edward and Wallis dined with the Bismarcks at the German embassy at lavish parties hosted by the German ambassador, Leopold von Hoesch. Indeed, the first occasion provided the Germans with an embarrassing moment regarding protocol. The initial guest list did not include

Wallis, and Edward telephoned Hoesch and asked him to invite Mrs. Simpson. After consulting Berlin, he did so willingly.

There were other invitations too, some from the Bismarcks, others to superb parties at the elegant Carlton Terrace home of Hoesch, which he had refurbished in the highest and most expensive taste with the design assistance of Albert Speer. These parties were not infrequent. The ambassador, whose London posting was recognized by Berlin as one of their most important, was provided with the resources to entertain the British aristocracy in a manner and style that would enhance their view of the Third Reich. The flattery of influential people, and the Prince of Wales and Mrs. Simpson in particular, became a matter of prime importance. Ribbentrop was even given to sending Mrs. Simpson red roses without reason. The various Fascist influences surrounding the Prince of Wales were beginning to build up. Indeed, captured German documents would indicate that the prince's sympathies toward Hitler's Third Reich had already been molded to a dangerous degree by the start of 1935. The German ambassador reported to the Führer in April that year that the prince had been critical of the British government's stance in Anglo-German talks which Hitler hoped would give him greater flexibility in his ambitions. Hoesch reported further:

> The fact that he [the prince] had come to realise the reprehensible character of clashes of arms . . . by no means meant he was a pacifist. Far from it . . . and he understood very well that the Reich Government and the German people were inspired by a similar desire.
>
> He fully understood that Germany wished to face other nations squarely, her head high, relying on her strength and conscious that Germany's word counted as much in the world as that of other nations. I told the Prince that what he had just said corresponded with the opinion of our Führer.

In addition to private conversations he was having with German officials, the prince was similarly indiscreet in public. Earlier in the year, the British Legion had approached him, as their patron, to attend their annual conference and at the same time had spoken to the Lord Privy Seal, Anthony Eden, about the possibility of a delegation from the BL visiting Germany. While Eden warned that the visit might be used by both sides for propaganda purposes, in the main he did not see there could be any objections. In June, at the Legion's conference, the Prince of Wales, though aware of the delicate situation regarding the Legion's plans, spoke strongly in favor: "I feel that there could be no more suitable body or organization of men to stretch forth the hand of friendship to the Germans than we ex-servicemen who fought them and have now forgotten all about it and the Great War."

Just as Eden had said, the propagandists pounced on the speech immediately. In Germany, the Goebbels machine went into operation and the headlines spelled out: "The British Friendly Hand—An Appreciative Gesture by the Heir Apparent." The Berlin *Morning Post* commented that the declaration by the Prince of Wales "is regarded in Germany as being the seal to the friendship agreement between the two countries."

Edward was immediately summoned by the king and severely reprimanded, doubtless at the instigation of the cabinet. Not only were the views he expressed contrary at that time to government policy, but the prince had no right to involve himself in political issues and certainly not without first seeking the approval of the prime minister.

While the prince's controversial remarks had come at a critical and embarrassing time for his government, they couldn't have come at a better time for the Germans; in fact, for them they were heaven-sent. Only a week earlier, discussion had begun in London of the naval treaty in which Germany was seeking to extend the limits on her air and sea armaments. Ribbentrop led the German delegation and angered the British straight away with his excessive demands. The discussions would continue for some time, but in the middle of this diplomatic activity came the prince's address to the Legion.

There were further troubles on the foreign front for the British government during that month. The Italians were on the point of invading Abyssinia, and Anthony Eden had flown to Rome for talks with Mussolini in an effort to resolve what had become an extremely tense situation which threatened to explode in Eden's face. It wasn't long after that the Prince of Wales decided to make plans for his summer holidays, and suddenly announced to the king that he intended to go cruising off the coast of Italy. "Don't you ever read the papers?" the king stormed. Once more, the prince had showed his favor toward the Mussolini Fascists.

Despite the king's protestations, Edward and Mrs. Simpson sauntered off into Europe once again for their holidays in 1935, using the alias of Lord Chester, which fooled no one. His intentions were twofold: to get Mrs. Simpson away from the prying eyes of his enemies in Buckingham Palace; and to dabble in a remarkably open manner in a finely balanced political situation which he felt, through his Italian connection, he could influence.

They headed first by rail to Cannes where they partied, swam, and holidayed. By September they had moved to the Duke of Westminster's yacht off Corsica. From there, they went to Budapest, stopping briefly to meet political contacts in Switzerland. The following day, Hitler made his most outrageous anti-Jewish speech yet during the Nuremberg rally which had attracted the presence of several of the prince's aristocratic associates from London.

In Budapest, the prince—allegedly on holiday—had meetings and lunches with leading government figures and, out of earshot of his annoying ministers, was able to say exactly what he damn well pleased about the international tension now mounting minute by minute.

From Hungary, he and Wallis moved to Vienna, Munich, and finally to Paris. It was no coincidence, either, that they were lunched there by Armand Gregoire, a lawyer and Nazi spy, the man who would become Mosley's banker in Paris. Through Gregoire, thousands of pounds were collected in various currencies to finance the BUF. Gregoire received cash from high places in England and from Mussolini. Starting in 1936, he would be used by Hitler to channel funds toward Mosley. He was an evil collaborator and a link man between covert alliances. Wallis hired him as her lawyer in Paris and Ernest had used him on shipping business. The links, as we shall see, would deepen.

On that visit also, the prince was—with Wallis at his side—at a luncheon at the British embassy given by Sir George Clark for the premier of France, Pierre Laval. It was indeed a scandalous situation: the Prince of Wales, with his mistress, was lunching with a man who was a sworn enemy of Britain and talking openly and seriously about major political affairs. At his trial after the war, Laval would state that during that luncheon, Edward spoke totally in support of Laval's pact with Mussolini, which, as far as the French were concerned, gave him carte blanche to invade Abyssinia.

There were further meetings between Edward and Laval at which Wallis and Madame Laval were sometimes present, and there could be no doubt, Laval would say, where the prince's enthusiasms lay. He supported Mussolini to the hilt.

Two months after Edward's meetings with Laval, his old friend, the British foreign secretary Sir Samuel Hoare, accepted what became known as the Hoare–Laval pact for ending the Abyssinian war. They suggested that two-thirds of the territory of Abyssinia should go to Italy, while the rump of the Abyssinian empire would receive a corridor to the sea. When details of the plan were revealed in the French press, there was uproar in Britain. Hoare was sacked, and Anthony Eden became foreign secretary. The damage to Baldwin and the League of Nations would be permanent, and Baldwin was well aware that in the background to it all, he could lay much of the blame at the door of the Prince of Wales and his meddling mistress Wallis Simpson.

That year 1935 had slipped by and most of Edward's spare time had been spent in the company of Wallis. When, in May, the Simpsons were at Buckingham Palace for the Silver Jubilee State Ball, Wallis danced for most of the evening with the prince once again, in full view of the king and queen. "As David and I danced past," she wrote. "I thought I felt the King's eyes searchingly upon me. Something in his look made me feel all this graciousness and pageantry were but the glittering tip of the iceberg that extended into unseen depths that I could never plumb."

The king, the following day, raged once more that his son had invited such an unsuitable person into the Palace. "In my home," he kept saying, "in my home." Before that outburst, Edward was already contemplating telling his father of the seriousness of his relationship with Mrs. Simpson. Her total domination of him was clear to see; in August he took her away on a Mediterranean cruise without Ernest, and in his absence Dr. Cosmo Lang joined the king at Balmoral for a "long and intimate talk" about Edward's current obsession.

Lang confided: "The King believes that this affair is more serious than the others. This is what is worrying him." It worried Ernest too. He had gone to Washington and would seek Aunt Bessie Merryman's advice. "No woman," she told him, "could possibly resist the attentions the Prince is paying Wallis . . . there is no possible outcome except unhappiness for the three of you."

Edward and Wallis returned to an apprehensive circle awash with gossip and rumor. He seemed unaffected by it and was in high spirits at a party at Bryanston Court, where he was to be found wearing a German helmet and goose-stepping around the living room.

In his memoirs, he wrote that throughout the latter part of 1935, he intended to tell his father of his feelings, perhaps removing himself from the line of succession to the throne to pursue his ambitions toward her. He had formed in his mind a plan to present his position to the king, though King George's biographer, Sir John Wheeler-Bennett, doubted that he ever had the courage to do so. Mountbatten disagreed. "He would have mustered the courage if the King had lasted one more year . . . then he could retire from the succession and leave the Duke of York in the sidelines to take over." But as it happened, he did not have a chance to do any of the things he had planned.

In November, there was his brother Harry's wedding to Lady Alice Scott. Then came a general election, in which Stanley Baldwin returned as prime minister. On the day the House of Commons was due to reassemble, however, the king's sister, Princess Victoria, died, and the formal opening of Parliament was canceled.

Events moved quickly. The king canceled all engagements and went into mourning for his sister. He caught a chill and retired to Sandringham for Christmas. His health went into rapid decline, with a recurrence of the chest problems that had been troubling him for some time. Edward went to London to tell Stanley Baldwin of the situation and to warn him that the king was not expected to last. Baldwin, while duly sympathetic, in addition was very upset that the death of his cousin, Rudyard Kipling, "a great Englishman," seemed to have gone largely unnoticed in the welter of press attention to the king's health. The following day, January 20, 1936, George V died shortly before midnight and Edward, Prince of Wales, became King Edward VIII.

Years later, Edward recalled the events leading to King George's death to his friend the Duke de Grantmesnil:

I had been down at Windsor for a day's shooting when
a rider came bearing a message from my mother. She
suggested I propose myself for Sandringham. When I
arrived, his physician, Lord Dawson, was present and
escorted me to the King's bedroom; he was slipping in
and out of consciousness and Dawson said there was little
hope.

Later that evening, after dinner, Dawson came in to
see my mother and myself and said to both of us, "You
would not wish him to endure any undue suffering?"
My mother said that we did not and I concurred; only
very much later, as I reflected upon the situation, did
it occur to me that Dawson intended to ease my father's
departure from this earth. I was truly horrified when
I discovered that Dawson had administered not one but
two lethal injections. It was certainly not my intention
to give him such authorisation when I agreed that my
father should not be subjected to a great deal of suffering.

Lord Dawson's notes of that night indicated that he
injected the king with three-fourths of a gram of morphia
and shortly afterward one gram of cocaine into the dis-
tended jugular vein. "Intervals between respirations
lengthened and life passed so quietly and gently that it
was difficult to determine the actual moment," Dawson
wrote.

From those notes it was clear that Dawson did not
inject to relieve the king's pain—he was already in a
comatose state for much of the time—and the action
could therefore be seen merely as a shortening of the
king's life. Further, Edward's own view that his mother
was aware of what Dawson intended is borne out by the
physician's additional notes, which stated that it would
also ensure that news of the king's death should receive
"its first announcement in the morning papers rather than
the less appropriate field of the evening journals," a statement which sounded exactly as if coming from the mouth

of Queen Mary herself. "Effectively, Dawson murdered my father." Edward said in recollection.

The monarchy then moved into a new and dramatic phase. The old king had written in his diary, "When I am gone, he will ruin himself within a year." It would not take quite that long. Everyone around him could see disaster ahead and it became a favorite topic at parties, trying to predict what would happen now that Edward was at Buckingham Palace. His friend Chips Channon wrote in his diary for that day, "My heart goes out to him. He will mind so terribly being King. His loneliness, his seclusion, his isolation will be almost more than his highly strung and unimaginative nature can bear. Never has a man been so in love . . . how will they rearrange their lives, these people?"

On January 28, King George's body was taken from Westminster, where it had been lying in state, for burial at Windsor. On the day of the funeral, Edward had arranged for Mrs. Simpson and her friends to take part of St. James's Palace to watch the procession. Edward slow-marched before the coffin, head bowed, a few paces ahead of his brothers and the remainder of the funeral party. As they came to St. James's, he looked up at the window, his eyes seeking those of Mrs. Simpson. Even as he was burying his father his thoughts flickered to her.

Stanley Baldwin, farther back in the procession, was doubtless thinking about the problems that faced him, now that Edward was king. Charles, the Duke of Coburg, was there, ready to take advantage of the new opportunity now emerging. Hitler had already given instructions that the new king should be coaxed into the strongest possible friendship with Germany. It was an incredible situation.

For the new monarch to show any sign of favor to Germany and the Nazis would be quite outrageous, since it would indicate Britain's support for the dastardly happenings unfolding at the hands of the Third Reich. On the day before the old king died, the Duke of Coburg

had made contact with Edward, telling him that he would
be Hitler's personal emissary to the palace and that the
Führer was anxious for friendly relations. It would be
the first of several meetings Coburg would have with the
king, minutes of which were sent direct to Hitler, suitably embellished, where necessary, in Germany's favor.
Among the quotations noted in the interviews on the
question of friendship with Germany, Edward is pur-
ported to have said: "Who is King here, Baldwin or I? I
wish to talk to Hitler and will do so here or in Germany.
Tell him that, please."

The king could not have been unaware of Coburg's
true affiliations. During the First World War, the duke
had suffered the shame of being taken off the role of
British Peerage and having his Order of the Garter removed because he sided with Germany and not his British homeland. In the late twenties and early thirties he
moved into every area of Nazism that was springing up
in Germany, including the Brownshirts in which he played
a major role. So when Hitler was seeking the personnel
to spread the word of friendship in Britain, Coburg was
an obvious choice. Although he had been stripped of his
British status, he had by now made himself acceptable
in London social circles, even though his membership
in the Nazi party was well known.

In his reports back to Hitler, Coburg wrote of the
king's observations during their meetings in "carrying
out the Führer's commission." The remarks he attributed to Edward during these conversations included the
following: "An alliance between Germany and Britain is
[for the king] an urgent necessity and a guiding principle
for British foreign policy. The League of Nations is a
farce . . ." Coburg also claimed in his report that the
king is

> resolved to concentrate the business of government on
> himself. For England, not too easy. The general political
> situation, especially the situation of England herself, will

perhaps give him a chance. His sincere resolve to bring Germany and England together would be made more difficult if it were made public too early. For this reason, I regard it as most important to respect the King's wish that the non-official policy of Germany towards England should be firmly concentrated in one hand and at the same time brought into relations of confidence with the official policy.

The King asked me to visit him frequently in order that confidential matters might be more speedily clarified in this way. I promised—subject to the Führer's approval—to fly to London at any time he wished.

When the Coburg documents were eventually discovered after the war, Edward—by then Duke of Windsor—denied he had ever said such things. There was, however, evidence from many other sources, revealed only in later years, that would give support to the view that it was quite likely he expressed opinions which could be taken in this manner. He had had, for example, many similar conversations with Lord Mount Temple who formed the Anglo-German Fellowship and became its president in 1935. Coburg was president of the fellowship in 1936, and like the duke, Mount Temple was given to long eulogies about the Germans, despite the fact he had two half-Jewish daughters. Unlike Coburg, Mount Temple repented and denounced the Nazis before his death in 1939. However, Coburg paid the price for his convictions. He was captured by the Americans and imprisoned at the end of the war, spending his last days in severe pain and poverty.

There were other examples: even as his father lay dying, Edward summoned German Ambassador Hoesch, whose documents would show that again Edward expressed sympathy with what was happening in Germany, and said he fully intended to visit the Olympic Games during the summer. He also asked the ambassador to tell a delegation of German exservicemen to keep two hours free for an audience with him, since he wanted to speak to them personally. He would also try to attend a dinner the ambassador was arranging for them.

Furthermore, Mrs. Simpson was under constant watch by MI5 and Scotland Yard, separately and independently of each other. In a top-secret memo to Baldwin, J.C.C. Davidson, the security liaison minister, warned that Mrs. Simpson was "in constant touch with the Germans and she has, if she likes, access to secret documents and cabinet papers." Such reports would be supported by Alec Hardinge, who was disturbed by the king's blatant disagreement with his government on foreign policy and the fact that he made no secret of his admiration for Mussolini and Hitler. Helen Hardinge wrote, "Alec much concerned over HM's irresponsibility."

Then there was the Mosley situation. Apart from his own intelligence, Hitler was kept well informed of Edward's views by the increasing contact of Mosley and his wife-to-be Diana with the Third Reich, and through the developing friendship between Hitler and Diana's sister Unity. She had totally penetrated into the Führer's inner circle, attended major social events, dined and talked with his hierarchy, and would be branded by history as a fanatical Nazi and Hitler lover.

Albert Speer himself recalled the scenes. "Quite often a select group of guests would wait for Hitler, and very often, the likeable Lady Unity Mitford was present. In good weather, we sat in a small courtyard . . . Hitler gave the owner and the waitresses a jovial greeting . . . and everyone ordered what they liked—cutlets, goulash, Hungarian wine from the cask. In this circle there was a sense of privacy, and one tacit agreement was that no one must mention politics, and no one did. The sole exception was Unity Mitford, who even in later years of tension persistently spoke up for her country; she did not abandon her efforts through all those years."

What was Unity Mitford's role in those deep, private discussions of Hitler's innermost circle of friends and advisers? In London, her brother-in-law to be, Tom Mosley, was now under almost twenty-four-hour surveillance by MI5, as his black-shirted racist thugs stormed around Britain mimicking the brutality of their German counterparts. Increasingly Mosley was using the king—"our caring new Monarch"—as a theme for his speeches, which were being monitored by police shorthand writers.

Mosley and the king were still in correspondence, in spite of the growing violence and Jew-baiting that surrounded the Fascist rallies. Further, Mussolini had been financing Mosley's party to the tune of £3,000 a month, although this figure had dropped to £1,000 by mid-1936. At this time, Hitler, aware of Mosley's contact with the king, began financing the BUF with cash channeled through secret bank accounts in Paris via Armand Gregoire, the French lawyer.

Whether or not Mosley's connections with Mussolini would have been known to the king is uncertain. In the spring of 1936, however, Edward was once again the cause of grave embarrassment to his government over the Abyssinian crisis. The Italians had just invaded, and after Marshal Badoglio's troops entered Addis Ababa, Emperor Haile Selassie made his escape through French Somaliland to the Red Sea, where a British light cruiser was waiting to take him and his family to safety.

The emperor was brought to London, whereupon Anthony Eden sought an immediate audience with the king to implore him to receive Haile Selassie at Buckingham Palace. The king argued, however, that by allowing the emperor shelter in this country, Britain had given notice to the world that she did not intend to abandon Abyssinia.

"It would be a popular gesture," Eden persisted.

"Popular with whom?" asked the king. "Certainly not with the Italians."

Edward wrote: "Sorry as I was for the Ethiopians, I nevertheless maintained that my action in receiving the Emperor might well have given unnecessary offence to Mussolini and drive him closer to Hitler." In the event,

the king agreed to send his brother the Duke of Gloucester to visit Haile Selassie at his hotel. But the king himself
recognized that he was totally at odds with his government over Italy. He wrote: "They [the government] had
embarked on a futile policy of coercing Mussolini which
utterly failed in its purpose and was only forcing him
into closer relations with Hitler. While I would be the
first to condemn aggression, and to advocate any forceful
measures to put it down, I could see no point in indulging
in half measures. It was more important to my eye at
this stage to gain an ally [Mussolini] than score debating
victories in the tottering League of Nations."

Edward, in regular conversation with Anthony Eden,
continually called him a fool for his support of the League
of Nations, and through all the delicate discussions with
the Italians over the Abyssinia problem, the king's own
contact with the Italians had reached dangerous levels.
He had dined with the Italian ambassador, Count Grandi,
whom he met first through the Metcalfes, and later at a
cocktail party at Bryanston Court, given by Mrs. Simpson. Grandi was also entertained at the Fort for intimate
conversations.

A note of these conversations was forwarded to the
German ambassador to Italy, which read: "About a week
ago an exhaustive conversation took place between the
King of England and the Italian Ambassador . . . the
King expressed profound regret that such serious tension should have developed in Anglo-Italian relations.
For peace in Europe, he was convinced that two great
nations, Germany and Italy, should be afforded full satisfaction by granting them, with full realisation of their
needs, the necessary colonial markets."

So while the critical negotiations were in progress between Britain and Italy, the king was staging his own
private accord with officials of the Italian government.
They would presumably have been in official contact
with the British Foreign Office and then gone on to cozy
little chats with the king. Edward tried to impress his

own views on Anthony Eden, not to mention the prime minister. It was a dangerous dabbling that the monarch was indulging himself in!

The prime minister was also gravely concerned about leakages of state papers which had been traced back to the king himself . . . and "while the Government was trying to bluff Mussolini over Abyssinia the King was secretly telling the Italian Ambassador that the League of Nations which was trying to impose sanctions was considered by Britain to be dead."

Hitler was giving similar thought to the Italian problem. He had even considered joining Britain in a campaign of sanctions against Mussolini over the invasion. "If I go in with them, then everything is over for good between Italy and us," he mused at a meeting of his high command. "Afterwards the English will drop me and we'll sit between two stools." The question was discussed over and over again, until at the point when the League of Nations, under Britain's leadership, agreed to impose the sanctions, Hitler decided to ally himself to Italy. For days after making that crucial decision Hitler would describe in somber tones the situation that had forced him to take that step. Albert Speer tells us in his memoirs, "He was all the more gratified when it turned out that the sanctions were relatively mild. From this Hitler concluded that both England and France were loath to take any risks and anxious to avoid danger."

This view was confirmed when German troops marched into the demilitarized zone of the Rhineland on March 7, 1936. This was an open breach of the Locarno Treaty, which Hitler feared might provoke military countermeasures from Allies. Nervously he awaited the first reaction to what he would later describe as his most daring of military undertakings, for he knew Germany at that time was in a relatively weak position. He would say, boasting of the Rhineland invasion, "We had no Army worth mentioning; at that time it would not even have had the fighting strength to maintain itself against the Poles. If the French had taken any action, we would have been easily defeated." And he waited in anticipation, as Albert Speer recalled:

> The air was electric aboard a special train carrying Hitler and his entourage towards Berlin. He paced up and down the carriage, sitting briefly and then moving about again. His most senior aides were around him, talking quietly and watching him with some apprehension. The train slowed as it approached a small station, Hitler rose to his feet and stood smacking the fist of one hand into the palm of the other.
>
> The train stopped and a guard came aboard carrying a wire message for the Führer and with some impatience, he snatched the piece of paper and read it. He smiled with relief upon those before him. "At last," he said. "At last. The King of England will not intervene. He is keeping his promise. That means all will go well."

The day was March 11, 1936, four days after Hitler had ordered German troops into the Rhineland. What inspired Hitler's statement of relief was a report from London by Leopold von Hoesch. An account of the events in Britain is on record from Fritz Hesse, who was then a German press attaché in London and a representative of the German News Agency. According to Hesse, Hoesch used his long friendship with the king to appeal to him to intervene and make sure that the British took no action over the Rhineland. He had an audience at Buckingham Palace where the king is said to have promised Hoesch he would send for Baldwin, which indeed he did.

The following day, Hesse reports, he was with Hoesch when the phone rang. Hesse goes on: "von Hoesch whispered 'The King' and handed me a second receiver so that I could listen to the conversation.

" 'Is that Leo? David speaking. . . . I sent for the Prime Minister and gave him a piece of my mind. I told the old so-and-so that I would abdicate if he made war. There was a frightful scene but you needn't worry. There won't be a war.' "

Four days after the Rhineland invasion, Hoesch wired Berlin: "Today I got into direct touch with the Court . . . the directive given to the government from there is . . . complications of a serious nature are in no circumstances to be allowed to develop."

Historians would say that nothing the King of England could say or do would ever have any bearing on world events, in politics or war: nor could he be blamed if Hitler acted on reports of Britain's friendliness toward Germany, emanating from the king himself. Captured Nazi documents would show, however, that the Führer took heart and encouragement from reports of the king's views which he took to mean that Britain wanted peace, not war. Hitler's expansionist ambitions were underway, and the evil of Nazism was unleashed on an unprecedented scale. Those who have tried to whitewash the role of Edward VIII cannot ignore the facts. His was a stupidity beyond belief to flirt with Fascist dictators over the head of his own government.

Tom Mosley's role was also becoming more sinister. In March he staged a massive rally at the Royal Albert Hall and in June, he and his followers began a concerted campaign against British Jews. He and William Joyce led a huge march of thousands of their supporters, chanting, "The Yids, the Yids. We've got to get rid of the Yids." From now until the beginning of the war, there would be countless street battles, the Cable Street riots and many Nazi-style rallies. As his campaign in London's East End intensified, anyone who looked Jewish would be attacked by his marauding Blackshirts, hundreds were injured and arrested, and on Sunday afternoons baton charges by the police became a regular feature of London life as thousands turned out to hear the British Führer. Mosley truly thought at this point that he had the following of the British masses behind him, and certainly, the number who came to his rallies was growing at a frightening rate.

People forget—and as the years have passed so has diminished the specter of this man who brought so much anguish, violence, and racial hatred into British life during the thirties. Though Mosley always denied he would take such measures, concentration camps in Britain would have been an easy step if Hitler had invaded. The gangsterlike thuggery and extremism of the man who wanted to rule the nation has been largely forgotten in the passage of time, but those who saw him in those days would never forget.

By that summer, Mosley's contact with Hitler was increasing. He and Diana went to Berlin, where they were secretly married in Goebbels's office. Coincidentally, the Nazi intrigue surrounding Edward was further intensified. Hitler had sent one of his top agents, Colin Ross, to London with the specific brief to make contact with politicians and those around the king, to help encourage friendship with Germany.

Another German spy had already made contact with Mrs. Simpson. She had been entertained at the German embassy by Herr Albert Treck, who owned a superb country house in Guilsborough, Northamptonshire, just down the road from The Old House, where the Duke and Duchess of York stayed occasionally with their daughters, Elizabeth and Margaret.

Under the guise of a country gentleman, Treck, who had as his hostess Ribbentrop's friend, Baroness Violet von Stroder, was able to carry out spy missions throughout the Midlands and gather information on airports, important installations and Army depots. It was probably Treck who gave Goering the graphic details of Coventry that enabled German bombers to attack with such accuracy. Treck disappeared from Guilsborough in August 1939, and the house was taken into the stewardship of the Trustee of Alien Property. Treck was arrested in Germany just after the war and his documents captured.

Whether she knew it or not, Wallis Simpson had been entertained by a most dangerous German spy, and there were many such people operating in Britain at that time. Edward's friend, Brigadier "Critch" Critchley, recalled an incident after a visit he made to Berlin: "A German countess was our hostess and I said out of politeness afterwards, 'You must come to England and let us return your hospitality.' Two weeks later I received a call from her to say she had arrived. It was quite a shock. I put her up in my London flat but, after about ten days, it was apparent she was asking too many questions and I got her out. Germany employed many such people to gain information. During a crossing from New York in the *Bremen*, I encountered another, a baroness. But this time I wasn't going to fall into the trap."

Joachim von Ribbentrop, who took every opportunity of meeting friends of the monarchy, knew Critchley was a good friend of the royal brothers and together they went to a boxing match at Harringey. Critchley arranged to meet him at the German embassy and as he waited in the anteroom two ADCs came into the room. "They began to tell me in a hostile manner that the German colonies should be restored to the Fatherland. That was enough for me; I had lunch with Ribbentrop once after that and I never saw him again until Nuremberg in 1945, in the dock."

In the meantime, Ribbentrop would become Hitler's ambassador to London, an announcement which came as quite a surprise to everyone. Chips Channon was in Germany at the time as Ribbentrop's guest at the Olympic Games, and wrote in his diary, "No one quite knows why he has been selected. Is it because his power is waning? Or is it because London is so important a post that the best man had to be sent? Or is it that there is simply no one else?"

The answer to those questions would be found after the war in Ribbentrop's own writings on the subject. He conceded that the only reason Hitler gave him the job was because of his friendship with Mrs. Simpson, whom he could influence, and through her, ultimately, the king. If she was not then an agent of Germany, she was at least a very special friend.

Hitler's last words, as Ribbentrop left Germany to go to London to present his credentials, were, "Ribbentrop, bring me an Alliance." The key, as Hitler and Ribbentrop saw it, was the king himself. "In the ordinary way, of course, the Sovereign could do little to influence politics or his Government, but if he were to give his support to the idea of an Anglo-German friendship, it would greatly help," Ribbentrop wrote.

Before all this could happen, Hitler first had to dispose of Leopold von Hoesch, the incumbent ambassador. Although known to be a friend of the king and Mrs. Simpson, he was no Nazi but an old diplomat caught up in the whirlpool of Hitlerism—and he wasn't much keen on it. Conveniently, he died. It was a heart attack, according to the German embassy. The truth, however, was that Hitler had Hoesch murdered to make way for Ribbentrop, who would be moved in after a suitable period of time had elapsed. There can be no doubt that the main reason for Ribbentrop's appointment was his closeness to the king's circle, and Mrs. Simpson in particular.

With the undercover surveillance of these associates of the king, Edward became the first monarch in British history whose documents had been screened by the security services before being shown to him. After Anthony Eden, the foreign secretary, noted that there was disquiet in the Foreign Office about the king's involvement in politics and foreign affairs, it was decided that all sensitive documents should be kept from him. The daily boxes of secret cabinet minutes, dispatches from around the world, reports of government departments—they were all screened, and classified information taken out.

As it happened, the king regarded his paperwork as a daily drudge, since his personal problems weighed heavily on him, and it became a task in itself for his staff to get him even to open the boxes, read anything, or sign documents. Urgent work was left lying around for days and confidential papers were left unattended at the Fort. Never had such important affairs of state been so badly neglected and ignored by a monarch.

The state of his work was noted by Alec Hardinge, who wrote: "Confusion in the King's affairs because he is impractical." His erratic hours, late nights, were giving his courtiers major headaches in the administration of Palace work and his duties as king. There was a mixed reception for Mrs. Simpson, too, whose control over the king was now almost total. Hardinge again: "It was scarcely realised at the time how overwhelming and inexorable was the influence exerted on the King by this lady. As time went by, it became clear that every decision, big or small, was subordinated to her will . . . it was she alone who mattered and before her, affairs of state sank into insignificance."

Mrs. Simpson's associations were also noted by Lady Hardinge, who recalled for Richard Thornton, "She seemed a heaven-sent opportunity [for those seeking] to enter Royal society . . . diplomats, especially German diplomats, sought her company . . ."

Ribbentrop, especially, was a frequent visitor to Bryanston Court. In her autobiography, Wallis said she met him only twice; but like many other aspects of her life about which she commented, her recollections were patently faulty.

Ribbentrop was close enough to Wallis by the middle of 1936 for American intelligence to record their own observations on the situation, noting that Ribbentrop was clearly passing on state secrets that emanated from Edward through Mrs. Simpson. Paul Schwartz, of the German Foreign Office, would also record that secrets from the British cabinet were common knowledge in Berlin and his description indicated that they too could have been passed on through Mrs. Simpson.

The Ribbentrop contact within the king's circle would be remembered after the war was over; surprising facts would emerge—and remain secret—as he was interrogated by the Americans before his execution at Nuremberg. Among other things, Ribbentrop maintained that in the months prior to abdication he had had long talks with the king on the question of a British alliance with Germany.

·SIX·

EVERYONE IS TALKING

Alice Keppel, the long-serving mistress of Edward's grandfather, King Edward VII, knew her place and never exploited her situation in public; she was the king's mistress, and it was the best-known secret in the nation. She was a gentle, sweet woman who had been taken advantage of by the king just as cruelly as he had humiliated his beautiful wife, Alexandra.

King Edward VII included Mrs. Keppel among his most trusted advisers. Lord Hardinge wrote: "I used to see a great deal of Mrs Keppel and I was aware that she had a great knowledge of what was going on. I would like to pay tribute to her wonderful discretion." She had no desire for greater things; the king already had a queen anyway.

Wallis Simpson's position was different. The throne next to her king was vacant; she could see the chance of position and power and she went for it. Discretion never was her strong point and she had no use for it now. For instance, she could have declined to take such a forward role in the king's life and affairs; he would have listened if she had declared her misgivings (which she later claimed to have) at being constantly at his side and on public view while still married to Ernest.

There was little doubt left in the minds of those closest to them that Edward would settle for nothing less than marriage to her, now he was easing her into the upper echelons of court and government circles and showing her off to the most important dignitaries in British life. In May, she was at a dinner the king gave for Prime Minister Stanley Baldwin, the Mountbattens, and Colonel Charles Lindbergh, who shared the monarch's enthusiasm for developments in Germany, among others. As yet, he dared not exclude Ernest from the gathering, especially in front of Baldwin's prim wife, Lucy. However, it was made clear to everyone that Wallis had planned the dinner down to the most intricate detail.

A month or so later, Edward attempted to promote the affection of the Duke and Duchess of York toward his mistress when he made them guests of honor at a glittering dinner party at York House which they attended with another gathering of high-ranking dignitaries. Wallis sat at the head of the table, and again everyone was made aware of the fact that she had planned the dinner herself. This time Ernest was not present, and according to Lady Diana Cooper, the whole thing was an unmitigated disaster. She recalled that the Duchess of York hardly acknowledged Wallis's existence. "She was cool and remote from first to last, both from disapproval of paraded illicit love, and also from the dreaded possibility of finding herself Queen."

The court circular the following day published a list of the king's guests, and made no attempt to hide the presence of Mrs. Ernest Simpson. Thereafter, and with the help of the two queens of the London social scene, Emerald Cunard and Sybil Colefax, the king lost no time in introducing Wallis Simpson into influential circles of the highest order, where she would meet and converse with those prominent figures in public life centered around Westminster. Anyone who failed in their total acceptance of Wallis would be cast out of the king's circle: that included his longest-serving palace staff and oldest friends.

Fruity Metcalfe, who had spent years in Edward's shadow at great personal cost, often helping him home after too much drink, was soon out of the king's favor. Wallis did not at all care for him; she thought he was a hanger-on and too fond of the king. In fact he had been Edward's nursemaid long before she arrived on the scene.

Brigadier G. Trotter, the king's comptroller, was fired simply because he refused to cut Thelma Furness. The king told him, "I am through with Thelma and am very keen on Wallis," at which Trotter replied, "Sir, I do not sack my friends."

Another loyal supporter, Admiral Sir Lionel Halsey, was dismissed when he protested at the soaring bills on Mrs. Simpson's account and for venturing to warn the king that she would never be accepted by the British public as his wife.

Edward, however, had already secretly set out on a course from which there was no return—to take Ernest Simpson's wife and marry her.

The point at which there was a serious discussion between himself and Simpson is not clear, but there are well-publicized and -recorded interviews at which Simpson, in front of witnesses, asked Edward what his intentions were toward his wife. He pressed the king: "Do you intend to marry her? She must choose between us." He wanted the matter brought to a head.

Things were not immediately resolved, however, and heated discussions took place on two or three further occasions. An agreement had to be reached by May if Mrs. Simpson was to be divorced before the coronation, which had been set for May the following year. It would take six months for the divorce to come through, and a further six months before it was made absolute.

The king and Mrs. Simpson were also insisting that in the eyes of the judge she should be the victim in the divorce and not the guilty party. This, they foolishly believed, might help the situation they would eventually have to face if they were married.

Simpson must have found the whole idea preposterous. He was the injured party, not Wallis. Everyone knew it. Everyone in every nightclub and at every dinner party in London had seen him humiliated. Whatever discussion followed to persuade Ernest Simpson to accept their proposal will never be known; but it was suspected by Simpson's friends that he would not have done it out of pure chivalry. The divorce costs were high, and as the guilty party he would have to pay them. There were other arrangements to be attended to, such as the hiring of a professional corespondent in the case, who would be caught in bed with Ernest at a Paris hotel by a waiter serving breakfast.

If Wallis plotted the whole thing, the king stage-managed it. He also made a substantial payment to Ernest Simpson to cover not just the expenses but compensation for the loss of his wife. The money was made over to Mrs. Simpson by Edward on March 28, 1937, five weeks before the Simpsons' divorce was made absolute. Wallis passed the money to Ernest via a bank account in Paris.

The divorce had to be carefully and meticulously arranged to avoid any suspicion of collusion. Ernest would be seen to be the adulterer, and although it was true that he was already having an affair with Wallis's best friend in America, Mary Kirk Raffrey, it had been by courtesy of Wallis herself, who, on one of his trips to America, had suggested that Ernest visit Mary, who had recently separated from her own husband. Not content with making the suggestion, Wallis even wrote to her friend to tell her that Ernest would be visiting her and asked, "Would you please look after him?" Mary and Ernest, each realizing their own marriages were all but over, fell into Wallis's trap, and into love with each other.

Dr. Cosmo Lang seemed to have had a premonition about it all, and in deeply somber and formal tones requested an audience with the king. His mood was a mixture of concern and anger, and he began the interview by saying he had often discussed Edward's "conduct" with the old king. Not surprisingly, Edward was angered, particularly at the reference to his "conduct." The interview proceeded in an icy vein. Mrs. Simpson was not mentioned, but the king knew then that the archbishop was against his friendship with Wallis and would oppose with all his might any attempt by the king to marry her.

The romance was coming out into the open, although the British public were largely unaware of it. Since the newspaper barons had agreed that for the moment they would remain silent on the subject, only obscure mentions of Mrs. Simpson had appeared.

But now their discretion was weakening. The couple were together as often as Edward's official duties would allow, Wallis appearing all the time in new clothes and jewels. His spending on her, despite the austerity of the thirties, was in itself a scandal, with so many depressed areas in Britain under the shadow of deep poverty.

An even bigger scandal was looming over the king's summer holiday, for which he had chartered the steam yacht *Nahlin*, at a cost of almost £5,000. With him were Wallis Simpson and his friends Duff Cooper, the war minister, and Lady Diana. It was to be a partly official and partly private cruise, but with Europe volatile, the government sent two destroyers to accompany *Nahlin* as she set out down the Dalmatian coast. At each stop the party was besieged by reporters and cameramen from the American press, and suddenly the whole world—except Britain, that is—knew of the king and his American moll.

The *Nahlin* holiday also had substantial political overtones, orchestrated entirely by the king and without the knowledge of his government. The aim was the furtherance of appeasement, a cause which was increasingly being advocated to the king by his aristocratic friends back in London. In Yugoslavia, for instance, a meeting with Prince Regent Paul, the homosexual friend of Chips Channon, was carefully and secretly prearranged so as to look like a casual encounter. Only a few weeks earlier, Prince Paul had been engaged in high-level talks with the Nazis over the supply of armaments. Mussolini had similar ambitions in that quarter. Prince Paul was able to assure the king that appeasement with the two Fascist leaders was in his view the most suitable and necessary course, not just for countries such as his own in the heart of Europe, but also for Britain. (Though his beloved Chips Channon could never believe Prince Paul would turn his back on Britain, in the end he would, and be branded as a traitor. When the news came early in 1941 that the regent—"the person I love more than anyone else in the world," wrote Channon—had signed a pact with the Axis forces, the British took immediate action. A coup d'etat, organized and backed by the British special operations executive under Hugh Dalton, was staged in Belgrade; Prince Paul fled the country. "I was relieved yet anxious for my poor Regent," wrote Channon.)

Another port of call on the *Nahlin* cruise was Vienna, where, as well as visiting the Vienna Fair hand in hand with Wallis, the king met Chancellor Kurt von Schuschnigg and Austrian President Wilhelm Miklas, who three months earlier had formed an alliance with Hitler. Conversation of political affairs could not be avoided; the king did not argue against the Austrian pact with the Fascists. And if the king's holiday—with War Minister Duff Cooper taking notes—was still supposed to be nonpolitical, *The New York Times* had already indicated the underlying trend: that the four countries visited might well have reached the view that a combination of Edward and Hitler could give them better protection than the League of Nations.

On their return to England, though "worried about the rumblings abroad," the king had still done nothing, nor said anything, to indicate his intention to marry Mrs. Simpson. That would be saved until her divorce was through in a few weeks' time; but by September the prospect must have been on the minds of his entire family, who had gone to Balmoral for the annual holiday.

His mother, his brother, their wives, and members of the court were all there. The king turned up with Wallis and Herman Rogers and his wife, Wallis's American friends who had entertained them at their villa in the South of France. It was the prospect of this family get-together that suddenly brought Wallis down to earth with a jolt. What had she got herself into? The whole situation was now galloping along; soon it would be out of control. Her divorce was due to be heard on October 27. Then there would be no stopping David.

She had received a letter from her Aunt Bessie, who was horrified at the publicity she was getting in America. "Please consider your position," Bessie warned her. "I'm scared for you." It hit Wallis like a thunderbolt from the blue and suddenly she was in a blind panic. She saw it all, the trouble, the politics, the press. Could she ever be queen? Once, in her wildest dreams, she had thought it possible and had played her hand for the position she lusted after. Now the reality was facing her. The sensational coverage in America of her holiday with the king would be only a shadow of what would follow in Britain.

She saw it all, and on a day in September she sat down and wrote Edward a note. They had had lovely, beautiful times together but she felt she must return to her husband. She and Ernest were poor and unable to do all those attractive things which, she confessed, she loved. But at least they would have a "calm and congenial life." The king, she added, must go on with his job.

The king's response was the usual one that emerged in times of crisis. He broke down and cried. Why was Wallis "saying such harsh things to David?" he wrote. "I love you . . . madly, tenderly, adoringly." They would see it through together, side by side, hand in hand. Wallis argued, reassured, but finally gave in. But neither knew how they would meet the crisis that would not be long in coming.

The divorce was the signal. *Simpson v. Simpson* was heard at Ipswich, out of the way and out of the limelight.

Wallis sued on the grounds of Ernest's adultery with Buttercup Kennedy, the professional adulteress used in the case. The *decree nisi* was granted, and it would be made absolute in May.

Still the press did not link Mrs. Simpson's name with the king. The court action was reported in a normal, straightforward way, without sensation, thanks to the plotting of Rothermere, Beaverbrook, and Esmond Harmsworth, son of Lord Rothermere, the chairman of the Newspaper Proprietors' Association.

Two weeks later, it all began to get out of control. The king's private secretary, Alec Hardinge, had left Edward a note at the Fort where the king and Mrs. Simpson had gone to stay for the weekend. It was his humble duty to report that the prime minister and members of the government were to discuss the king's friendship with Wallis: A serious situation was developing and it was hardly possible to contain a public outburst.

Hardinge suggested that Mrs. Simpson should leave the country immediately and that the king should seriously consider his position. Edward was shocked, angered, and ready to sack Hardinge. In a peculiar way, he blamed Hardinge for the crisis now approaching, as if he had started it all. Then he thought about it and decided Hardinge had been put up to it by Baldwin; that angered him even more. They had struck at the "roots of his pride."

He was in a state of near panic. He believed they were plotting against him. Convinced he could no longer work through Hardinge as his contact with Downing Street he contacted his old friend Walter Monckton and arranged to meet him secretly that Sunday at Windsor Castle.

It was during that meeting that the king faced the truth: he would have to tell Baldwin that if the government were to stop him marrying Wallis, he would go. He would resign the monarchy. "They will fight you," Monckton warned. "What they want is for you to give up Mrs. Simpson and let that be the end of it."

"I cannot do that," said the king. "I will not give her up. We shall be married." Monckton agreed to act as his go-between in the negotiations that would follow with the government. Baldwin was summoned to the Palace the following Monday evening. His view was exactly as Monckton had surmised. He believed the British people would not tolerate such a marriage. Nor would the Archbishop of Canterbury, who had great hopes that the forthcoming coronation of King Edward VIII would lead to a Christian revival. For him to marry a divorcée—an American divorcée at that—would be out of the question. Baldwin left without any sign of a resolution to the problem being found.

Later that night, Edward told his mother of his plans and implored her to meet Wallis Simpson. Queen Mary spoke sympathetically, then reminded him of the duty of kingship. She could not, she said, agree to meet her son's intended bride. To her surprise and astonishment, Edward told her he would abdicate if that's what would be necessary to marry Wallis. "Won't you just see her, talk to her?" Edward begged his mother.

No. She would not, could not, bring herself to do that; nor would she ever receive Wallis Simpson. Wallis was, in her eyes, an adventuress and she called her as much. Mrs. Simpson was as much to blame as her son in what she told Baldwin was "this pretty kettle of fish." Edward's decision to give up the throne for "this woman" caused her great pain and grief. Nothing in her entire life had caused, or would cause, her so much distress and humiliation. As events would unfold, she would totally support Baldwin's view that for a woman with two husbands still living to marry the King of England was out of the question. Throughout her life Queen Mary had put her duty to her country above all else, even above her children and her inner emotions. Her son the king should do the same. She implored him not to turn his back on that duty and to give up Mrs. Simpson.

It was with this on his mind that the king set off the next evening, Tuesday, November 16, for his tour of South Wales to see for himself the stark reality of the problems out in the real world that was Britain in 1936. The crowds cheered, waved, cried. His compassion for them touched the hearts of the miners and their families as he toured the mining valleys. Everywhere he went, he repeated that now famous phrase, "Something must be done."

In London, Wallis had enough jewels on her person on any given evening to keep an average Welsh mining family in sustenance for a whole year. She had also settled on the idea, despite denials in her autobiography, that somehow or other she was going to be queen; anyway, Edward kept telling her so. An American friend received a letter in which she wrote, "Strange as it may seem, I am going to be Queen of England." There were also reports that she had tried to order new underwear bearing the royal insignia; and in a powder room when she was told that she was being rude to another woman whom she had pushed out of the way, Wallis replied, "You won't talk to me like that when I'm Queen."

Chips Channon, who met her at the opera in November, noted her attire—"a simple black dress dripping with emeralds. Her collection of jewels is the talk of London." But occasionally she lapsed into pensiveness, sometimes misery. Many people were asking her to do the right thing and leave the country. Although some said she should have done it months ago, she always responded in the same way: "They do not understand . . . the King would come after me regardless of anything."

About the same time, the king was telling his brother, the Duke of Kent, that he was going to marry Wallis. (Kent was still the most supportive member of Edward's family. He had good cause; the king had personally taken steps to make sure his brother was kept virtual prisoner in a remote house while he was cured of his increasing addiction to drugs.)

"What will she call herself?" asked Kent, expecting a minor duchess title for the king's twice-married consort.

While the king was away, Wallis had lunched with Esmond Harmsworth, which resulted in the *Daily Mail* publishing a leader article so sycophantic and exaggerated in its praise of the king as to be almost laughable. During the lunch, Harmsworth suggested to Wallis the possibility of a morganatic marriage, a suggestion she wasn't at all keen on when she heard what it would entail: a marriage in which she would not be queen, only the king's wife—nor could any children of the marriage have any rights to succession, or claim on the king's estate. "It sounds strange and almost inhuman," Wallis said when she discussed the suggestion with the king. But they agreed it was a possibility.

Harmsworth also put the thought to Baldwin, who saw the king and asked if he wanted to pursue that path. This would mean seeking not only his government's approval, but also the agreement of the dominions. Now Baldwin would have formally to raise the issue of the king's marriage to his entire cabinet; so far he had restricted his discussions to senior ministers only. Personally, Baldwin was against a morganatic marriage and saw only two choices: give up Mrs. Simpson and remain king; or abdicate.

Wallis, who was now convinced that Baldwin wanted Edward out, was furious and unwell. She was exhausted from the recent pressure of it all and had had to move permanently to the Fort for security reasons. On November 28, she told Edwina Mountbatten over the telephone, "I am lying here making all kinds of important decisions."

On that day, Baldwin, who spent an hour and forty minutes at Buckingham Palace, finally gave Edward the ultimatum: unless he could have the king's assurance that he would not press the issue, his government would resign. Furthermore, Clement Attlee, the leader of the Labour party, had given his assurance that he would not form a new government.

The king asked for time to consult his friends: Lord Beaverbrook, Winston Churchill, Monckton. Baldwin agreed, but warned that the press was getting nervous. Breaking point was almost reached; and the great sleeping British public, still unaware of the turmoil at the Palace, would have it thrust upon them in a great crescendo of words.

That bombshell came two days later, from a totally unexpected source. The Bishop of Bradford, the Right Reverend A.W.F. Blunt, publicly criticized the king for his attitude to the church and his poor attendance. The *Yorkshire Post* used the issue to link it with the sensational reports about the king in America.

The following day, the agreement that had kept the king and Mrs. Simpson out of the British press collapsed. The king prepared himself for the onslaught, which came in the morning papers of December 3 with massive headlines: "The King and Mrs. Simpson."

The Duke of York, returning from Edinburgh that morning, saw the posters. The shock, the realization, was brought home to him there and then that the one thing he dreaded most might soon now happen. He and his wife Elizabeth might be King and Queen of England.

Wallis was in tears. The publicity was much worse than she had feared. "I can't stay here another day," she insisted. "I must leave England this afternoon." The king agreed, after having had a long and tortuous examination of what lay before them.

Perry Brownlow, Edward's lord-in-waiting, agreed to accompany Wallis, who would go immediately to the South of France to the home of her American friends Herman and Katherine Rogers. They traveled together across the Channel on a steamer under the names of Mr.

and Mrs. Harris. That night, crowds had gathered outside Wallis's home in Cumberland Terrace and windows were broken by a chanting mob.

The king kissed her good-bye before driving to Marlborough House to see his mother, in response to a letter she had sent to him that day: "The news in the papers is very upsetting, especially as I have not seen you for ten days. I would very much like to see you."

The Duke and Duchess of York were there when he arrived, and exhausted but emboldened by drink, he explained to them all why he could not live without Mrs. Simpson, why he must give up the throne.

All her life, Queen Mary had been somewhat reserved toward her eldest son; cold was how Edward himself described her. Like Baldwin and all the others, she had kept putting off a confrontation over Mrs. Simpson, though she had warned the prime minister as early as February that she feared for the future. In this crisis her emotions for him were unchanged. She was bitter and unswerving in her view that Mrs. Simpson could never be accepted into the family. Edward left Marlborough House that night, saying that this was something he would have to handle alone.

As crowds gathered at all points of action—the Palace, Downing Street, Westminster—so too did the placards, and a new and menacing tone appeared in the crisis. An orchestrated campaign made its debut: "Abdication means revolution." Tom Mosley's Fascist machine was at work, trying to make capital out of the situation. With the leaders of all parties adamantly refusing to form a government if the king went ahead and married Mrs. Simpson, Mosley could see an opening. Special Branch surveillance of Mosley and his racist propaganda had noted that his speeches made continued references to the king as a compassionate hero who could save Britain. The Home Office and Baldwin would not have been unaware that Mosley might try to group his Fascist movement around the king if Edward decided to fight the government and go ahead with his marriage plans. The idea that Churchill, Beaverbrook, Harmsworth would support the King's party was unthinkable. A political party headed by the monarch would be against all that the constitution of Britain stood for. It would scuttle democracy; it could lead to the start of Fascist rule in Britain.

Why not? The king didn't dismiss the idea lightly. Germany, Italy, and Spain had succumbed to similar doctrines. Who were these people who wanted to gather around him? Edward wrote that there was no visible leader, but that "scattered groups of people in cars toured the streets of London and other big cities, with home-made signs and loudspeakers shouting, "Stand by the King." Slogans were chalked on walls, and an uprising seemed imminent. This, however, was no spontaneous act. Tom Mosley had planned it.

Nor was the Mosley organization the only group fighting to keep the king on the throne. Quietly and behind the scenes others of varying political persuasions had similar intentions. Among the most influential was the ubiquitous Imperial Policy Group founded some four years earlier by Sir Reginald Mitchell-Bank, with leading financiers and industrialists among its members. The king's friend Kenneth de Courcy was its secretary and also doubled as the group's head of intelligence. The IPG was campaigning through the highest channels of Western European governments to stay out of Hitler's way and allow him and Mussolini in due course to move against the Soviet Union. Hitler should be allowed to reclaim his territorial rights; Britain and France should not intervene. Their views were shared by an equally pro-Hitler lobby in America, with many supporting the view that Hitler's economic miracle should be allowed to develop, affording them huge investment opportunities.

De Courcy and the IPG remained convinced that Edward should stay on the throne, and they were equally certain that if Baldwin could be forced to resign through

Edward's refusal to abdicate, a new government could be formed behind Winston Churchill. But however much Churchill might have wanted revenge from those who had helped keep him in the political wilderness in previous years, a traitor to democracy he was not.

At the other end of the political spectrum, the Labour party leader Clement Attlee was under similar pressure. There were those in the Labour party who were suggesting that now was the time to make Britain a republic. If Baldwin resigned, then Attlee should grasp the opportunity to form a government and use the whole constitutional crisis now unfolding as a basis for the dissolution of the monarchy. Attlee refused, and Baldwin, as we have seen, was able to tell the king that if he did not abdicate, his government would resign and no political party would come forward to take over.

Except, perhaps, Mosley. That thought had given Baldwin sleepless nights.

Clearly Edward had to decide if he would encourage Mosley. There seems to have been a point at which this decision became critical to him. He wrote: "Had I made a move to encourage the growth of his movement, it might have grown. . . . I shall go further and say that had I remained passive while my friends acted, the result might have been the same. . . . It was a night of soul-searching. While I paced my bedroom floor, my mind retraced the myriad paths of my life. In the end . . . I put out of my mind the thought of challenging the Prime Minister. By making a stand I should have left the scars of civil war."

Edward's "friends" had obviously warned him that civil war could be the result. On that night of December 3, 1936, Britain came close to a catastrophic course of action that, if successful, could have put Tom Mosley in the seat of government.

As Lady Diana Mosley noted some years later: "If the King and my husband had been in power, there would have been no war with Hitler." And presumably, Fascism would have taken over Europe completely; Hitler would have ruled supreme, and his murderous, racist regime would have thundered on through Europe, unhindered by, and copied in, Britain.

Edward concluded that had he stayed to fight, the concept of the monarchy being above politics would have been shattered and the party system "fatally hurt." He knew that the forces of Fascism were ready to pounce, and in self-congratulatory terms he recalled in his autobiography how a close friend in the Lords wrote to him that it would be realized eventually that his "nobility in refusing to test your popularity was a sign of true greatness and probably saved the very existence of the Empire. The advent of a 'King's Party,' brings within your power to create civil war and chaos."

The relevance of these words may well have been overlooked when Edward wrote his autobiography in the 1950s; he seemed almost rambling in his reflections. Their importance became clear, however, when read together with the MI5 and Special Branch files on Mosley which were not released until 1985–86; even now some are held back for release in later years.

Mosley wanted power in Britain; and the abdication crisis could have provided a springboard. Hitler himself, however, was low-key about Mosley's efforts, and believed he had misread the situation in Britain by trying to impose on the nation a copy of the Führer's Third Reich. Mosley had no original or new ideas; he merely imitated German methods slavishly, and because of that Hitler thought the British Nazi party would come to nothing. In every country, Hitler argued, you had to start with a different premise and change your methods accordingly.

If Mosley was involved in a conspiracy to center Fascist politics around the king, another group of conspirators was trying to get Mrs. Simpson off the hook and out of the abdication crisis, at least until its intensity had eased. Lord Beaverbrook, Lord Brownlow, now in France with

Mrs. Simpson, and Walter Monckton had discussed a plan to persuade Wallis to renounce all intentions of marrying the king. While Beaverbrook and the others desperately wanted Edward to stay on the throne, Baldwin, and most of his cabinet, were of the view that the king should go, regardless of Mrs. Simpson's position. It is highly probable that Beaverbrook, in trying to get Wallis to renounce the king, had an insight into the action Baldwin might yet take, if he was forced to. The IPG was told by an MP with intelligence contacts that Baldwin still had a trump card. He had the China Report on Wallis Simpson, commissioned by King George V, and the top-secret security memos on her Nazi friendship and suspicious associations. The contents were revealed to Kenneth de Courcy, and the IPG realized immediately that these allegations, embellished or not, would certainly damage their case. They surmised too, that if he was forced to, Baldwin would bring the reports into play and give the king no real alternative.

Now it was clear: the love story that history would dub the greatest romance of the century was surrounded by seediness, suspicion, plot, and counterplot. A weak-willed king, of flawed intellect, had fallen into the grasp of manipulative politicians—and of Wallis Simpson. Together they turned his head toward ambitions of power that could never be his. It was an infatuation of mammoth proportions and no woman, particularly not Wallis, would have been able to ignore the vision of wealth and importance that could be hers. Wallis Simpson was not in love with Edward VIII. She had been consumed absolutely by the one thought . . . that she might be queen.

·SEVEN·

THE WOMAN I LOVE

"Please, Perry, please get me out of here. I cannot stand this another moment." The time was 3 A.M, in a small hotel at Blois, France. They had stopped en route, and suddenly the place was besieged by a score of newsmen who had just discovered their whereabouts. The commotion in the lobby awoke Mrs. Simpson and her party.

"Please hurry, Perry," she said to Perry Brownlow, who was escorting her on the drive south. "I cannot take any more of their incessant questioning." They prepared to leave quickly; herself, Brownlow, a chauffeur, and a detective.

"This way." Brownlow indicated the servants' stairs. They passed through a musty corridor, went downstairs to the rear of the hotel, and slipped out through a door which had not been opened in years. The car was waiting to speed them away.

Later that day, at Vienne, south of Lyons, reporters caught up with them again, and to pacify their requests for a statement, Mrs. Simpson said: "I would like everyone to understand that I need calm and rest. I have no plans of my own. The King will be the judge. While waiting for his decision I am going to withdraw into silence."

She had stopped for lunch in a small but well-known gourmet restaurant at Vienne, and she spoke of her journey: "I have not slept a wink for two nights," said Mrs. Simpson after she had finished lunch. "I will come back in better times."

After the detective had signaled that it was safe to move, Mrs. Simpson ran out through the kitchens, up the cellar steps to her car parked in a quiet side street —and soon she was on her way again, speeding away farther from the eye of the storm in London.

It was almost midnight before she reached her destination, the Rogers's villa near Cannes. There, newspapermen had to jump for their lives as the big black sedan carrying Mrs. Simpson sped up the long narrow lane leading to the villa. Eight trunks and five suitcases containing Mrs. Simpson's clothes had arrived at Cannes on the Blue Train the previous day. Mrs. Simpson was out of the way and here was the opportunity, if one was needed, to let things cool down.

On Thursday, December 3, Mr. Baldwin had a forty-minute talk with Queen Mary; the Dukes of York, Kent, and Gloucester met; the prime minister was summoned to the Palace; and the king left Fort Belvedere for London, and drove back at 1:30 in the morning. Baldwin had told Attlee in the House of Commons that he had "no statement to make today"; Winston Churchill had hoped that "no irrevocable steps" would be taken and that night went himself to see the king at Fort Belvedere.

Although outside Buckingham Palace the crowds shouted, "We want King Edward," and "He's a Jolly Good Fellow," and a banner was marched from the Marble Arch which read: "After South Wales You Can't Let Him Down," it became increasingly clear that public opinion was moving over to the side of the government.

Of that, there was absolutely no doubt among the rest of the royal family. Even the Duke and Duchess of Kent had moved against Wallis, and once the marriage declaration was made, Kent declared, "He is besotted with the woman. One can't get a sensible word out of him," while Baldwin said, "He is bewitched."

Wallis was still influencing him as the crisis reached its critical stage. The monarch's most senior financial adviser, Sir Edward Peacock, recalled that in her daily, sometimes hourly, telephone calls to the king from the South of France, Wallis was urging him to stand up for himself. Peacock had no difficulty in hearing the telephone conversation, since the king felt it necessary to shout, and he noted "the insistence over the telephone of the lady was that he should fight for his rights. She kept up that line until near the end, maintaining that he was King and his popularity would carry everything."

Wallis was playing a double game; about that there can be no doubt. While appearing to indicate she was willing totally to withdraw from the king's life, she was in fact urging him toward a challenge to the government and to the British constitution. Everyone around him at the time conceded that he seemed incapable of making up his own mind; although he sought the advice of his various so-called friends, in the end, he did what Mrs. Simpson told him to. Further, during the run up to the abdication, he was drinking to the extent that his brain must have been permanently in a confused state.

That Saturday night in London, Winston Churchill, who had become King Edward's father figure and was risking his political career in the process, tried to bring a halt to the seemingly unstoppable sequence of events that would lead to the king's abdication. On that Saturday, December 5, 1936, he implored the government and the public: "I plead for time and patience. If an Abdication was to be hastily extorted, the outrage so committed would cast its shadow across many chapters of the history of the British Empire." He asked: "What has the King done? He has proposed legislation to his Ministers [which would allow him to marry Mrs. Simpson] which they are not prepared to introduce. If the King refuses to take the advice of his Ministers, they are free to resign. They have no right to put pressure on him by soliciting beforehand assurances from the Leader of the Opposition that he will not form any alternative government.

"I plead, I pray that time and tolerance will not be denied."

Time and tolerance there would not be. Prime Minister Stanley Baldwin, and his greatest ally Geoffrey Dawson, editor of *The Times*, were determined to force the issue, down the road and as quickly as could now be achieved, toward abdication.

Those newspapers supporting the king implored him not to go, the *Sunday Pictorial* for instance.

> For three days the nation has been storm-tossed in its emotions, but out of it now emerges this considered view that in this modern world the King need not be sacrificed.
>
> Following his long years of service as Prince of Wales he has been a splendid King. We want him to remain King, and he will be just as good a King when this unhappy affair has blown over and assumes its proper perspective as an unusual chapter in the domestic story of the British Crown. It was a shock to the nation at first, but that aspect has passed, and more and more we are seeing the King as a man who has not allowed even this unexampled explosion of publicity to deflect him from his desire to marry Mrs Simpson.
>
> Few of us could stand such a test as that, and it is another admirable quality to add to the long list of excellencies we have always attributed to the King. To so keep up Government pressure that he feels his only way out is abdication would be a crime, and a heartless one. The King wants to marry Mrs Simpson, and we want the King. Our Government, and the Governments of the Dominions, will be best serving the happiness of the whole British family if they approach the problem solely from the point of view of making the best of it.

Dawson of *The Times*, however, knew probably more than anyone about the background to this crisis. He was Baldwin's confidant and the man about whom Lord Beaverbrook would later write: "But for him, Edward VIII would still be King."

Dawson pushed the issue to the limit in his leader articles, and on the Monday the headlines rang out again.

The front page of the *News Chronicle* on December 7, 1936, told the story of a nation in suspense during the weekend that preceded the abdication of King Edward VIII.

> THE KING MUST TAKE
> THE NEXT STEP
> Cabinet and Parliament
> Awaiting His Decision
> Cheers and Boos in
> Downing Street
> TODAY'S WEATHER: Cold
> AUSTRALIA ALL OUT 234

On a cold, damp Sunday evening, mounted police cleared the crowds from Downing Street and drew a cordon across the Whitehall entrance as cabinet ministers left No. 10. At Buckingham Palace crowds sang the National Anthem. Women were in tears at the Guildhouse, where Dr. Maude Royden ended her sermon with the words "God Save the King!" Crowds gathered outside Windsor Castle, hearing rumors of preparations for the king to broadcast.

That weekend was the dramatic pause in the tragedy of Edward VIII. The first act had been played to an electrified audience in London and relayed all over the world. The last act was still to come. The world was moved and shocked, took sides and argued, guessed at the end . . . and waited.

Just as it seemed the abdication crisis was nearing its

end, the Beaverbrook plan came into play. Perry Brownlow prepared a statement that would be flashed around the world: Wallis would withdraw and renounce the marriage.

The following day, Mrs. Simpson issued her first statement during the whole crisis. Lord Brownlow read it to the reporters of the world's newspapers at Cannes. Wallis had "no wish to hurt or damage the King or the Throne." The headlines said:

MRS. SIMPSON OFFERS TO
WITHDRAW
"Her Situation Rendered Both
Unhappy and Untenable"

Two other headlines:

MANCHESTER CORONATION
WORKERS LOSE THEIR JOBS

MR. CHURCHILL TOLD TO
"SIT DOWN"

In the House of Commons where Mr. Baldwin was cheered repeatedly, it was evident that the House was now "overwhelmingly behind the Government."

On Wednesday, December 9:

MR. BALDWIN'S FIVE
HOURS WITH THE KING

SOLICITOR AND DOCTOR
FLY TO MRS. SIMPSON

1 A.M. VISIT OF DUKE OF KENT TO FORT
BELVEDERE

The pace was quickening. The arrival of a doctor at Wallis's hideaway gave rise to rumors that she was pregnant. The official explanation was that she was suffering a nervous breakdown, though years later a nurse would say that Wallis had had an abortion. No evidence has ever been discovered to confirm this statement.

Baldwin called in Theodore Goddard, Wallis's solicitor, and asked him what was going on. Goddard knew no more than he and was dispatched by special plane to the South of France. Wallis told him she would stand by her decision, come what may, and then she telephoned Edward to tell him that.

The king would not budge from the course he was set on. The abdication documents were being drawn up; the cabinet was ready to meet. The king pleaded with Wallis not to withdraw: "You can do whatever you wish, go wherever you want, I will follow." So the process rolled on toward its climax.

Secretly, however, Wallis had no intention of calling a halt; she had discussed with Herman Rogers the possibility of boarding a ship to Peking, which would have put her out of reach of the king until all tension had died down. She had written him a farewell note and reckoned she was all ready to leave France for the voyage east.

Sir Kenneth Peacock didn't believe that for one minute. His view was this: "She apparently began to think of her own unpopularity and a statement was suggested which the King approved, well realising that it would divert some of the criticism from her to him, the very thing he wanted." The Duchess of York and Queen Mary regarded the withdrawal statement as a "piece of face-saving sham." The royals believed Wallis was playing for high stakes, all or nothing, and if her final actions were anything to go by, they were right. She actually telephoned the king, at a most critical hour, to recite the farewell message she had written him, knowing full well that it would be rejected. The analogy, as someone put it later, was that she was threatening to gas herself in an electric oven.

The king also read something to Wallis from papers

being drawn up by his solicitor, George Allen: "The only condition I can stay here is if I renounce you for all time." Allen repeated the same words to her, to which Wallis responded, "For all time is too long for me."

Thursday, December 10, and the king signed the instrument of abdication in front of his brothers; Bertie would become King George VI later, although it was for him, Edward wrote, "a terrible blow." He was petrified at the thought of becoming king.

That night Edward was joined by his mother and brothers for a last dinner at the Fort, a tearful, morose scene. He made his final broadcast to the nation . . . and was gone. It was, wrote the queen, "a dreadful goodbye. The whole thing was too pathetic for words."

Edward, King of England, had become Duke of Windsor, and the shout of "Long Live the King" would now be for George VI.

Edward's farewell message to the empire, broadcast around the world, went as follows:

> At long last I am able to say a few words of my own. I have never wanted to withhold anything, but until now it has been not constitutionally possible for me to speak. A few hours ago I discharged my last duty as King and Emperor, and now that I have been succeeded by my brother, the Duke of York, my first words must be to declare my allegiance to him. This I do with all my heart.
>
> You all know the reasons which have impelled me to renounce the throne. But I want you to understand that in making up my mind I did not forget the country or the Empire, which as Prince of Wales, and lately as King, I have for twenty-five years tried to serve. But you must believe me when I tell you that I have found it impossible to carry the heavy burden of responsibility and to discharge my duties as King as I would wish to do without the help and support of the woman I love.
>
> And I want you to know that the decision I have made has been mine and mine alone. This was a thing I had

to judge entirely for myself. The other person most concerned has tried up to the last to persuade me to take a different course. I have made this, the most serious decision of my life, upon a single thought of what would in the end be the best for all.

This decision has been made less difficult to me by the sure knowledge that my brother, with his long training in the public affairs of this country and with his fine qualities, will be able to take my place forthwith, without interruption or injury to the life and progress of the Empire. And he has one matchless blessing, enjoyed by so many of you and not bestowed on me—a happy home with his wife and children.

During these hard days I have been comforted by my mother and by my family. The Ministers of the Crown, and in particular Mr Baldwin, the Prime Minister, have always treated me with full consideration. There has never been any constitutional difference between me and them and between me and Parliament. Bred in the constitutional tradition by my father, I should never have allowed any such issue to rise.

Ever since I was Prince of Wales, and later on when I occupied the throne, I have been treated with the greatest kindness by all classes, wherever I have lived or journeyed throughout the Empire. For that I am very grateful.

I now quit altogether public affairs, and I lay down my burden. It may be some time before I return to my native land, but I shall always follow the fortunes of the British race and Empire with profound interest, and if at any time in the future I can be found of service to His Majesty in a private station I shall not fail. And now we all have a new King. I wish him, and you his people, happiness and prosperity with all my heart. God bless you all. God Save the King.

Dickie Mountbatten, who offered a hand of friendship in the last few days before the abdication, wrote: "I feel there is nothing I can do to help except bite off people's heads who have the temerity to say anything disloyal about their king . . ."

But when on December 10, he went to the Fort where the rest of Edward's family had assembled for the final rites, Mountbatten quickly assigned his allegiance to the new king and on December 11 wrote: "Dear Bertie, Heartbroken as I am at David's departure and all the terrible trouble he has brought on us all, I must tell you how deeply I feel for Elizabeth and you having to shoulder his responsibilities. . . . You will have the sympathy of us all except a few extremists (be they communists or fascists) who may use this to stir up trouble . . ."

That night Scotland Yard flooded London with plainclothes policemen, mingling with the crowds outside Buckingham Palace and Downing Street. Special Branch officers feared a "public uprising" spearheaded by Mosley's Fascists; but although uniformed and plainclothes members of his Blackshirts were out in force, only five arrests were made.

Mrs. Simpson, meanwhile, was listening to the events on radio.

"I was shocked to learn," she recalled, "that David was planning to take up temporary residence in a hotel in Switzerland. I telephoned our friends, Baron and Baroness Eugene de Rothschild who had a castle, Schloss Enzesfeld near Vienna to ask if they could invite David to visit them. They consented instantly."

Later, as the king's speech of abdication came over the radio, she lay on a sofa, her head buried in cushions and her hands over her eyes. The woman who would be queen had lost. Harold Nicolson recorded in his diary: "We are all staggered with shame and distress. I never dreamt it would come to this."

Nicolson might also have recalled an earlier diary warning, some months before the crisis blew up, when he wrote, "I have an uneasy feeling that Mrs. Simpson, bejewelled, eyebrow-plucked, virtuous and wise, is getting him [Edward] out of touch with the type of person with whom he ought to associate. Why am I sad? Because I think Mrs. Simpson is a nice woman who had flaunted suddenly into this absurd position."

The duke sped away by car to Portsmouth to board the destroyer *Fury* and sailed immediately for the French coast. *Fury* reached Boulogne late the following afternoon after fourteen hours at sea, having been slowed down in the Channel by fog. From early in the day, strong forces of armed police were drafted into the town from the neighboring stations. The news that the duke was expected soon leaked out, and thousands flocked toward the waterfront to catch a glimpse of him.

It had been arranged to attach a special Pullman to the Boulogne–Basel express, which also went on to Zurich and was due there at 1:05 P.M. The duke remained on board *Fury* till darkness fell, when he took a stroll on the quay with his Scotch terrier. Then his forty-three trunks were loaded onto a train for the transcontinental journey.

As he left, the Archbishop of Canterbury, in a radio broadcast, poured vitriolic scorn on the former king and his social circle whose way of life was alien to all that was best in British traditions.

There were the "rats," too, who were coming out of the woodwork with disapproving words about Edward, whom they branded insane, and Wallis, whom they had never really liked. Perry Brownlow, back in London, sprang to her defense whenever possible and said she had done all she possibly could to halt the abdication. But the talk in the nightclubs and at dinner parties would be endless and argued over interminably. Did she really love him, or was she merely taken in by the fantasy of it, the jewels, the glittering social world she had entered? Others were less sympathetic and were saying she had schemed her way into the king's heart, that she pushed her hand to the limit and lost.

That forthright critic, Alec Hardinge, who had resigned over the king's association with Mrs. Simpson, was back at the Palace to become King George's principal private secretary. Other staff loyal to Edward were eased out, or simply asked to resign. Perry Brownlow was one; his resignation as lord-in-waiting at the Palace was accepted even before he had offered it, upon his return from escorting Wallis through France. Wallis's name was mud. Even the Duke of Kent, now suspected of having returned to his drug habit during the abdication crisis, was walking around saying, "I could kill that woman." Author Hector Bolitho brought out a revised edition of his biography of Edward in which he attacked his stubbornness, his conceit over his popularity, and his fantastic vanity and described him as a distraught, unreasonable man—an assault which Compton Mackenzie and Churchill criticized heavily, for the way Bolitho had suddenly turned somersault in his views.

The Churchills continued to defend the former king at every opportunity, even Clemmie Churchill, who had strongly disagreed with her husband and was of the view that Edward should have set aside his personal feelings and performed his inherited duty.

At a dinner soon after the abdication (when she heard Lord Granard attacking the former King and Mrs. Simpson), she turned instantly upon him, with the reply, "If you feel that way, why did you invite Mrs. Simpson to your house and put [her] on your right?"

Yes, it was being said that Wallis had tormented the king in the final forty-eight hours with the prospect of withdrawing from his life. Maybe that would have forced him to stay and remain king, and given the help of a new political party, influenced by Wallis's Fascist friends, then the specter of a Führer-style monarch might have become a reality.

If that is what Baldwin had feared, then it would have been a basis for disposing of the king, whatever the cost. Baldwin, too, had pushed his hand to the limit in threatening to resign, secure in the assurances of other political leaders that they would not form a new government. If at the last, the king had stayed, what then? Baldwin could have handled the situation if Mrs. Simpson had indeed withdrawn totally. But with her still around in whatever role—king's mistress, occasional dalliance, long-distance lover in a South of France hideaway—the problem would remain. Anyway, his evidence of her affiliation with the Nazis would have heavily influenced his handling of those final forty-eight hours of the crisis.

Edward himself, in retrospect, was convinced Baldwin and Dawson had plotted to get rid of him. But there was no plot. The prime minister's stance was shared by his cabinet, and whatever evidence they had against Mrs. Simpson, whatever they thought of the king's antics, Baldwin played his hand to perfection, forcing Edward day by day into a corner from which he could not escape. It had to be that way. The dangers which only years later would begin to be realized by the public, but of which Baldwin was aware even then, were too great to allow Edward to stay on the throne.

Ribbentrop was certainly of this view when he cabled to the Führer: "I have worked for friendship with England for years. . . . I was sceptical about the likelihood of success, but because of Edward VIII, it seemed a final attempt should be made. . . . Today I no longer have any faith in any understanding . . . Baldwin has already apprehended this, and Edward had to abdicate since it was not certain whether he could cooperate with an anti-German policy."

·EIGHT·

HEIL HITLER

———◆———

In a castle in Austria, long hours of reflection, contemplation, and yearning for his beloved Wallis provided no great or calming diversion for the Duke of Windsor as he stood on the edge of a new and different life.

So many years in the service of his country, so many years in the company of flatterers and sycophants, so many years of being able to snap his fingers and watch people jump: it would all change now.

He saw the months ahead as being a temporary exile from his country. When he was married to Wallis and the dust had settled, he would return to the joyous welcome of his friends, and to his family as the Shadow King.

Churchill wrote to him almost as soon as he left to voice a note of optimism on that score:

> I was so glad to learn that Your Royal Highness had found a convenient agreeable shelter for the moment. I know your charming hostess well, having been a guest with her at Maxine's villa.
>
> From all accounts the broadcast was successful, and all over the world people were deeply moved; millions

wept. The Government were grateful. They certainly ought to be.

From words I had with Neville [Chamberlain], I gathered that what he attached great importance to was your living absolutely separate until everything is settled and the new Civil List is voted. He was rather grim and bleak, but I am sure he is right on this point.

I suppose, Sir, you saw that the Attorney-General in the Debate on the Abdication Bill declared formally that there was no obligation upon Your RH to reside outside the British Dominions. So I earnestly hope that it will not be very many months before I have the honour to pay my respects to you at the Fort.

References to the Civil List gave a clue to another problem taxing the duke's mind at that point: money. When he left England, he had a personal fortune of £800,000. He had no property or other earnings. His houses were handed over to the new monarch, and his income from the Duchy of Cornwall ceased upon his resignation. His only other asset was his ranch in Canada, which provided virtually no income.

That fortune he had, though large by normal standards, was in fact a most modest sum, bearing in mind he would now have to finance himself for the first time in his life. In fact, he felt he was in quite a precarious state. There would be a home to set up, servants to hire, not to mention Wallis's wardrobe, their entertaining, traveling and so on. Eight hundred thousand pounds would not provide an investment income sufficient to finance all that.

For the rest of their lives, the Windsors would consider themselves constantly on the brink financially, leading Edward into the most dangerous of money-making ventures, and leading both into writing their life stories and earning money from press and television interviews.

When the duke passed everything over to George VI, the new king said he would guarantee Edward an allowance of £25,000 a year if nothing was to be forthcoming from the Civil List, that is, the taxpayer. The latter proved intractable. No money was voted to the duke by Parliament after he had abdicated, and it seemed that the king's government were advising the king that no money be paid to the duke at all, unless he agreed not to return to England without prior approval of the royal family.

Three months after the abdication, this delicate situation had still not been resolved. The duke was constantly on the telephone to London about it; speaking to the king, his brothers, his sister, Churchill—anyone who would listen.

On April 25, 1937, Churchill made notes on the subject:

> I understand that the allowance, apart from certain business elements, was a matter of family affection arising out of the King's promise to the Duke before the latter's abdication. It is altogether a personal and brotherly affair. It would not be right for Ministers to advise the King to make the payment of this allowance contingent upon the Duke not returning to England without the King's permission.
>
> Such advice would tend to involve the King in what might become very distressing publicity. Above all, Ministers should not advise that such a condition should be presented to the Duke through the lawyers. The Duke would have no option but to refuse to receive such a communication; for otherwise he would put himself in the position of bartering his right to return to his native land for pecuniary advantage. It is to be hoped therefore that Ministers will not persist in such advice to the King.

Churchill himself eventually negotiated an undertaking from the king that the £25,000 a year would be paid from the monarch's own resources. The government was, in this way, saved the embarrassment of a public discussion on whether or not the duke should receive an official income.

In his long wait for Mrs. Simpson's divorce to be made absolute the duke, becoming impatient, wanted to leave his castle and move to France. His solicitors, however, warned that they must stay apart until the decree was confirmed, otherwise they might invalidate the divorce.

During these months, hardly a day went by without letters being exchanged or long telephone conversations held at night. Edward was also telephoning Buckingham Palace, to discuss plans for his marriage once the divorce had come through.

The duke had become a problem, as *The Daily Mirror* recorded in a leader article, which also highlighted the now much-discussed question of the time that would elapse before the Windsors would be allowed home.

The Daily Mirror was quite adamant in an editorial that the duke and his bride would soon be back:

> Daily the Royal Family is receiving 'phone calls from Austria. Not content with causing a pretty serious change in Coronation plans, Edward, Duke of Windsor, has been calling up members of his family to discuss the revised proceedings.
>
> Talk of years of voluntary exile for the Duke is so much nonsense. As much as he loved dashing abroad for his holidays when duties chained him here for most of the year, now that lack of duties keeps him chained abroad he is straining to return.
>
> England is dear to the Duke and already Fort Belvedere is being prepared for his home-coming, which will be not so long after the Coronation.

Churchill himself, however, had made known his view of an early homecoming. Shortly after the abdication, he wrote to Geoffrey Dawson, at *The Times*. After speaking of the "sledge-hammer blows *The Times* dealt the late King" he went on:

Now, of course, the only thing is to look forward and repair the damage that has been done to the Throne. I am hoping that the Duke of Windsor will soon be able to come back and live here quietly as a private gentleman. For this purpose the dust of controversy must be laid, and the new reign established on unshakeable foundations. I am sure he has no other wish but to live quietly in England, and it seems very hard if he should not be allowed to do this.

May I enlist your chivalry in trying to bring this about, after a suitable lapse of time? Perhaps the Newspaper Proprietors' Association might be induced to give him the same kind of immunity as was such a comfort to Colonel Lindbergh. Perhaps you will let me have a talk with you about this later on.

Only history would show how wrong Churchill was in his view. The duke would never return to live in England; nor would he be welcomed by the royal family.

Now, at the castle, the duke was like a caged lion, pacing about, drinking often, going on private trips, and dealing with business matters and mail. And he was refusing to speak English. Fruity Metcalfe, who had joined him at Enzesfeld in January, wrote home to his wife: "He has become very foreign, talking German all the time. All he is living for now is to be with her. I have never seen anyone so madly in love. It's pathetic."

The mail was enormous, three hundred letters a day sometimes. They came from all over the world, and many of them abusive—"but we don't show him those." The duke spoke often of "the rats" back home, and noted those who had turned against him once he'd left.

As the weeks went on, so the tension mounted, and now it was beginning to show itself in the relationship between Wallis and Windsor. Fruity Metcalfe wrote, "He's on the line for hours every day to Cannes. . . . I don't think these talks go so well sometimes. . . . She seems always to be picking on him and complaining about something she thinks he hasn't done or ought to do . . ."

And Mountbatten noted an occasion when he overheard a telephone conversation between the two of them when Edward said to Wallis, "I've just spent the happiest day of my exile. Dickie's here." There was a pause, and then he said, "Oh no, darling, I could never be really happy with you not here, but this was the nearest thing to not being unhappy."

The money situation was preying on the duke's mind, too, and Metcalfe noted: "He won't pay for a thing . . . it's becoming a mania with him. It really is not too good . . ."

In fact, money seemed to be the only touch of realism in the duke's thoughts. When Mountbatten came to the castle to visit, there were long conversations about the forthcoming wedding to Mrs. Simpson. Mountbatten offered to be the best man but the duke dismissed the suggestion. He wanted his two younger brothers as his supporters and he was expecting most of his family to be there. In the event, it would be Mountbatten who would have to tell him by letter that "others had intervened," and not only would Dickie himself be unable to attend, the duke's brothers and sisters would be barred from attending.

Expecting that any single member of his family would attend the wedding showed a remarkable naiveté on the part of Windsor. He either did not know or had simply ignored the wide gulf that existed in the family, which was obvious to those callers at Buckingham Palace who were able to get into conversation with the king over his brother. "HM is anxious that the Duke should *not* return to this country," noted the wife of Lloyd George after the former Liberal prime minister had been to the Palace. She also wrote that the king was of the view that Mrs. Simpson "dare not come back here" and "she has no friends."

In the latter case, the king was right. Most of those who had been so keen to capture the attendance of Mrs. Simpson at dinner parties in 1935 and 1936 would now rather cross the street than talk to her if perchance they met her walking down the Mall.

On May 8, Wallis Simpson would change her name by deed poll as if to wipe away all record of her past; she resorted to her maiden name, Wallis Warfield, in a vain attempt to look unsullied.

Meanwhile, as has been seen from the newspaper comment, the duke was constantly on the telephone to Buckingham Palace, as if although temporarily out of the country, he was still in charge. Walter Monckton was sent by the Palace to point out, with all due diplomacy, that the king could no longer take the constant verbal contact, since he was extremely busy. The telephone calls must cease. It was a difficult task for Monckton, and it left the duke with a bitterness that would remain and fester.

The king had to be consulted on one more issue, the location of the wedding of the duke and Mrs. Simpson. She had suggested a villa in the south of France called La Croe at Antibes, which would become their first home together. The king, however, felt that the Riviera was hardly the right location: too flashy and associated with the socialite gaiety of the thirties. The search for another place for the wedding led the duke and duchess straight into Nazi hands, and here began a new contact with Nazi Germany that would lead to grave disquiet in London.

All this came at a time when senior Special Branch and MI5 officers were recording their growing concern over Tom Mosley's activities, in particular the way he was still aligning his speeches with the former king. Police shorthand writers taking down Mosley's speeches recorded many references to the monarchy, but the Fascists were saying that although they were loyal to the crown, that did not necessarily mean to George VI.

All of the British security services were well aware of

the Mosley plan and kept tabs, not only on him, but Diana, the Windsors, and others, by constant observation. It was at this point, in mid-1937 and beyond—that the Home Office in London considered the prospect that Mosley might at some point try to regroup around the Duke of Windsor. It was resolved in the security services that if he should attempt to do so, the Fascist leader would be arrested for sedition. But contact with the Duke of Windsor would come not from Mosley but from Charles Bedaux, friend of the Nazis and anxious to please them. He had heard from the Rogerses that the Windsors were looking for somewhere to hold their wedding, since the king had ruled as "totally out of the question" the ceremony's being held in the South of France. That was far too garish and gossipy, even for the Windsors' wedding.

But in refusing this venue, King George played into the hands of Bedaux, who put his superb Château le Cande at the Windsors' complete disposal. What a coup for Bedaux: Berlin would be delighted; in London there would be grave disquiet. Charles Bedaux had been anxious to do all he could to keep in the Germans' good books. They had confiscated one of his businesses and he wanted it back. He was a man solely devoted to his own self-interest, yet he was highly dangerous. The extent of his eventual contact with the Nazi regime would become clear only in 1943, when he was captured by the Americans while working on a German project in North Africa. In his possession would be found papers signed by the German High Command and letters of sanction from Vichy France. He would eventually commit suicide in a Miami prison.

To Wallis Simpson, here and now in the spring of 1937, Bedaux and his wife Fern were a charming couple; indeed Wallis was thrilled and went early to Le Cande, leaving the South on March 9, 1937, with her maid and some twenty-six pieces of luggage.

The château was the kind of place she would feel at

home in; the kind of place she could envisage as befitting the wife of such an important world figure, though she would never afterward quite achieve the style and elegance of Bedeaux's home. Two dozen blue-liveried flunkies were lined up as a guard of honor to welcome her when she arrived. Fern Bedeaux had been fussing around for days; everything was perfect, from their monogrammed silver cutlery to their pure Oriental silk bedsheets; the finest of foods to the latest in evening entertainment after their regular dinner parties. The magnificence of the thousand-acre estate at Tours made even Wallis gasp. It was the perfect setting, she said to Fern, for their marriage.

The duke, meanwhile, was becoming increasingly agitated for her, fearing lest there be some final hitch in Wallis's divorce. Back in England, a legal clerk named Francis Stephenson had already lodged with the attorney general's office an allegation that there had been irregularities of a serious nature in the Simpsons' divorce. If his complaint had been pursued with any vigor, irregularities would certainly have been discovered: Collusion among all parties; payment of money; perjury. But for reasons known only to himself, when the day of the divorce came to be made final, Stephenson would confirm that he had withdrawn his complaint. Whoever had put him up to halting the Simpson divorce in its tracks twenty-four hours before the abdication had now decided it was not worth pursuing.

Wedding plans were well advanced when Wallis telephoned the duke on May 3 with her special news: "It's through, David," she screamed down the mouthpiece. "My divorce is through." He already knew, having been telephoned from London earlier by his solicitors. Already he was packing, ready for the dash from Austria across France to Tours.

She came down the steps to greet him. He took both her hands in his and kissed them. They said a few words to the press and then retired to a quiet room she had prepared to welcome him, decorated with azaleas, roses, and lily of the valley. They had so much to talk about.

But there were still unhappy problems looming that would cause them both anxious times. First, Wallis discovered that under French law, she would have to produce a birth certificate, which of course she could not do. Hurried arrangements were made through her Aunt Bessie and local American consular officials to arrange for a sworn statement of her arrival on this earth to be taken from an American doctor who claimed he had been present. This was promptly conveyed to Paris to avoid Wallis's having to go through the embarrassment of making her own sworn statement regarding her birth.

For the duke himself, family matters were a cause for concern. He had already been told that he would not be welcome at the coronation of King George VI on May 12. The day before, he did something that can only be seen as an attempt to distract some of the attention being focused on his brother's great event, calling a press conference to announce formally his engagement to Wallis and that the wedding would be held on June 3. Even the date would be seen as something of an insult to his family. It was his father's birthday.

Despite all this, he still retained the expectation that at least his brother the Duke of Kent would be present at his wedding. But after the coronation, this hope would be shattered. No member of the royal family would attend. It was naive of him to think otherwise. But the most wounding aspect of the whole business came on May 29, when the *London Gazette* carried the official announcement that the Duke of Windsor would be entitled to "hold and enjoy for himself only the title of Royal Highness . . . his wife and descendants, if any, shall not hold said title style or attribute."

The duke immediately fired off a letter of protest to his brother, convinced that he would have a change of heart, and in the meantime he would insist that his fiancée be accorded the same recognition as himself at any gathering at which they were present. And so here on foreign soil, in the home of a Nazi agent, the former King of England formally rejected his heritage and turned his back on his country.

All day Tours was in a state of excitement. Thousands of French sightseers, who'd arrived by bus and private car early in the morning, gathered in the streets outside the hotel to watch the guests departing for the château, while the villagers of Monts, to whom the duke, in accordance with French custom, had distributed a gift of money in honor of his wedding day, went out to the château in a body. The weather was brilliant, but although the duke was out early, the bride did not leave her room until just before the wedding.

There were two ceremonies—a civil service conducted in French by Dr. Mercier, Mayor of Monts, and a religious ceremony conducted in accordance with the rites of the Church of England by the Reverend R. Anderson Jardine, Vicar of St. Paul's, Darlington, who later resigned from the church in the ensuing furor.

The civil service was brief and informal. Only the two witnesses, Fruity Metcalfe and Herman Rogers, along with W. C. Graham, the British consul-general at Monts, who represented the British government, and five members of the press, were present. Cecil Beaton took the pictures.

At the civil ceremony, held in the small salon of the château, the only decorations in the room were two large vases of pink carnations and red peonies. The duke entered the room at 11:33, the bride some minutes later. The duke was dressed in a black morning coat and striped trousers, a white and gray striped shirt and a gray tie. A white carnation was pinned in his buttonhole. The bride's wedding dress was a close-fitting, ankle-length, two-piece gown of powder blue crêpe. It was cut along very simple lines. Over it was a close-fitting short jacket of the same material as the dress. Her high-brimmed blue straw hat had a stiff veil turned upward from the brim. Her only jewelry consisted of a pair of diamond and sapphire earrings and a bracelet of square-cut diamonds and sapphires, the gift of the duke.

The bride and bridegroom and the two witnesses took their places in armchairs in front of the table. There were said to be 2,000 telegrams and 20,000 letters to the duke and duchess from all over the world; gifts too from the king and queen. Clearly, though, there were still those who showed some animosity. British film directors decided not to circulate in Britain the film of the Windsors' wedding, which was being shown in most other countries. They stated that this had been done without pressure or guidelines from the government.

Was it worth it? Was this what Wallis really wanted, just him, isolated and cut off, and not a king? There were no great signs of her love, nor any of her emotion. Ba-ba Metcalfe wrote that Wallis was unmoved by his obvious infatuation for her, showed not a glimmer of softness, and never took his arm or looked at him as if she loved him. Lady Metcalfe wrote that day: "Let's hope that she lets up on him in private, otherwise it must be grim . . . no one will ever know to what extent Wallis was at the bottom of everything. Baldwin is supposed to say that as a schemer and intriguer, she is unsurpassed. My opinion is that she must have hoped to be either Queen or morganatic wife. . . . I loathe her for what she has done, though I am unable to dislike her."

Walter Monckton arrived carrying a letter from the king: On no account should the duchess be termed "Her Royal Highness," nor should she be curtsied to, or enjoy any other of the traditions of respect that surround a person of HRH status. The duke was furious and insisted he would fight it. He ignored the instruction of the king and told his staff to address the duchess as HRH.

It was a bad start and the bitterness was very evident as they drove off for their three-month honeymoon in Austria, where they had been loaned another castle, which had been made ready with all the comforts the new-lyweds could possibly desire. It seemed a most charming, innocent choice for a honeymoon; but it did not please the heads of British intelligence. The owner was Count Paul Munster, who had, during the past few years, divided his time between Austria and England. He was under general observation because of his association with known backers of Mosley's BUF. Even before they left for Austria, the duke had been talking enthusiastically to Charles Bedeaux about a possible visit to Germany, about which Bedeaux had already been in touch with Hitler's aide, Fritz Weidemann. Through him, the Windsors established direct contact with the Führer. Weidemann was instrumental in setting up the arrangements for the visit, and toward the end of their honeymoon, the Windsors joined Charles Bedeaux at his shooting lodge in Hungary to finalize everything.

Bedeaux had already announced to American contacts that he was helping the duke to become involved in the study and development of industrial and housing projects, both in Europe and America. The duchess recalled: "David's curiosity was immediately whetted. The idea had already been evolving in his mind that he might carve out a career fostering large-scale housing developments." Bedeaux himself had indicated that the duke's interests lay particularly in the field of housing for the underprivileged, and when mention was made that this might in time take him back to Britain to encourage developments there, British security pricked up their ears again. Was it just coincidence that Mosley, in his current speeches, was continuing the theme of support for the caring, courageous Duke of Windsor? Further, from the feelers Bedeaux was putting out, it appeared that the German visit would be followed up by a tour of American cities. It was not difficult for the British to imagine an international scenario in which the duke would be hoisted back into the world's headlines, first with a visit to Germany, followed up by a tour of the United

States. In the crescendo of publicity and press coverage he would achieve, the next step, that of returning to Britain under the guise of his supporting the cause of the working classes, could be difficult to refuse.

After the honeymoon, the Windsors returned to Paris, where they took an apartment at the Hôtel Meurice until they found a more permanent home. Almost immediately, they were contacted again by Bedeaux, who had arranged to bring two important Nazis to discuss their forthcoming tour.

It was purely by chance that British intelligence learned of the duke's plans to tour Germany. According to a report published in 1966, MI5 agents had been following Errol Flynn, the Hollywood actor who was suspected of working for the Nazis. Flynn was believed to be an important link between them and the IRA in the late thirties, and there was concern over the aid the Republicans were getting from Germany. Indeed the strength of the IRA as war loomed prompted Chamberlain to note: "IRA forces seem strong enough to over-run the weak Eire forces." He advised that Britain must be ready to send forces to southern Ireland. British agents kept watch on Flynn, who met Bedeaux and the duke and duchess in their apartment. MI5 noted that they discussed the German tour and "connections to be made with the Germans."

Flynn was followed on a train, where he was seen talking to known Nazi agents. He was observed again in Berlin by British agents three days later in the company of Rudolf Hess, Hitler's deputy, and Martin Bormann. The three men then went directly to Paris, going straight to the Windsors' suite at the Meurice.

Hess also had a private meeting with the duke and later made personal notes of conversations between them. The deputy Nazi leader wrote that the duke was proud of his German blood, that he was more German than British, and that he was keenly interested in the development of the Third Reich and its policies in Germany.

Hess added, "There is no need to lose a single German life in invading Britain. The duke and his clever wife will deliver the goods."

While all captured German documents have to be read with a degree of scepticism, it has been noted by many that the duke, in his mood of dissatisfaction over his treatment at the hands of his family and the British government, was quite likely to have spoken in such terms.

One thing is quite certain. By the time the honeymoon was over, the duchess was beginning to wonder whether she had done the right thing. Two previous husbands were never at home during the working day: her third husband had no work in view. She had an apparent dislike of having him fussing around her and assuring her that every whim, need, and wish would be complied with. It was too overbearing for her, and they both were getting fed up with the almost unavoidable situation whereby every conversation led, at some point, back to the abdication to such a degree that they themselves were now arguing about it and disputing the whys and wherefores over and over again. Wallis became extremely bored with the whole topic. She was also already bored with the slowness of the life they were thrust into. The glamour, the excitement, the social whirl, and the importance had all suddenly gone from their lives. There was, and it takes little imagining, an emptiness that neither was used to or could adjust to overnight. Walter Monckton wrote. "She could not easily reconcile herself to the fact that by marrying her, he had become a less important person." According to Monckton, she was already pushing the duke toward his reemergence as a public figure.

Two days after the meeting with Bedeaux was recorded, the duke announced on October 3 that he would begin his ten-day tour of Germany almost immediately. He also revealed that upon his return he would visit the United States for a tour of housing and industrial projects. So while he and the duchess went east, Charles Bedeaux headed west, across the Atlantic where he would spend the next nine days trying to fix a tour of America.

Churchill was utterly dismayed when he heard, but apparently made no move to stop the duke from embarking on a tour which, in the eyes of most British politicians of all parties, amounted to crass stupidity at a time when Hitler's sinister and menacing Nazis were involved in increasingly despicable anti-Semitic deeds. Lord Beaverbrook, by contrast, pleaded with the duke not to go.

The Americans had already given much thought to how to treat the duke's request to visit the U.S. Telegrams, eventually in code because of embarrassingly frank comments about the duke and duchess from European diplomats, had been flashing between Washington and the U.S. European embassies. Cordell Hull gave instructions that he did not want the State Department publicly to be seen to be acting in any way insulting to the duke, who was a popular figure with millions of Americans. At the same time, British fears over the political nature of the visit should be taken into account.

In London, Sir Robert Vansittart, permanent undersecretary at the Foreign Office and soon to become chief diplomatic adviser, called in Sir Ronald Lindsay, the British ambassador in Washington, Vansittart had now assembled a substantial security file on the Windsors, which made shocking reading: leaks; dubious meetings; casual discrediting remarks; agents' reports— all logged and top secret. Those on the duchess were particularly damaging. Lindsay's view was clear; he felt quite positive that the duke would attempt to return to England after an anticipated highly acclaimed tour of America.

Lindsay was also summoned to an audience with the king, at which Queen Elizabeth was present. The Palace insisted that if the tour went ahead, the Windsors should receive absolutely no official recognition of co-operation from any British embassy, nor from any British diplomat. Vansittart had already given that instruction to all European British embassies, and when the duke and duchess arrived in Berlin to begin their tour of Germany on that mid-October day, they were surprised to find that they would not be greeted by the British ambassador, Sir Neville Henderson, who had conveniently taken leave. The duchess would recall with disdain: "The attitude of the Foreign Office was clearly evident . . . as soon as we got off the train at Berlin . . . only a Third Secretary from the British Embassy was there to meet us. He brought a note from the British Ambassador stating that he had been directed to take no official cognizance of our visit."

The Germans, however, were going to make the most of the visit. Dr. Robert Ley, the infamous Nazi labor leader, took them in his huge black Mercedes to his home in Berlin, a twenty-six-room mansion once owned by a Jewish banker. The place was surrounded by twenty of Hitler's own black-suited guards from the S.S. Inside, they were greeted by Ribbentrop and Goebbels.

Then, amid cheering crowds, the duke and duchess began their tour of factories and housing projects that were the pride of Hitler's new Germany, culminating in a meeting with the Führer himself. Standing in the brilliant sunshine on the balcony of his mountain home at Berchtesgaden, Hitler, dressed in the Nazi uniform, greeted his guests with an upraised arm. Then he and the duke went off to talk in private, leaving the duchess in the company of Rudolf Hess. Recalling the meeting, the duchess wrote, "The interview was supposed to last half an hour but when an hour had passed, with no sign of David, Hess became agitated and went off to telephone. While he was away, David and Hitler returned, talking energetically. Since Hitler spoke no English, David insisted on continuing in German. I could not take my eyes off Hitler, who at close quarters gave one the feeling of a great inner force. His hands were long and slim, a musician's hands, and his eyes were truly extraordinary, intense, unblinking, magnetic, burning with some peculiar fire."

They all walked through a large drawing room overlooking the Bavarian Alps and then the meeting was at an end. Hitler shook the duchess by the hand, then turned to the duke and gave the Nazi salute, to which the duke responded with "*Heil*, Hitler."

He gave the salute three times during the two-week visit, and apart from the continual attention of Dr. Ley, whom they both hated for his lewd, boorish, and often drunken manner, the Windsors enjoyed their visit. They appeared to have done nothing more than cooperate with the German publicity machine which was geared to make the most out of the presence of the most talked-of couple in the world; and there were many influential Britons in Germany at that time who were perhaps involved in more reprehensible activities.

Windsor himself would never admit, however, that his visit at such a critical period of international affairs was a most irresponsible and foolhardy act. Although he openly praised the high standards of social development reached under Nazi rule, and admired Germany's industrial surge, he did not seem to understand the sinister backdrop to it all. But neither did many other European and American visitors to Germany at that time.

Hitler and his henchmen went out of their way to be good hosts, and the Führer commented about Wallis that "she would have made a good Queen." There is no public record of the conversations between Hitler and the duke. The duchess' own recollection was that the duke spoke little about the discussion, other than to say that it was about stopping the spread of communism. The Germans' own records are known to have included an account of the conversation—and the file was among captured German documents on foreign policy. Its whereabouts would become something of a mystery, but the probability is that the file, which would undoubtedly have wounded British pride further had it been released after the war, is now somewhere in the royal archives, along with many other sensitive reports concerning the activities of the Duke and Duchess of Windsor.

The duke must have picked up certain clues to Hitler's ambitions during that visit but, as far as we know, he never reported them to the British Foreign Office. Hermann Göring for example, showed him a map of Europe on which Austria was already shown as part of Germany. Göring joked about it when the Windsors questioned him, but if any alarm bells rang, the Windsors were deaf to them all.

They were overwhelmed by the attention they received, especially at a glittering gala dinner given for them by Edward's cousin the Duke of Coburg. It pleased Wallis especially because there, in front of her, was the place name bearing the prefix Her Royal Highness. Thus, the Nazi Coburg became the first member of the royal family to afford her such recognition.

In the final hours of the German trip, the Windsors were surrounded and fêted by the top men in the Third Reich. Goebbels, Göring, and Hess, particularly the latter, were in close conversation with them. In such mounting European tension, mere pleasantries could not have been the sum of their exchanges; and the duke set off back to Paris with his head swimming with Nazi propaganda.

Charles Bedeaux, meanwhile, had almost completed his arrangements for the tour of America. It would be a major event, involving a dozen cities. Wallis was totally enthralled, anxious as she was to get back to her homeland, and was overjoyed when Bedeaux told her the mayor of Baltimore had promised a huge welcome for the city's now royal daughter and the ex-king. To Wallis, it all sounded so wonderful; to the duke it presented at last an opportunity to get back into worthwhile and, perhaps, gainful employment. They had both either ignored and dismissed the sinister side of Bedeaux's arrangements.

As soon as news of the trip was announced, the Windsors were flooded with invitations from the New York elite who wanted to land the social catch of the season. Since Washington had decided that if the visit went ahead, it would not give official recognition, the duke would go as a private citizen. The Americans could see that they faced a ticklish situation. The king and queen, the British government, and large sections of British opinion were against the duke setting foot on American soil.

The king, as Sir Ronald Lindsay told Sumner Welles early in November, had not in any way yet achieved the popularity of Windsor, whose years in the public eye would not easily be forgotten. There was enough concern being expressed at all levels of government and the intelligence communities of Europe and America over Windsor's willingness to be used as a glamorous front man for those who supported the Fascist leaderships. Even Windsor himself could not have been blind to the criticism of his allegiances, yet he continued to court the limelight and to associate with those very people who were inspiring public concern.

When the itinerary for his tour was announced, there would be further speculation as to its purpose. Some of the factories he was to visit had strong existing German connections, including DuPont, Eastman-Kodak, Standard Oil, and General Motors. From any viewpoint, it seemed that once again Windsor's gullibility had led him to form an alliance with friends of the Nazis who would doubtless be somewhere close by on his tours. He had been set up by Bedeaux to help further the German cause, both in terms of propaganda and to give his hangers-on a unique intelligence opportunity as the Windsors met high-ranking officials in host countries.

Trouble was already building up for the U.S. tour.

Four days before the Windsors were due to depart, Churchill wrote to the duke, pointing out the dangers of traveling in a German ship:

> The American journey I feel sure will be prosperous and you will get a reception from that vast public which no Englishman has ever had before. There is only one point on which I would presume to make a suggestion. Would it not be wiser to cross the Atlantic in the *Normandie* rather than in the *Bremen* or *Europa*? Nothing can beat the *Normandie* for comfort; but what makes me write is the importance of not running counter to the overwhelming anti-Nazi feeling in the United States. As you know, the mob in New York a few months ago actually raided the *Bremen* and tore down the Swastika flag. There are millions of Jews in the United States, and they have a great deal of influence there. I do not think that your tour of Germany will be a serious impediment, but if you arrive in a French ship, you will have effectively made a gap between the German and the American tour. Moreover, travelling by the *Normandie* would enable you to pay a compliment to France, which after all is the country with whom our fortunes at the present time are bound up.
>
> I hope, Sir, you will forgive me for venturing to put this point before you, for I, like your many friends in England, have only one desire, namely for your continued happiness, good fortune, and influence for good.

In America, hostile reaction was emerging. *The New York Times* said in a leading article:

> Ex-Kings have interested themselves in making crops, in gambling, in drinking, in social life, and in trying to get their throne back. The Duke of Windsor is perhaps the first King to undertake a study of housing.
>
> Unless he is a good deal wiser than our own housing experts, he may find that brief visits to Germany and the

United States will not teach him much. He might learn more by visiting Great Britain if the state of affairs permits him to return.

Yet he must be given credit for wanting to use his time in a constructive way. The ex-King is, after all, in the same boat as other victims of technological unemployment. He must acquire new skills if he is to lead a normal useful life . . .

He was welcomed here in his earlier years—he himself only knows whether they should be called his happier years.

Some of the adulation with which he was then received was no credit to our supposedly democratic society, and some of the curiosity which will greet himself and his Duchess, if he returns again, will be no credit to us either.

The newspaper followed that up three days before the duke was to sail, stating:

The Duke's decision to see for himself the Third Reich's industries and social institutions, and his gestures and remarks, have demonstrated adequately that the abdication did rob Germany of a firm friend, if not a devoted admirer, on the British throne.

There can be no doubt that this tour has strengthened the regime's hold on the working classes.

The Duke is reported to have become critical of English politics and is reported as declaring that British ministers of today and the possible successors are no match for the German or Italian dictators.

There was concern in London, too, when as the duke continued with his plans he made a surprise speech at a dinner for foreign correspondents in Paris later that year. His tone was threatening:

I am naturally not criticising anyone present, but direct my remarks to the Press as a whole. Some of the recent misstatements concerning the Duchess and myself have caused us considerable concern and embarrassment and might well lead to dangerous consequences. I wonder if inaccuracies of the kind I mean are worthy of the great industry for which you work.

Our visit to Germany has been very interesting, and we are now looking forward to our tour of America and to further opportunities of making a study of the methods which have been adopted in the leading countries of the world, in dealing with housing and industrial conditions.

In this connection, I would wish to make it perfectly clear that any journey I have undertaken or may plan in the future I do as a completely independent observer without political considerations of any sort or kind and entirely on my own initiative.

We all know the circumstances that led up to the events of last December and the forces which influenced my final decision.

I am now a very happily married man, but my wife and I are neither content nor willing to lead a purely inactive life of leisure.

We hope and feel that in due course the experience we gain from our travels will enable us, if given fair treatment, to make some contribution as private individuals towards the solving of some of the vital problems that beset the world today.

The hostility toward them in the American press continued, and international labor movements, telling "the truth" about the previously unpublicized and devious background of Bedeaux, launched a worldwide protest.

One of the founders of time and motion study Bedeaux, whose fortunes had risen on the back of a widely criticized industrial system, thus became the target and enemy of the labor unions. The New York longshoremen said they would boycott the Windsors' ship when they arrived.

The furor grew by the hour, until Bedeaux decided

he could rescue the situation only by withdrawing from the project himself. From New York, he sent a telegram to Windsor: "Because of the mistaken attack on me here, I am convinced that your proposed tour will be difficult under my auspices. I implore you to relieve me completely of all duties in connection with it."

Bedeaux slipped away through the rear of his hotel and from Canada made his way back to Paris, but the duke agreed to go ahead with the tour, even in the face of such vitriolic opposition.

Sir Dudley Forwood, who was making the arrangements for him, was convinced he knew the real reason. "He wanted to prove to his wife he had lost nothing by abdicating; that as a Duke he was as important and influential as he had been as king." It was also quite obvious to Forwood, however, that the duchess was pushing him on toward this strange goal.

When their bags were packed and ready for transportation to the ship, the British ambassador in Paris, Sir Eric Phipps, gave the Windsors a farewell lunch. Then, suddenly, at the eleventh hour, it was all off. Canceled. The instruction, it is said, came directly from King George, whose displeasure at the commotion surrounding his brother had reached the point where he was bursting with anger.

With his arrangements in ruins, Bedeaux arrived back in Paris to find a message awaiting him from the duke. He was summoned to the Meurice; there were no recriminations and the duke did not for a moment blame Bedeaux for the fiasco. It was, he said, the result of a successful and slanderous campaign mounted by Communists and Jews.

The Windsors were still blind to the dangerous liaisons this man could have drawn them into, which would have resulted in an even more rapid discredit in both political and personal terms than the duke would eventually himself achieve. Bedeaux, on the other hand, had reaped the benefit of his association with the Windsors and had become an important industrial collaborator with the Nazis. For the next two years they would meet and dine regularly, even after the commencement of World War II.

When the Americans landed in North Africa, Bedeaux was arrested by the Free French in Algiers and held in a military prison at El Biar. The FBI was given the task of unraveling his company associations with the Nazis, and their investigations provided a mass of material sufficient for Bedeaux to be considered as a serious traitor. He was flown to Miami while a decision was made to try him for treason. The sentence could have been hanging—or alternatively he might have been sent back to France to be shot.

The Windsors remained his friends; even when he was in his death cell, they wrote letters of condolence to him.

·NINE·

UNWELCOME VISITORS

With the American tour halted, the Windsors decided to apply their minds to finding a permanent home. They wanted to return to England, but that was, apparently, still out of the question, and they did not seem to have any idea of what the future would hold for them or where they would eventually settle.

Money was forever on the duke's mind. By December 1937, the question of his financial settlement with his brother had clearly not been resolved to his satisfaction, as was shown when he wrote to Neville Chamberlain, who had now succeeded Baldwin as prime minister. "If my understanding of the present situation is correct, it is now proposed that my personal freedom . . . be linked with a private family arrangement on financial matters which my brother, the present King, made with me the day before I abdicated, in such a way that he would be permitted to break his private agreement with me if I were to exercise my right to visit my country without first obtaining approval. . . . I regard such a proposal as both unfair and intolerable as it would amount to accepting payment to remain in exile . . ."

The duke and duchess were hoping to make a short visit to England during 1938, but the responses they obtained from such letters of complaint about their status were hardly encouraging.

Walter Monckton, on one of his occasional visits, noted with dismay the effect this turmoil was having on the duke's mental state. He appeared to have lost his confidence and harbored a terror of displeasing the duchess in any way. His feelings of isolation and misery heightened when a British newspaper featured the declining state of the duke's beloved Fort Belvedere which had remained unattended since his departure and was a depressing picture of dilapidation. The king had promised Edward the use of the Fort upon his eventual return, but the current condition of the house that Edward had spent so many hours renovating indicated that an imminent return was not contemplated.

In the spring of 1938, Wallis's insistence on a home of their own to replace the rented rooms they occupied at the Hôtel Meurice inspired them to take a lease on the Château de la Croe at Antibes. It was also entirely necessary for them to leave Paris as soon as possible. The British ambassador had relayed to the Windsors an order, veiled as "a request," that they should not be present in the French capital for the forthcoming state visit to France by the king and queen.

At the same time, the duke had taken steps to sound out his mother's feelings toward him, as a possible ally in his quest for a return to England. Her response did nothing to give him hope when she wrote: "You ask me in your letter of 23rd of June to write to you frankly about my true feelings. . . . You will remember how miserable I was when you informed me of your intended marriage and abdication and how I implored you not to do so for our sake and for the sake of the country. You did not seem able to take in any point of view but your own. I do not think you have ever realised the shock which the attitude you took up caused your family and the whole nation. It seemed inconceivable to those who had made such sacrifices during the war, that you, as their King, refused a lesser sacrifice. My feelings for you as your mother remain the same and our being parted and the cause of it, grieve me beyond words. After all, all my life I have put my country before everything else and I simply cannot change now."

The despair of the Windsors, and of the duchess in particular, was only enhanced by the reception of the king and queen in Paris. Wallis could hardly contain herself as she read the headlines about her sister-in-law Elizabeth's considerable impact in the city where she had been fêted for the past six months. The Queen of England had won the hearts of the French nation, while in Berlin, Hitler, watching the newsreels of the visit, declared that she was "the most dangerous woman in Europe."

That spring also, the duke's favorite of all the European countries, Austria, collapsed into Hitler's arms. It was just as had been sketched in on Göring's map; the Nazis had goose-stepped into Vienna in March. Windsor did not join the ranks of the worldwide protestors against this action, though many of his friends, including Chancellor Schuschnigg and Baron Louis de Rothschild were caught up in the mess and interned by Hitler.

There was one faint British voice among those cheering the arrival of Hitler in Vienna; Unity Mitford had hurriedly caught the train from Munich to witness her Führer's triumphant arrival. She saw him the following day and shook his hand. Hitler said to her, "They said the English would be here to stop me, but the only English person I see is on my side." Unity wrote to Churchill to tell him her honest view of the Austrian situation; that Hitler had been welcomed by the majority. Churchill's response was terse and to the point. It was because Hitler feared expression of free opinion that "this dastardly outrage" had occurred.

With so much to depress them, the Windsors set about making their home in La Croe a palace fit for an exiled monarch. Despite his constant worry about finances, the duke could hardly refuse the duchess anything as she began to prepare a suitable domicile whose magnificence would match anything they might have had in London.

All that summer of 1938, the Windsors busied themselves settling into the villa and hiring staff, some twenty servants in all. They joined the Riviera playground set in the casinos of Cannes, Nice, and Monte Carlo and entertained old friends from London. Churchill, recalling one dinner at La Croe where he was staying, wrote "The Windsors are pathetic, but they seem happy . . . the poor duke, gay and charming, now has to fight for his place in conversation."

For the first time, Wallis could become the homemaker for them, and no expense was spared. As well as the duke's own furniture, silver, and porcelain shipped over from England, the duchess spent weeks on her excursions, buying antiques for La Croe, pictures, ornaments, more furniture and silverware, monogrammed table linen, silk sheets, and pillow cases, all hand-embroidered with the Windsors' initials. The best interior designer was hired from Paris. Wallis would also add immensely to her wardrobe.

The vexed question of a permanent home for the Windsors remained not just in their own thoughts, but in those of the British government too. Wallis herself, although fluent in neither French nor German, was heard to suggest that they might even consider taking up permanent residence in Germany, "since we are clearly not wanted elsewhere." Nor was it merely a question of the feud between them and the rest of the royal family on which the matter rested. Chamberlain was well aware of the MI5 and Scotland Yard reports on the speeches of Tom Mosley, who continued through 1938 and 1939 to refer to the ex-king. Security reports would continue to indicate that Mosley still viewed a regrouping of British Fascists around Windsor as a possibility.

British intelligence would not have been unaware of the activities of other Britons, some associated with Mosley, whose visits to Germany were causing more than a raised eyebrow. The Mitford sisters always visited there, as did their parents, Lord and Lady Redesdale.

Journalist and travel writer Robert Byron, attending the last big Nazi rally in Nuremberg with Unity Mitford, made some illuminating observations in his diary:

> September 5, 1938, Lunch at the Osteria [Bavaria], a little *burgerlich* restaurant which the Führer got into the habit of using when the Party Headquarters were nearby and where Bobo [Unity Mitford] first met him. . . . We made a detour to see if the Führer was back. No—she can tell by there being no one outside.
>
> . . . I start on foreign policy; she says she is confident there will be no general war because it would be the ruin of the Führer's whole life and policy. . . . She would not admit and could not begin to see that a diplomacy which in two or three years had raised the whole world in potential coalition against Germany is, from the German point of view, faulty.
>
> Of course, what England was waiting for was a man with a brain, though she admitted it might take 100 years to find one. Diana Mosley, she said in passing, has staked her life on being linked with the Dictator of England. If he fails to attain dictatorship, she will commit suicide . . .

How often must British intelligence, Chamberlain, and the cabinet have been presented with material that indicated Mosley's intention to grab power by any means possible—and if that meant utilizing the name of the Duke of Windsor, then so be it. Chamberlain could not be at all sure at this moment that Windsor would not, if presented with the right situation, go along with Mosley. Although some of the protagonists have denied there was ever a plot between them, Tom and Diana Mosley would say that if Edward had remained on the throne there might not have been a war.

Could it really be the case that the only reason Chamberlain continued his firm refusal of the duke's request to return to England for a visit was his wish not to upset the king? No. The truth was that Chamberlain faced such intense opposition from within his own party to suggestions of the duke's return that he abandoned the idea completely. That opposition was inspired not just by the king's feelings on the issue, but by the common belief among politicians that Windsor's mere presence in the country constituted a danger, and that danger was linked quite positively with Mosley.

So in exile they continued their pretense of running a royal court at La Croe. The lavish, almost vulgar, elegance was sufficient to make even the most socially experienced guest gasp with surprise. Wallis, who had furnished her last home at Bryanston Court on a few hundred pounds, now gave not a second thought to spending £8,000 on one single Meissen piece. The servants were dressed in a personal livery designed by the duke. They wore scarlet coats with gold cuffs for formal occasions and black suits with red striped waistcoats during the day. Every possible service, from hairdresser to manicurist, was available to visitors. The expense of it all must have made a substantial dent in the duke's remaining funds; yet they continued their lavish spending in total disregard of the clouds of conflict growing ever darker. In London, Tom Mosley was saying: "What on earth does it matter if Germans unite with others of that race?" Mosley was persisting with his campaigns "Mind Britain's Business" and "Britain Fights for Britain Only." In other words, he wanted the British government to stay out of the troubles in Europe and fight only if they were attacked. He saw no point in resisting Hitler simply because what he was doing was immoral, and he kept insisting there should be no war with Germany.

By the end of November 1938, Mosley's racist speeches and anti-Semitic rallies had reached fever pitch, particularly following the new surge of attacks on Jews throughout Germany following the murder by a Jew of a German official in Paris.

By March 1939, Hitler had invaded Czechoslovakia in total contempt of the Munich agreement that had been argued over and thrashed out amid such criticism a year earlier. Already, Hitler's claims that he was only interested in bringing former German territory back under his national banner had become a mockery.

Mosley went out on the hustings and pursued his "mind our own business" ranting. It had nothing to do with Britain. Stay out of it. Remember the horror of the last war; the millions killed; the poverty it brought. Not surprisingly, then, at the end of March, when the British government gave a guarantee to Poland that it and the French government would give Poland support if its independence were threatened, Mosley immediately wrote: "Any frontier incident which excites the light-headed Poles can set the world ablaze: British government places the lives of a million Britons in the pocket of a drunken Polish soldier."

If Mosley was looking for support for his ravings, he got it, and quickly. In May, the Duke of Windsor was back in the spotlight with words that closely echoed so much of what Mosley had been saying. "I break my self-imposed silence now only because of the manifest danger that we may all be drawing nearer to a repetition of the grim events that happened a quarter of a century ago. Peace is a matter too vital for our happiness to be treated as a political question."

So declared the duke in a speech broadcast from the historic World War I battlefield of Verdun in France to ninety million listeners in America, and a worldwide audience of four hundred million. The BBC refused to relay his message in Britain and denied there was any pressure from the government.

The duke's mother, Queen Mary, listened as her son, alone but for the radio engineers, sat before a microphone in the sitting room of his suite in the Hôtel Coq Hardie,

Verdun, and told the world: "I speak simply as a soldier of the last war whose most earnest prayer it is that such cruel and destructive madness shall never again overtake mankind.

"For two and a half years I have deliberately kept out of public affairs, and I still propose to do so. I speak for no one but myself, without the previous knowledge of any government."

His travels, his study of human nature, had left him with a profound conviction that there was no land in which the people wanted war.

"International understanding does not always spring up spontaneously of itself. There are times when it has to be deliberately sought and negotiated, and political tension is apt to weaken that spirit of mutual concession in which conflicting claims can be best adjusted."

For the first time his voice betrayed the emotion he felt when, after denouncing "poisonous propaganda," he said: "I personally deplore, for example, the use of such terms as 'encirclement' and 'aggression.' They can only arouse just those dangerous passions that it should be the aim of us all to subdue.

"It is in a larger interest than that of purely personal or purely national interest that peace should be pursued. Somehow I feel that my words tonight will find a sincere echo in all who hear them. It is not for me to put forward concrete proposals—that must be left to those who have the power to guide the nations towards closer understanding. God grant that they may accomplish that great task before it is too late."

Political commentators were asking: What could possibly have inspired the duke to make such a speech at such a critical time?

The broadcast was made as the king and queen were leaving England for a goodwill visit to America. In the two weeks preceding, President Roosevelt had made a direct appeal for peace to Hitler and Mussolini. Hitler had responded with a pro-British speech in which he spoke of a genuine and lasting friendship between Germany and Britain and once again insisted that the return to Germany of its colonies could never become the cause of military conflict. On the same day of his speech, however, he ended the Anglo-German naval pact, which, as Churchill correctly perceived, permitted him to build many new submarines; and on that day also, he ended the German-Polish Declaration of 1934, thus signaling the invasion of that country.

This time, American commentators were in praise of the duke for his speech. He had succeeded in what he had set out to achieve: stealing the thunder, and to some extent nullifying the propaganda effect, of his brother's visit to the United States.

Hitler, as some in London observed, could not have stage-managed the duke's interception at this point better if he had planned it himself. Those of suspicious nature suggested that perhaps his agents had; certainly there was mounting concern over the duke's motives and surprise at his continued pro-German sympathies as war loomed.

Under close scrutiny, his words contained little that could be held controversial; but his insistence that the speech was made "without reference to any government" seemed to imply that he expected criticism and even suspicion that there had been prior contact between him and the Third Reich.

After all, he could be accountable to only one government—Britain's—and the words *encirclement* and *aggression* were adjectives used more in sympathy with Germany, it seemed, than with his homeland.

Back in Britain, Mosley's last big meeting before the war started was in mid-July, when he hired Earls Court in London. Twenty thousand turned up to hear him, to watch the Nazi-style fanfares and the parade of Blackshirts carrying their flags to the stage through the center of the massive hall. Banners around the walls declared the familiar message: "Mind Britain's Business." Then

Mosley himself marched in alone down the center aisle to a tumultuous roar, climbed to the top of a high platform, and ranted nonstop for two hours with much misguided passion and feeling.

Looking down at the vast sea of faces before him, cheering, shouting, and then falling silent as his voice rose to crescendos, he cried, "I am told Hitler wants the world. In other words, I am told he is mad. What evidence have we got that this man who has taken his country from the dust to the heights after some twenty years of struggle, what evidence have they got to show that suddenly he has gone mad? Any man who wants to run the whole of the modern world with all its diverse population—such a man is undoubtedly mad. I challenge them to produce one single shred of evidence about the singularly shrewd, lucid, intellect whom they ventured to so glibly criticise. Why is it a moral duty to go to war if a German kicks a Jew across a Polish frontier . . . ? to be prepared to fight a world war over a few acres that don't belong to us . . . ? Suicide . . . insanity!"

The following month, August, only a couple of weeks before the outbreak of war, Diana Mosley went to Germany to see Hitler for the last time before the conflict began—the last time ever. The Führer told her that war with Britain was now inevitable because of the guarantees the government had given to Poland. Diana gave Hitler a report on her husband's speeches, about which he showed great interest. Though she knew now that war was only a short time away Diana still maintained her adulation of Hitler—keeping a framed picture of him beside her bed. There was also one of Goebbels on the mantelpiece.

She returned to England to find her husband's speeches, which seemed beautiful to her, being denounced as outrageous. He said, on the day Hitler marched into Poland on September 1, 1939, "Stand fast, my comrades and companions. Come what may, you have lit a flame in Britain which all the corrupt Jewish money-power cannot extinguish."

Then he went on the attack again over appeasement: "Britain nor her Empire is threatened . . . therefore Britain intervenes in an alien quarrel . . . we must demand peace . . . the British Union will continue our work of awakening the people until peace is won and the People's State of the British Union is born."

Fewer people were attending his meetings now, but his violent, thumping oratory, inflaming the remaining crowds into mass hysteria, remained as strong as ever. In Hackney, he shouted: "Put your hands up, those who will fight for Poland." Only two in the vast crowd did so, and they were immediately set upon.

Unity Mitford was still in Germany when war was declared on September 3. One hour after Neville Chamberlain's final ultimatum to Hitler had been disregarded, Unity faced a crisis of conscience. The story that has gone into the history books gives the commonly held view of her dilemma: so torn was she between her infatuation with Hitler and her love for her native British Isles that she took an envelope to the Bavarian Interior Ministry in Munich, then walked into a nearby park and shot herself through the head.

The envelope was opened by an official at the Ministry and was found to contain Unity's Nazi Party badge, a picture of Hitler, signed and dedicated, and a letter to the Führer. The official at the Ministry, who knew Unity, is said to have sent out an officer immediately to tail Unity as she walked into the Englischer Garten, and it was he who saw Unity shoot herself with a small pistol. He summoned assistance from a nearby Luftwaffe building.

This is the story that has been perpetuated by historians and the Mitford family alike. But there are a number of discrepancies. In their version of events Jonathan and Catherine Guiness (in *The House of Mitford*) state that Unity first fired one shot into the ground and then a second shot into her head. Another witness present at the time, though only a boy, was a Mr. H. W. Koch, who later came to live in England and wrote his account in the *Radio Times* in 1981. He had been walking in the park with his mother and brother when "a young fair-haired lady walked towards us, clad in a greyish costume. Hardly had she passed when behind we heard a sharp report . . . my brother caught in his arms the lady that had just passed us. Blood streamed from the side of her face." Within minutes, men in military uniform, possibly from the Luftwaffe building, were on the scene, followed with remarkable speed by the Gestapo.

The main discrepancy between the stories is the number of times the pistol was fired. The Guinesses say twice, Koch recalled one shot. But there are other unanswered questions. Is it likely that Unity would shoot herself almost in view of a mother with two small children? How did the Gestapo arrive so promptly on the scene and instruct the Koch family never to talk about the incident? Why didn't the man said to be tailing her halt her suicide, if that is what he suspected she would attempt? But most important, it seems strange indeed that she was not killed outright, if the shot was fired at such close range.

What we do know is that Unity survived the bullet wound, and upon Hitler's personal instructions was given the best possible medical care. Furthermore, the order was immediately given that Unity's shooting should be classed as a state secret, an aspect that would be rigidly enforced by the Gestapo.

But is this the truth concerning Unity's near-fatal injury? The author has heard of this contrasting version, which casts totally new light not just on that incident but also on Unity's own activities in the run-up to World War II. Almost a year before the outbreak of war, Unity was recruited as an agent for British intelligence by her then lover, Janos Almasy, the last member of a dying Hungarian aristocratic family, who appeared outwardly to be an ardent Nazi but by late 1937 was working for the

Edward, the Prince of Wales—a handsome, slight young man whose charm and poise would conquer so many. *(Camera Press)*

The closest of friends: the Prince of Wales and his cousin Lord Mountbatten at play during the Empire tour of 1920, in a bath slung between the guns of HMS *Renown*. *(Central Press)*

Wallis Simpson (center) in Oriental costume, 1926. A top-secret background check conducted by the Crown discovered that Wallis had earlier been active in the brothels of Hong Kong and Shanghai. *(UPI/Bettmann News Photos)*

Freda Dudley Ward, Edward's friend, confidante, and first real love, was abruptly dropped when Wallis took over his affections.

Timothy Seely, son of Freda Dudley Ward's sister Vera. The evidence that he is also the son of the Duke of Windsor goes well beyond the striking physical resemblance.

Fruity Metcalfe was Edward's aide and minder for half his lifetime, until the duke, dashing to be with his duchess, deserted Fruity in Paris as war broke out. *(Associated Press)*

The Duke and Duchess of Windsor on their wedding day. *(Camera Press)*

The duke and duchess visit the Führer, October 1937. *(Popperfoto/Pictorial Parade)*

Britain's answer to Adolf Hitler and Benito Mussolini, Sir Oswald "Tom" Mosley, founder of the British Union of Fascists, here in civilian clothes. His more familiar dress of the era was a black Nazi-style uniform and jackboots. *(Daily Mirror)*

Lady Diana Mosley was Mosley's mistress at twenty-two and married him in Germany in 1936, with Goebbels and Hitler witnessing. She became the Duchess of Windsor's closest friend. *(Universal Photos)*

Gold miner extraordinaire, Sir Harry Oakes was one of the world's richest men when he was murdered in 1943. The Duke of Windsor tried to keep the ensuing investigation quiet. *(Daily Mirror)*

A founding member of Murder, Incorporated, and one of America's most ruthless mobsters, Meyer Lansky was also the richest, leaving a fortune estimated at $400 million. He would host the Duke of Windsor in Havana. *(Daily Mirror)*

Count Freddie de Marigny escaped the gallows by the skin of his teeth after being wrongly accused of Oakes's murder. *(Associated Press)*

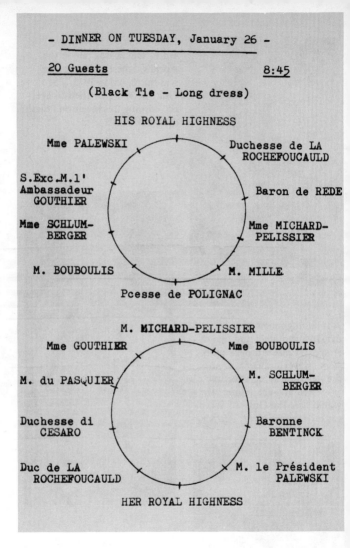

- DINNER ON TUESDAY, January 26 -

20 Guests   8:45

(Black Tie - Long dress)

HIS ROYAL HIGHNESS

Mme PALEWSKI   Duchesse de LA ROCHEFOUCAULD

S.Exc.M.l' Ambassadeur GOUTHIER   Baron de REDE

Mme SCHLUM-BERGER   Mme MICHARD-PELISSIER

M. BOUBOULIS   M. MILLE

Pcesse de POLIGNAC

M. MICHARD-PELISSIER

Mme GOUTHIER   Mme BOUBOULIS

M. du PASQUIER   M. SCHLUM-BERGER

Duchesse di CESARO   Baronne BENTINCK

Duc de LA ROCHEFOUCAULD   M. le Président PALEWSKI

HER ROYAL HIGHNESS

A typical seating plan for dinner with the Windsors, meticulously arranged by the duchess, who, it will be noticed, is described as Her Royal Highness, disregarding the Buckingham Palace order that she should not use the prefix.

The duke arrives in Paris after a trip to the United States in June 1969—a few days before the investiture of Prince Charles as Prince of Wales. *(Keystone)*

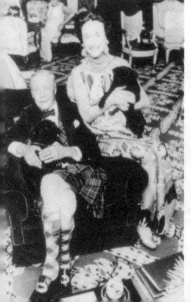

The duke and duchess in France in 1967. *(Camera Press)*

Meeting the family: This was the one and only time the Duchess of Windsor was photographed with the Queen, Prince Philip, and Prince Charles—after the funeral of her husband. *(Sunday Mirror)*

Their home, my home. Georges Sanegre, the Windsors' butler for most of his working life, was photographed after the death of his mistress, whose portraits hang in every room. *(Sunday Mirror)*

British. Almasy had long been friendly with other members of the Mitford family, who had visited his castle, Berstein, a half-empty relic of earlier wealth. In the gathering storm, he was intimate with certain members of a family whose contact with the Nazis, by and large, could only be described as enthusiastic. But Almasy's power over Unity, who had fallen deeply in love with him, was such that he persuaded her finally to his cause: spying for the British.

Himmler began to suspect Unity and went directly to Hitler to insist that she would be liquidated because of the obvious danger to the Third Reich and her closeness to the central seat of power. The Führer would not even contemplate the situation and dismissed the very idea that his friend Unity could be anything other than she appeared, a loving and firm supporter of him. Himmler persisted, and devised a plan to have her shot in the Englischer Garten on that day. The bullet that hit her was fired from a distance, not by Unity herself, according to the author's source.

She was taken away in a Gestapo car to a clinic, where she was placed under guard. Her flat was placed under the immediate control of Himmler's men and no one was allowed inside. Hitler himself would visit Unity on two occasions, but it would become clear both to him and to Himmler that she was now no danger to them, since the wound had severely damaged her brain.

Hitler himself arranged for her to be repatriated to Britain. She was to be taken to Berne in late December, and on to England through France. Janos Almasy escorted Unity on the journey into Switzerland. She was also accompanied by two nurses, who were nuns; one of them was Hungarian.

There was great confusion and rumor surrounding Unity's shooting; she herself, even in the better moments of her mental state, apparently never admitted to attempting suicide, though it is clear from some earlier statements prior to the outbreak of war that she had talked openly of the possibility if hostilities became certain.

The story of Unity Mitford's intelligence work was recorded by another British agent, David Edge, who had been working in Hungary at the time. His account seemingly surprised MI6, since Unity's activities had been known only to the highest level of intelligence. The Mitford family have always maintained that Unity's shooting was by her own hand. She was never able to set down the exact details of the incident. She died in 1947 when the bullet, still lodged in her brain, shifted and killed her.

Mosley's former aide, William Joyce, was also in Germany when war broke out. They had fallen out and Joyce, an Irish-American, became a naturalized German. He stayed, and became the infamous Lord Haw Haw, the hated and evil wartime broadcaster, who spent the rest of the war taunting the British—for which he was justly hanged.

Mosley's sister-in-law, Ba-ba Metcalfe, had motored down to La Croe with her husband Fruity that summer to join other houseguests of the Windsors. On August 22, they began to run for cover after the sudden announcement of the Nazi-Soviet pact, which came as something of a thunderbolt to the duke. He had become convinced since his conversation with Hitler that the Germans would move to the East, that their real target was the Soviet Union and not Britain.

The prospect of war would become his preoccupation for many days. He sent two telegrams, one to Hitler and one to King Emmanuel of Italy, pleading for peace. At 2 A.M. on the morning of September 1, the duke was woken by the local postmaster who carried what he insisted was a highly important telegram. It was from the Führer. If there was war, Hitler declared, it would be England's responsibility, not his. At dawn, Germany invaded Poland.

Fruity Metcalfe did not rejoin his wife and the other summer houseguests of the Windsors on the journey back to Britain. It was said at the time he was feeling unwell and unable to face the long trip home, but really he was beginning a new tour of duty.

He'd been contacted by Buckingham Palace, on the direct and secret orders of the king, to remain at Windsor's side and act as his ADC. Windsor himself was unaware that the Palace had been in touch with Fruity, whose agreement to become unofficial watchdog and informer to the king was done out of his sense of concern for his closest friend.

The first air-raid warnings were being sounded over London when Walter Monckton landed at Antibes in a small plane. His mission was to bring the duke and duchess back to England. They'd been expecting a plane of the King's Flight to fetch them, but Monckton brought news that this had been withdrawn and that they must travel in the government plane. This the duchess positively refused to do. "It looks as if it is tied up with string," the duke remarked angrily.

He was further deflated when Monckton indicated that there were other conditions: before setting off the duke must undertake to accept one of two posts which would be offered to him, that of deputy regional commissioner in Wales, or liaison officer with the Number One British Military Mission in Paris. The duke reluctantly agreed, but still refused to travel in Monckton's plane, so Churchill, at the Admiralty, was contacted with the request that he send a ship to any French port and the duke and duchess would be waiting.

They set off on September 8, the duke and duchess, Fruity Metcalfe, and the Windsors' three Cairn terriers. The duchess recalled: "I packed the car with certain valuable possessions, because of the danger of France being overrun."

It took three days to get to Cherbourg, where Lord Louis Mountbatten and Churchill's son, Randolph, were

waiting to take them aboard the destroyer *Kelly*, which
was standing by to sail to England immediately the couple were safely below. Randolph handed the duke a letter
from his father: "Welcome home! Your Royal Highness
knows how much I have looked forward to this day."

As he was piped aboard, the duke whispered to his
wife with some joy: "We're going home at last."

The few belongings that the duchess had collected
together were humped up the gangway by ratings, and
quickly HMS *Kelly*, which later achieved fame off Crete
while still under the command of Mountbatten, set sail
for Portsmouth. The skies darkened in the cool autumn
evening and it was pitch black when the destroyer reached
the other side of the Channel. Blackout was enforced,
but there was a token attempt at the red-carpet treatment
for the homecoming, with a small naval guard of honor
and even smaller crowd of sightseers, mostly workers at
the naval dockyard.

The Windsors stayed overnight in naval accommoda-
tions and drove the next day to Fruity Metcalfe's home
in Surrey. The duke went straight on to Buckingham
Palace for the first meeting with his estranged family for
close on three years.

It wasn't an easy occasion for either side. Queen Mary
showed her true compassion for which she was well known,
but there was still a coolness on the part of the king.
Even before his new job could be discussed, the duke
pressed for some recognition by the royal family of his
wife, by pleading "I really am disappointed that she can't
use our title, be called Her Royal Highness." He also
wanted to bring the duchess to the palace to present her
to the king and queen, and had the idea that he and his
wife could take on certain public duties to relieve the
pressure on the royal couple. The king would have none
of it. There was no question at that time of the divorcée
being accepted into the family, with or without the title
HRH. Indeed the king read the riot act. Britain was at
war; there would be no more speeches, no more public

statements that embarrassed either him or the government. Britain's future now depended on the alliance of
the dominions and friendly nations. They must not be
upset, and certainly not by the duke.

Windsor traveled back from London to the Metcalfes'
home that night in a blind rage, a seething anger that
took some days to subside. He sat brooding in Surrey,
waiting to hear from his brother what job he was to be
offered. As he waited, he began to take the duchess on
trips to London, visiting their old favorite haunts or just
walking through the streets, being stopped for the occasional handshake when recognized by a passer-by, or
the occasional cheer, an echo of former days. Once they
went back to Fort Belvedere, but it was with some sadness that they both saw the house, now run-down, overgrown, with a thousand memories trapped behind the
shuttered windows. The duke's thoughts perhaps went
back to the spring of 1930 when his father agreed that
the Prince of Wales should have a home of his own. That
September day, as the duke and duchess drove from the
Fort, Edward turned and took one last look. Never again
would he go there. He waited several more days for word
from his brother as to what task he would be given, but
he never heard from the king again. Instead, he was
summoned to the War Office, where he was told by the
chief of the Imperial General Staff that he would be
drafted to the British Military Mission at Vincennes and
should report there immediately, with the rank of major
general—a far cry from his previous acceptance of military rank, when, as Prince of Wales, he became field
marshal. The king had made it clear to Leslie Hore-
Belisha that the duke should be given no option; he must
take the French post because the duchess might get a
"hostile reception" at the commands in Britain. The
duke made one last attempt to stay: he enquired of the
Welsh Guards, in which he held the rank of honorary
colonel, if they would have him back to serve. Yes, was
the reply. No, said Hore-Belisha.

In truth, the duke's archenemy, the security supremo Sir Robert Vansittart, had reinforced the king's own view that the Windsors should not be allowed back into Britain at present, and particularly not around the command posts, where Wallis would receive daily reports from her chatterbox husband. This was no idle fear. Vansittart was still convinced she was in touch with the Germans, and the duke was still courted by the various pro-Fascist factions that were operating in Britain.

It was a sensitive and difficult period, and top secret material still remains from that era under lock and key, as can be seen from the case of Dr. Arthur Albert Tester, prewar friend of Mosley and mystery financier of the British Fascists.

Tester fled London with his family under quite spectacular circumstances in 1939 and subsequently turned up in Rumania as head of the Gestapo there and using a special passport signed personally by Hitler.

The strange and mysterious movements of the monocled Dr. Tester can be traced back to the Britain of the 1930s, when he lived with his wife and five children in a beautiful mansion on the cliffs of North Foreland, the most easterly point of Kent. They also had a beautiful flat in Bayswater, London.

In the run-up to the outbreak of war, Dr. Tester was often seen in the close company of Tom Mosley, and according to some, was Mosley's closest adviser and largest benefactor. In the years immediately prior to the war, Tester provided much of the cash that Mosley required to keep going, as support on the home front began to dwindle. Other cash came from the secret bank account in Paris. The source of both lines of funding was approved by Hitler himself and, in the case of the Paris channel, was handled by Armand Gregoire. Tester was also involved at the same time in the setting up of a British news agency that in turn was being financed by a direct £110,000 contribution from the office of Dr. Goebbels. At the same time, Lady Diana Mosley had been commuting between London and Berlin, trying to raise German cash to support a radio station that would broadcast from an offshore base to Britain. Through the news agency and the radio links, there would be a ready-made propaganda service to flood Britain and the continent with Nazi-biased material. Hitler himself agreed to Diana Mosley's pleadings for cash to support the radio station, and it was halted only by the outbreak of war.

Tester, in the meantime, had bought a huge steam yacht, the 245-ton *Lucinda*, and this was to be his escape route once the time came for him to flee Britain when his true role as a leading Nazi agent was revealed. He sailed away to the Mediterranean and was tracked by the British to Naples. In 1940, he arrived in Belgrade and was said to be seeking business contracts. All the time, Tester was working for Hitler. Soon, Yugoslavia was invaded and Tester disappeared again. He turned up next in Athens, shortly before Greece fell to the Nazis, and was next discovered living in a luxurious suite at the Pallas Atheneè Hotel in Bucharest.

The truth of Tester's seniormost Nazi rank would be discovered when he became the head of the Gestapo in Rumania in 1942. He was last heard of as the war ended, trying to escape. He was apparently shot in Transylvania by a Rumanian frontier guard, and at the time was still carrying the passport signed by Hitler. But what were Dr. Tester's connections in Britain? Who were the business contacts and top people he associated with? What secrets did he take to his grave on that Transylvanian outpost? Britain will not know until his file is released by Scotland Yard in 2030.

The Windsors, meanwhile, moved back to France, this time in the destroyer *Express*, with Fruity Metcalfe once again as the duke's aide, in military uniform. The winter months passed quietly, with the duke performing his tasks at the Mission, where he had residential quarters, while the duchess checked into a suite at a small Paris hotel. She busied herself by joining the French Red

Cross and her reunions with the duke were frequent, as if he had been away for weeks, instead of days. This was the first time they had been apart since the wedding.

As with the First World War, the duke's role was unchallenging and well away from whatever enemy action might ensue. However, his contributions were not all banal. He wrote a comprehensive report on the Maginot Line in which he was highly critical of many aspects, an observation in which he would be proved totally correct.

In the meantime, Fruity Metcalfe moved into the Ritz, where he stayed for most of his time in Paris. Many wives would have resented this devotion: he was closer to the duke than any other man and had a good deal of influence over him. He was clearly suspicious of Charles Bedeaux, who had returned to Paris in October, when they all had long conversations. Fruity noted he was a "will o' wisp . . . I can't make him out . . . he knows too much."

There was another problem for Fruity, too. Before the duke left, Hore-Belisha insisted that he should not receive any payment for serving his country, a fact the duke wanted published in the newspapers. When, however, Hore-Belisha pointed out that the duke's brothers were also serving and were not receiving payment the matter was dropped. Fruity now had discovered he wasn't being paid either, nor did he have an official rank; just ADC to the duke. "What beats me," complained Fruity, "is that HRH is prepared to do nothing for me. I really think I can't stay on, and in lots of ways I won't be sorry."

In April 1940, Norway and Denmark fell to the Nazis. In May, the western blitzkrieg began and both Holland and Belgium fell. Winston Churchill, still at the Admiralty then, was embroiled in war politics in London, where Prime Minister Neville Chamberlain was attempting to form a National Government. Since, however, no members of the Labour party were prepared to serve under him, Chamberlain resigned on May 10 and Churchill was called to Buckingham Palace. The king asked him to take over the government: he wrote in his diary that day, "I knew at that moment there was only one person whom I should send for . . . and that was Winston."

The news was welcomed by all countries involved in the fight to beat Hitler, and one of Churchill's first tasks was to send a cable to President Roosevelt in Washington.

Although I have changed my office, I am sure that you would not wish me to discontinue our intimate, private correspondence. As you are no doubt aware, the scene has darkened swiftly. I think myself the battle has only just begun . . . the small countries are simply smashed up, one by one, like matchwood. We must expect, though this is not certain, that Mussolini will hurry in to share the loot of civilisation. We must expect to be attacked here ourselves, both from the air and by parachute and airborne troops . . .

If necessary we shall continue the war alone and we are not afraid of that. But I trust you realise, Mr President, that the voice and force of the United States may count for nothing if they are withheld too long. You may have a completely subjugated Nazified Europe established with astonishing swiftness.

All I ask now is that you should proclaim nonbelligerency, which would mean that you would help us with everything, short of actually engaging armed forces.

A most urgent need, Churchill felt, was action to support French morale, and on May 16, he flew to Paris for talks with the French War Cabinet and discovered the situation there was far more critical than he had imagined. Whether the duke managed to see Churchill on his visit to Paris is not known, but on that day, he dashed back to the house he and the duchess were renting and told her to start packing. He took leave from the Mission and drove his wife away from Paris and down to Biarritz, where he booked her into the Hôtel du Palais, before himself returning to Paris. The journey both ways had been long and hazardous. The roads were crowded with immigrant families from all over Western Europe traveling bumper-to-bumper with lines of cars, trucks, and carts conveying what few possessions they could carry tied to the roofs. Where they were going no one knew, not even the families themselves—perhaps to Spain or Portugal where the borders were already jammed.

In the middle of this critical stage of the war, the last thing Churchill wanted, or expected, was further intrigue involving the Windsors. But it was all starting up again. Nazi spies had throughout tracked the movements of the duke and duchess, to let the world know that they had agents everywhere, and the information that the duchess was in Biarritz was given out over German radio, with every detail of her arrival, even her room number at the Palais.

Within a week the Windsors were on the move again. The duke had left the Mission to head for Biarritz to pick up the duchess but there was some mystery as to whether he had been given permission to leave by his superiors. Churchill noted that there "was a great deal of doubt" over the circumstances under which the duke left Paris. It appeared he had bolted, the day after Oswald Mosley was arrested in London and interned.

In the north, the German advances continued and the British War Cabinet was discussing the evacuation of troops from the Channel ports. Churchill broadcast to the British nation that "once the battle for France abates its force, the battle for our island will begin. Side by side, unaided except by their kith and kin from the dominions and by the wide empires that rest beneath their shield, the British and French people have advanced to rescue not only Europe but mankind from the foulest, most soul-destroying tyranny which has ever darkened and stained the pages of history."

France was on the brink as the duke and duchess,

driven by a chauffeur, Ladbroke, headed south to their villa at Antibes. They arrived on May 29, the day the massive evacuation of British and Allied forces began from Dunkirk, with 150,000 men taken from the beaches by the historic flotilla of small boats.

·TEN·

LISBON INCIDENT

━━━━━━━◆━━━━━━━

While the drama of the duke and duchess was unfolding across the Channel, British security had taken no chances that there could be any counteractivity from Tom Mosley in London.

The day after an Emergency Powers Bill had been rushed through Parliament, May 22, Mosley was arrested and taken to Brixton Prison. A little over a month later, Diana too was arrested and held in Holloway. The eleven-week-old son she was breast-feeding and eighteen-month-old Alexander went to stay with relatives.

Though attempts have since been made by his family and supporters to play down Mosley's activities, there was no doubt that the War Cabinet feared his constant barrage of appeasing and defeatist speeches. Mosley claimed he didn't want Germany to win the war, but if they did, he did not think Hitler would destroy the empire. In later life he always insisted that Hitler would not have put him in a position of power; but in Brixton Prison he was heard telling his solicitor that Hitler had already appointed him as co-leader of Britain, ready for when the invasion came.

During his stay in prison, Mosley's cell was bugged by MI5, such were the fears of the security services.

Over the course of his detention he faced a sixteen-hour investigation by Norman Birkett, QC, which produced, initially, a rather chatty picture of Mosley and his Nazi friends. He had told Birkett that Hitler was a charming and emotional man with a great sense of humor. He boasted that the Führer admired his wife Diana, whom he treated seriously, and was entranced by her sister Unity, whom he constantly joked with.

While Hitler, like Edward, admired strong women with a dominant character such as Diana Mosley or Frau Goebbels, Mussolini, by contrast, said Mosley, was every inch a public man with a big personality. "Whenever one went to Rome, one was liable to be drawn out in public. It caused me immense embarrassment. On the first visit there there was a big march and Mussolini suddenly sent me a message, 'Would I stand in the tribune instead of him?' It was a ruse. I was photographed with him and I have been taunted about it ever since."

As Norman Birkett's questioning proceeded, Mosley's attitudes emerged.

> Q [Birkett]: On what grounds did you attack the Jews?
> A [Mosley]: Their whole influence upon national life. I should have said that. I had never looked into the problem in any shape or form. I always actually thought it was the work of cranks and always, although they were so opposed to us, overlooked it, but then I wondered "why are they so opposed to us?" We want to stop certain things. We want to stop international usury, we want to stop the whole money-lending racket. We do not like price-cutting. We do not like the sweating of labour. Gradually it dawned on me that certain people were very much engaged in these things. I was compelled to look at the Jewish problem by their opposition to us and, having looked at the Jewish problem, I developed what is called anti-semitism.
> Q [Birkett]: In what year did you first make your declaration against the Jews?

A [Mosley]: October 1934, the Albert Hall meeting. I think it was about October 1934. It will be recorded in the general papers. I previously quarrelled that summer with Lord Rothermere because seeing this coming he publicly demanded that I should adopt the Conservative policy and should not develop anti-semitism. We had correspondence which was published at the time on the subject, and my first initial attack on the Jews was October 1934. I had then never been in Germany except once when accompanying Mr Ramsay MacDonald in the spring of 1929, when I heard a funny man called Hitler had started a funny movement. I did not meet him.

Q [Birkett]: You would appreciate that a policy of hostility to the Jews at a time when Jews were being oppressed in Germany would not be very popular among humane people in this country?

A [Mosley]: I think that anti-semitism here has grown colossally in the last few years. When we began it hardly existed.

Q [Birkett]: Do you think the British Union fomented it?

A [Mosley]: Yes, I think it is partly them, and partly us.

Q [Birkett]: Again, part of the policy of the British Union is to stop all immigration, is it not?

A [Mosley]: Stop all foreigners coming in, but also gradually and humanely get rid of all foreigners who are here.

Q [Birkett]: That is to say this country would no longer be as it was in the old days, an asylum for the oppressed?

A [Mosley]: Oh, certainly.

Q [Birkett]: And those who were here would be expelled?

A [Mosley]: Gradually.

Q [Birkett]: And the Jews would be expelled too?

A [Mosley]: Quite right.

Q [Birkett]: Would they be allowed to take their possessions with them?

A [Mosley]: Yes.

Q [Birkett]: Even the "international racketeers" as they are termed?

A [Mosley]: They would be subject, naturally, to inquiry. They would get it like anybody else.

Q [Birkett]: They would come out of that inquiry very badly, would they not?

A [Mosley]: Some, very badly.

Q [Birkett]: And then they would not be allowed to take anything?

A [Mosley]: But we apply the same rule to our own people.

Q [Birkett]: The attitude of the British Union to the Jewish problems arose, I understand you to say, because they had attacked your meetings, so you thereupon gave the problem some consideration?

A [Mosley]: Not only attacked our meetings, but there was also the victimisation of our people employed by Jews.

Q [Birkett]: In what sense—in the "sweated" industries?

A [Mosley]: Simply dismissed: a girl known to be a Blackshirt was dismissed.

Q [Birkett]: By that time, 1934, the Jews in this country had seen how their co-religionists were being treated in Germany?

A [Mosley]: Very likely that was so.

Q [Birkett]: And they said, no doubt, "this Fascist Movement in Britain is the same type of movement existing in National Socialist Germany"?

A [Mosley]: Yes.

(Years later, there would be a chilling postscript to the Mosley bravado in front of Birkett, when it was revealed at a Nazi war-crime trial in Israel that even as he spoke, extermination camps were being prepared in Treblinka for British Jews who would, come the invasion, be rounded up from London's East End, from Leeds, from Manchester, and from other areas pinpointed by Mosley.)

The horrors to be perpetrated by Hitler and his increasingly evil Third Reich were then little known; but in contemporary France it was bad enough. The duke recalled, "There were endless lines of cars . . . judging by the licence plates, all of western Europe was on the run. We had a hard, slow trip, with many long waits . . ."

The Windsors were joined by a new ADC, Major Gray Phillips, who had hitchhiked from Paris, and for a week or so, in the south at least, there was relative calm; Maurice Chevalier even called in for a drink.

In the rest of France it was chaos. By June 10, half the country had fallen to the advancing Germans, and the Dunkirk operation was complete, leaving Paris abandoned. A week later, Marshal Petain made his incredible speech telling the French nation to lay down their arms, and France had capitulated.

After Gray Phillips warned the duke and duchess they ought to evacuate, preparations were made to close up La Croe and to pack into boxes and crates as many of their valued possessions as possible. They hired a truck and packed their belongings inside, taking with them some of the most precious—although many by now had been stored in a bank vault. The duke had contacted the American consul in Nice, who agreed to take the house under his care. Some of the duke's staff would also remain, but the Windsors would leave with a heavy heart this, the first home which they had furnished and reequipped, and only such a short time ago.

The Germans were now at Dijon and heading south at some speed, and the Italians were crossing the border at Menton and would soon be upon them, so the duke telephoned the British embassy at Bordeaux to request evacuation arrangements for himself and the duchess, if necessary by the Royal Navy. He was instantly told that this was impossible and that they would have to find their own way out of the danger zone.

There were only two options left open: a sea passage if they could find a ship, which seemed unlikely and would be hazardous, or overland to Spain, still neutral but unfriendly to Britain after the Spanish civil war. The Windsors made contact with other Britons in the south and prepared to make the perilous journey as the Italians swarmed toward them from the east, their planes commencing the bombing of Cannes as their party left. The duchess recalled: "The staff was grouped around the entrance to say goodbye. As I was about to enter the car, the gardener stepped forward to press into my arms a huge bunch of tuberoses. 'Your birthday present, darling,' David whispered. . . . In the confusion I had forgotten the date. Our staff wept as we left, so did I."

Joining the British consul general, Major Dodds, in Nice they set off on June 19 in a convoy heading for Spain and then Portugal. Ladbroke drove the duke and duchess in their Buick; Gray Phillips was in the car, with the Cairn terriers. The diplomatic Rolls Royce carried Dodds and his assistant, next were the Woods in their Citroën and, finally, came the duke's truck, also carrying the duchess' maid, Marguerite Moulichon.

Once again, it was a long and arduous journey. The roads were jammed with people all heading toward the border. After two days of traveling, the Windsors reached the Spanish border beyond Perpignan. There were long queues of refugees waiting for entry permits. Like many of them, the duke's party had no visas and were refused admission. The duke himself took over negotiations for their entry into Spain, which was achieved only after several hours and frantic telegraph exchanges between him, the Spanish officials, and the British ambassador in Madrid. However, the Windsors' truckload of possessions was barred and the driver was sent back to La Croe with instructions to store its cargo of valuables.

The convoy traveled on to Barcelona, where they rested for the night, and the following morning headed on toward Madrid. By now, London and Berlin were well aware of their movements. Churchill was kept informed of their progress in Britain, while Hitler and Ribbentrop were watching from Germany.

When the duke arrived in Barcelona, he went straight to the British consulate and sent a telegram to the Foreign

Office in London: "Having received no instructions have arrived in Spain to avoid capture. Proceeding to Madrid."

He was unaware that a British ship, the *Monarch* from Bermuda, was due at any time in Barcelona to pick up British diplomats evacuated to Spain from Italy. The British Foreign Office in London was not at all sure that they should tell him. As Walter Monckton noted, "The return of the duke and duchess to this country might raise certain complications. On the other hand, if he were to remain . . . he might run the chance of being captured by the Germans and another set of equally awkward complications would arise."

The duke journeyed on, unaware of the discussions in London as to his future. The following day, Buckingham Palace gave consent to the duke's return to Britain, and Sir Samuel Hoare, the British ambassador to Spain, invited "their Royal Highnesses to proceed to Lisbon," a communication that brought an angry response in London when the king saw a copy of it. His private secretary, Alec Hardinge, wrote immediately to the Foreign Office: the king had viewed with "extreme displeasure" the fact that the duke and duchess had been referred to as "their Royal Highnesses" and insisted that such an error never be repeated.

The Germans acted swiftly to capitalize on the situation, and their propaganda machine swung into action with stories that the duke had arrived in Madrid to negotiate Britain's withdrawal from the war. The skirmish of diplomatic activity was only just beginning and the duke had become caught in the crossfire.

There began a remarkable tug-of-war between the two countries, both seeking possession of the Windsors. But by some remarkable intelligence work, Churchill was able to discover what the Germans were planning, thanks to the British embassy's listening post in Lisbon. Most of the instructions were coming from Ribbentrop, although Hitler got involved at the last minute. They desperately wanted the duke and duchess to remain in Spain, and during that month they would do their damnedest to achieve it.

At that time Hitler was preparing for the invasion of Britain, and in both capitals, Berlin and London, tension was high. At the first sign of invasion there is no doubt that George VI and other members of the royal family would have been spirited away to Canada. So would members of other European royal families, such as the Queen of the Netherlands and the King of Norway, who had come to Britain after their countries had been invaded. Churchill's government would undoubtedly have gone, too. With the throne vacant, Hitler would probably have had no difficulty in persuading Edward to return with Wallis as his queen.

Many people might think that such a puppet monarch, supported by a pro-Nazi puppet government, would have failed, but this is not necessarily the likely outcome. It has to be remembered that if Britain had been beaten by Hitler, the whole of western Europe, excluding Spain, Portugal, Switzerland, and Sweden, would have come under his control.

Although it is true that there would have been a British underground resistance, such an organization would not have had the same hopes and advantages as the continental resistance groups that looked for encouragement and support from a Britain that was still fighting on against Hitler. In addition, most of the continental resistance movements did not get fully organized until after the Americans had come into the war in December 1941 when the prospect of an American-backed second front to liberate Europe, with plentiful supplies of equipment flown in to help, gave a tremendous boost to the resistance fighters in France and other occupied countries.

In Britain, under Hitler, this could not have happened. Even if America had come into the war in December 1941 (though perhaps Pearl Harbor would not have happened if Britain had been subdued earlier in the year), the prospect for a successful second front launched from across the Atlantic would have been very dim indeed. The people of Britain would have had to accept defeat with a heavy heart and try to make the best of it. Perhaps Hitler's rule would not be so bad after all. They at least would have had the reassurance that Hitler, in line with his racial theories, admired the British for their Aryan origins. The Jews would have been given a very bad time, but most of the British would probably have carried on their normal lives. In these circumstances, the reinstatement of Edward as king was quite a credible proposition. It also has to be remembered that it was less than four years since he had abdicated, and that George VI, though popular, had still not achieved the same love and loyalty that he was to enjoy by the end of the war.

On June 23, the ducal party drove into what remained of the city of Madrid, where the scars of the civil war that had ended fourteen months previously were still so evident. Rooms had been reserved for them at the Ritz Hotel by Sir Samuel Hoare, the duke's old friend from London, now British ambassador to Spain. He immediately reported to the duke that Churchill wanted him to return to England without delay. Windsor was not committed to that prospect and even now talked of doing so only on his own terms. He did not wish to be seen as a war refugee returning to Britain, and remembering the previous occasion in September 1939, he insisted that his wife be received at court. He also demanded a worthwhile job, and so Hoare wrote to Churchill on June 27, expressing his fear that the duke might refuse to return to England unless his conditions were met. He stressed that any indiscretion by the Windsors at this point would be picked up and reported to Hitler, thus helping to confirm Churchill's view that the Windsors were still Hitler's friends.

Such indiscretions were not long in coming. Alexander Weddell, the American ambassador to Madrid, reported to Washington that the duke had talked openly of his view that the war should be ended without delay. That could only mean appeasement. The duke had said that Germany had totally reorganized the order of its society in preparation for war; countries that were unwilling to accept such a reorganization should avoid dangerous adventures. The duchess chipped in more directly, expressing her view that France had lost because it was diseased internally.

Furthermore, while in Madrid the Windsors spent a great deal of time with prominent pro-Nazi Spaniards who, following the civil war, could hardly be described as friends of Britain. Understandably Hoare felt he should get the duke and duchess out of Spain just as soon as was possible. But now, as the original research by Michael Bloch tells us, a great furor began to unfold.

Telegrams between Hoare and Churchill followed, Hoare negotiating with the duke to try to pare down his demands, Churchill at the other end talking to the king and getting his view of what the rest of the royal family wanted. The duke gave up his insistence on a job in England but demanded that "in the light of past experience, my wife and myself must not risk finding ourselves being regarded by the British public in a different status to other members of my family."

He had already told the Spanish foreign minister Juan Beigbeder y Atienza that he would not return to England without that condition being met. Beigbeder, who was in touch with Germany, offered the Windsors a most beautiful palace which would be placed at the Windsors' indefinite disposal.

Churchill had other ideas, and he threatened the duke with a court-martial if he failed to follow instructions. He telegraphed the duke: "Your Royal Highness has taken military rank, and refusal to obey direct orders of competent military authority would create a serious situation. I most strongly urge immediate compliance with the wishes of your government." Churchill first showed a copy of his telegram to the king, who commented that it should have a "very salutary effect."

Two days passed, and the Windsors packed their bags and headed for Portugal, where Churchill had instructed that they should be picked up by flying-boats off the Portuguese coast.

While these arrangements were being made, Churchill had an audience with the king and, later that same night, confided to Lord Beaverbrook that the duke was to be sent to the Bahamas, although no official announcement was to be made for some days. Churchill also noted that of all the British colonies at that time, the Bahamas were the least important!

The Windsors arrived in Portugal on July 3, unaware of the plans being made in London. Their spirits lifted, for, compared with Madrid, Lisbon was an open, friendly city with plenty of food still and a hospitable local people.

They went straight to the home of a local banker, Ricardo Espirito Santo Silva. "Why there?" asked Sir Walford Selby, the British ambassador, since the duke's party had been directed to the Hotel Palacio at Estoril. However, they were diverted to the villa after Ricardo had offered personally to put them up, as they would all be much more comfortable there. Gloom descended on the British envoys when they were told, since Ricardo was an agent of the Germans in Lisbon whom they had been courting for months.

On July 4, the day they were due to fly back to England, Churchill cabled the duke with the Bahamas offer. The Windsors were both devastated that they were not being allowed to go home, but Churchill made it clear there was no alternative. The flying-boats were recalled while new travel arrangements were planned. Churchill cabled Roosevelt to tell him of the appointment, but although the duke himself had requested that they should be allowed to go to New York en route to Nassau, the Foreign Office opposed the suggestion with all the vigor it could muster.

As time dragged on, Churchill became increasingly concerned, particularly in view of top-secret information about the activities of the duchess while in Madrid. The king's private secretary wrote to Downing Street expressing the king's concern that, not for the first time, "This lady has come under suspicion for her anti-British activities and so long as we never forget the power she can exert over him in her efforts to avenge herself on this country we shall be all right."

Arrangements to get the Windsors out of Portugal and onto a ship for the Bahamas would take some time to set up, but they were kept under close scrutiny. Their every move was being recorded by two sets of secret police—MI6 from London and an overseas unit of the German S.S.

Back in Berlin, the plot to kidnap the duke and duchess, if they would not stay in Spain voluntarily, was maturing. On July 10, Baron Oswald von Hoynigen-Huene, the German minister in Lisbon, telegraphed Ribbentrop: ". . . the appointment of the duke to Governor of the Bahamas is for the purpose of keeping him away from England since his return would greatly strengthen the position of the English friends of peace whereupon his arrest at the instigation of his enemies could be counted upon. The duke intends to postpone his journey for as long as possible, at least until the beginning of August, in the hope of an early change in his favor. He is convinced that had he remained on the throne war could have been avoided and describes himself as a firm supporter of a peaceful compromise with Germany. The duke believes with certainty that continued heavy bombing will make England ready for peace."

The following day, Ribbentrop telegraphed Baron von Stohrer at the German embassy in Madrid: "We are especially interested in having the Duke of Windsor return to Spain at all events . . . from here it would seem best if close Spanish friends of the duke were to invite him back to stay for a short visit . . . after their return they must be persuaded or compelled to remain on Spanish soil. For the latter we would have to secure the agreement of the Spanish Government for the internment of the duke . . . at any rate, at a suitable occasion in Spain, the duke is to be informed that Germany wants peace with the English people, that the Churchill clique stands in the way of that peace, and that it would be a good thing if the duke were to hold himself in readiness for further developments . . . especially with a view to the assumption of the English Throne by the duke and duchess."

"Hold himself in readiness"! Hitler had big plans for the duke and duchess. Obviously they were an important link in his thinking. He wanted the duke to be a quisling, and in London, that prospect had already crossed Churchill's mind when he wrote: "If Great Britain broke under invasion, a pro-German government might obtain far easier terms from Germany by surrendering the Fleet, thus making Germany and Japan masters of the new world. This dastard deed would not be done with His Majesty's present advisers but if Mosley were Prime Minister or some other Quisling government were set up, what would they do . . . ?"

The threat of a German invasion of Britain was expected daily. "Everything should be brought to the highest pitch of readiness," Churchill wrote. He even instructed his top advisers to investigate the use of mustard gas, planning to drench the beaches with it if there was a real threat of the Germans' landing.

On July 16, Hitler issued a directive: "Since England, despite her hopeless situation, shows no sign of willingness to come to terms, I have decided to prepare a landing operation . . . and if necessary carry it out. The aim of this operation will be to eliminate the English homeland as a base for carrying on the war and, should it become necessary, occupy it completely."

Three days later, he called upon Britain to capitulate and ordered that the preparation for invasion must be complete by mid-August. The Battle of Britain had begun. Hitler gave Britain the choice between peace and "unending misery," but he sneered that Churchill would not be among those who would suffer, for "he will no doubt already be in Canada."

In the middle of all this critical diplomatic activity, the duke stepped back into the political arena with comments which, to many in London, would be considered treasonable. On July 21, he sent a telegram to King George arguing that he should step in to end the war. He urged his brother to set up a peace cabinet, headed by the elderly but still active Lloyd George, an action that would have meant the king dismissing Churchill as leader of His Majesty's Government. The duke was in favor of immediate peace negotiations if an honorable basis could be found.

Naturally, there was never any question of the king dismissing a government which had the wholehearted support of Parliament. It was just another example of the duke's crass naiveté.

Back in Berlin, Ribbentrop had called Walter Schellenberg, head of the Gestapo overseas counterintelligence, to talk about the Windsors, who were still languishing in Portugal. "What do you think of the duke? How do you evaluate him as a political figure?" Ribbentrop asked. Schellenberg asked for time to answer and check his files but made a few comments off the top of his head. Then Ribbentrop began to lecture him about the Windsors. The Duke of Windsor was one of the most socially aware and right-thinking Englishman he had ever met. It was this which had displeased the governing clique; the marriage issue had been a welcome pretext to remove this honest and faithful friend of Germany. All the questions of tradition and ceremony that were raised were completely secondary.

The Gestapo man's recollections continued: "Here I tried to object, but was silenced by Ribbentrop's abrupt gesture. 'My dear Schellenberg, you have a completely wrong view of these things—also of the real reasons behind the duke's abdication. The Führer and I already recognised the facts of the situation in 1936. The crux of the matter is that, since his abdication, the duke has been under strict surveillance by the British Secret Service. We know what his feelings are: it's almost as if he were their prisoner. Every attempt that he's made to free himself, however discreet he may have been, has failed. We know from our reports that he still entertains the same sympathetic feelings towards Germany, and that given the right circumstances he wouldn't be averse to escaping from his present environment—the whole thing's getting on his nerves.' "

Ribbentrop went on:

> The Führer feels that if the atmosphere seemed propitious you might perhaps make the Duke some material offer. We should be prepared to deposit in Switzerland for his own use a sum of fifty million Swiss francs—if he were ready to make some official gesture dissociating himself from the manoeuvres of the British Royal family. The Führer would, of course, prefer him to live in Switzerland, though any other neutral country would do so long as it's not outside the economic or the political or military influence of the German Reich.
>
> If the British Secret Service should try to frustrate the Duke in some such arrangement, then the Führer orders that you are to circumvent the British plans, even at the risk of your life, and, if need be, by the use of force. Whatever happens, the Duke of Windsor must be brought safely to the country of his choice. Hitler attaches the greatest importance to this operation, and he has come to the conclusion after serious consideration that if the Duke should prove hesitant, he himself would have no objection to your helping the Duke to reach the right decision by coercion—even by threats or force if the circumstances make it advisable. But it will also be your responsibility to make sure at the same time that the Duke and his wife are not exposed to any personal danger.

In the near future, the Duke expects to have an invitation to hunt with some Spanish friends. This hunt should offer an excellent opportunity for you to establish contact with him. From that point he can immediately be brought into another country. All the necessary means for you to carry out this assignment will be at your disposal. Last night I discussed the whole matter again thoroughly with the Führer. We have agreed to give you a completely free hand, but he demands that you let him see daily reports on the progress of the affair. Herewith, in the name of the Führer, I give you the order to carry out this assignment at once. You are ready, of course, to carry it out?

Schellenberg asked Ribbentrop: "Do I understand that if the Duke of Windsor should resist, I am to bring him into this "other country" that you speak of by force? It seems to me there's a contradiction in that. Surely the whole action must depend on the voluntary co-operation of the duke?"

"Well," answered Ribbentrop, "the Führer feels that force should be used primarily against the British Secret Service but against the duke only insofar as his hesitation might be based on a fear-psychosis which forceful action on our part would help him to overcome. Once he's a free man again and able to move about without surveillance by British Intelligence he'll be grateful to us. As far as the money to be placed at his disposal is concerned, fifty million Swiss francs by no means represents the absolute maximum. The Führer is quite ready to go to a higher figure. For the rest—well, don't worry too much. Have confidence in yourself and do your best. I will report to the Führer that you have accepted the assignment."

Schellenberg nodded, rose, and was about to say goodbye, when Ribbentrop said, "One moment—" and taking up the telephone asked for Hitler. He handed Schellenberg the second earpiece, so that he could listen in, and when Hitler's peculiar hollow voice came on the line Ribbentrop briefly reported the conversation. Hitler's replies were curt: "Yes—certainly—agreed." Finally he said, "Schellenberg should particularly bear in mind the importance of the duchess's attitude and try as hard as possible to get her support. She has great influence over the duke."

"Very well then," said Ribbentrop, "Schellenberg will fly by special plane to Madrid as quickly as possible."

"Good," Hitler answered. "He has all the authorisation he needs. Tell him from me that I am relying on him."

Ribbentrop rose, made a bow toward the telephone, and said, "Thank you, my Führer, that is all."

Schellenberg flew to Madrid by special plane on July 25 when Baron von Stohrer was already making plans to lure the duke and duchess into Spain. An invitation had been sent to them to stay with Spanish friends just over the Spanish border and the duke and duchess had accepted. Schellenberg telegraphed Ribbentrop: "Influence on the duke and duchess by a confidential emissary is already so effective that a firm intention by them to return to Spain can be assumed as in the highest degree probable. In order to strengthen this intention, a second confidential emissary . . . was sent off today, 26th July, with a letter to the duke very skilfully composed psychologically."

Schellenberg positioned himself in Lisbon, having flown from Madrid, and was joined by two Gestapo aides; the problem for his consideration now was to get the duke and duchess out of Lisbon from under the noses of the swarm of British agents who were already surrounding the couple.

Churchill, in London, had a good idea of what was going on, not only from the on-the-spot intelligence but also from the British listening post in Lisbon.

Lord Lloyd, the colonial secretary, viewed the situation with such gravity that he asked Churchill to send a telegram to the prime ministers of Australia, Canada, New Zealand, and South Africa and drafted a suggested note: "The activities of the Duke of Windsor on the continent in recent months are causing HM and myself grave uneasiness as his inclinations are known to be pro-Nazi . . . we regard it as a real danger that he should move freely on the continent. Even if he would be willing to return to this country, his presence here would be most embarrassing both to HM and to the Government. In all the circumstances it has been felt necessary to try to tie him down . . ." However Churchill did not accept the draft and wrote a watered-down version which was sent to the dominions.

Meanwhile, the duke was engaged in a running argument with Churchill, through a stream of telegrams. First he complained that the Foreign Office had refused permission for him to land in America en route to the Bahamas; Wallis was particularly angry and told her husband "to insist." The Foreign Office was equally adamant, and Churchill equally convinced, that they should go straight to Nassau, with a break in their journey at Bermuda to change ships.

There was one further exchange of telegrams before this could be achieved. The duke requested that he should take with him two young menservants who were of military age—a request which was refused. The duchess was furious about the ruling and again urged her husband to insist that they be allowed to keep the servants.

The king was kept informed of these developments and his response was short and to the point. "Tell him to do what he is told," he instructed Downing Street. Churchill, however, tried hard to defuse the situation and to avoid a public clash between the two brothers. He persuaded the War Office to release one of the men for service in the Bahamas as the duke's aide.

·ELEVEN·

A-HUNTING THEY WILL GO

Sir Walter Monckton was dispatched from London by plane on July 23 carrying a letter from Churchill to the duke wishing him a good journey and offering what he termed "serious counsel." "It will be necessary," the prime minister wrote, "for the Governor of the Bahamas to express views . . . which are not out of harmony with HM government . . . many unfriendly ears will be pricked up to catch any suggestion that your Royal Highness takes a view about the war, or about the Germans, or about Hitlerism which is different from that adopted by the British nation." That warning, however, would go unheeded, and the duke would not temper his views.

Monckton arrived in Lisbon to find the place awash with rumor, plot, and intrigue and found the duke in a troubled, nervous state. The Windsors by now had been made aware of the plans to get them into Spain. The duke's old friend, Don Miguel Primo de Rivera, Marques de Estella, had sent him by hand a long letter outlining the details of their arrangements. Don Miguel had previously been in touch with the duke and spoke of matters of "extreme importan[ce] to warn you of." He went on: ". . . we are dealing with something of extreme gravity which directly affects the personal safety of Your Highness and that of the duchess were you to manifest an opinion or act in some way contrary to a decision of the British Government."

Don Miguel then explained the plan, that on a date to be chosen by the duke, equipped with guns or hunting apparel for disguise, they would leave for Guarda, a small village located 250 kilometers northeast of Estoril. The Frontier Guards would be warned not to give the slightest difficulty. And once in Spain the duke and duchess would travel normally to the place arranged for them to stay.

The duke was handed the letter by a Spanish agent of the Germans, Don Angel Alcazar de Velasco. The duke read it again and again, and the contents clearly worried him. Some hours later, the duke was visited by another mysterious figure, recorded only by the code name "Viktor" by Schellenberg. One theory that has been suggested is that Rudolf Hess had now been dispatched personally to Lisbon to oversee the removal of the duke to Spain. This cannot be confirmed from any documents relating to the incident. But equally there are no mentions of the Duke of Westminster, who had also suddenly arrived in Portugal. Westminster was a prewar supporter of Hitlerites, but his mission now appeared to be of calming the Duke of Windsor. If Viktor *was* Hess, it seemed to have failed to persuade the Windsors to move to Spain. The duke asked him for forty-eight hours to reflect. One other piece of intrigue, which occurred in France, would have a bearing on the Windsors' actions. The duchess' thoughts kept turning to the possessions they had left behind in their two homes in France, La Croe at Antibes and the Paris house in Boulevard Suchet. She desperately worried that all her furniture, porcelain, silver, and linens, so recently acquired—as well as some treasures the duke had brought from England—should be lost in the pillage. She now decided that her most urgent task should be, somehow or other, to rescue those possessions and either have them safely stored, or brought to Portugal for onward transmission to wherever they settled. The rescue of the possessions at La Croe would not present a huge problem; but Paris was already occupied by the Germans. In both cases, however, Spanish help would be required for the rescue.

The duke got in touch directly with Juan Beigbeder y Atienza, the Spanish foreign minister, asking him to send a "confidential emissary" to discuss the problem of their belongings, and the Windsors were delighted when they discovered that it would be Don Javier Bermejillo, an old friend whom they called Tiger. They worked out between them how the pieces could be secured or brought to Lisbon, and made arrangements for the duchess' maid Marguerite Moulichon to travel to Paris to supervise the collection of some of the contents of that house.

Tiger also took the opportunity of discussing the whole situation with the duke, who was clearly not particularly discreet in the information he revealed. In a telegram from the German embassy Ribbentrop learned that "Churchill had threatened to court-martial W had he not accepted the [Bahamas] post. . . . He had been given one and a half month's grace . . . to get certain effects from the move from his Paris house."

A later telegram to Ribbentrop from Stohrer indicated that through Tiger the duke expressed thanks for cooperation over his Paris house and requested that a maid of the duchess be allowed to travel to Paris in order to pack up various objects and transport them by van to Lisbon.

Stohrer, while agreeing to the duke's request, saw it immediately as a chance to delay the Windsors even longer in Portugal, so that their removal, not to the Bahamas, but instead to Spain, could be effected. Mlle. Moulichon was allowed to travel to Madrid and, after many delays at the French border, on to Paris. The Germans were using the maid for further intrigue. When she reached Paris, Marguerite packed the luggage and trunks and was due to travel by train to Lisbon, hopefully to arrive before the Windsors sailed for the Bahamas. As she was waiting for a car from the Spanish embassy in Paris to collect her, however, two German Gestapo officers arrived at the Boulevard Suchet and told the distraught servant that she would not be allowed to leave France for the time being. Ribbentrop's plan was disintegrating fast, however, and Schellenberg reported back that the duke had decided after all to go to the Bahamas, which information had come direct from the duke. On July 30, Don Angel had returned to see the Windsors, and the results of that interview were contained in a telegram to Ribbentrop from the German embassy in Madrid. It said the duke had declared that the situation in England was by no means hopeless. "Therefore he should not now be in negotiations carried on contrary to the orders of the Government, let loose against himself any propaganda . . . which might deprive him of all prestige at the period when he might possibly take action. He could, if the occasion arose, take action from the Bahamas."

If that was an accurate report of the conversation between the duke and the German agent, he appeared to be saying that he would go along with the wishes of his government for the time being, but he could still change his mind, even in the Bahamas. (This prospect, as we will see, would soon come to fruition.)

Schellenberg, meanwhile, had to consider how or when he would carry out Hitler's personal instructions that if the duke wouldn't agree to go to Spain voluntarily he should be taken by force. The Germans had already, as a last-ditch effort, tried to scare the Windsors into leaving for Spain by warning the duke that his life was in danger, not from the Germans, but from the British.

Although the Windsors were already encircled by MI6, Walter Monckton had to put the duke's mind at rest and, as Monckton later recalled, "The duke was not satisfied until I secured the attendance of a Scotland Yard detective to look after them." Monckton cabled Churchill with the request; the prime minister agreed and a flying-boat

was ordered up especially to carry Detective Sergeant
Harold Holder of Special Branch on an overnight flight
on July 31. His role would be to act as the Windsors'
bodyguard on the journey to the Bahamas.

The next day, the Windsors were due to sail on the
SS *Excalibur* of the American Export Lines to Bermuda,
where they could pick up a Canadian ship for Nassau.
Would they be on it? The Germans hadn't given up yet;
but neither had Walter Monckton, whose sole task now
was to make sure they were. New instructions, however,
had arrived from Berlin. Ribbentrop fired off another
message to Baron von Stohrer in Madrid with instructions
to tell the duke that Germany was determined to compel
England to make peace by every means, and it would
be as well if the duke were to hold himself in readiness
for further developments. Germany would be prepared
to cooperate with the duke and to clear the way for any
desire expressed by the duke and duchess. Ribbentrop
added that Churchill intended to get the duke into his
power in the Bahamas and to hold him there forever. If
the duke insisted on leaving, there would still be a chance
that the Portuguese agent could remain in touch with
him, Ribbentrop went on; should the occasion arise, negotiate.

On the same day, Hitler called an immediate conference at the Berghol to make further plans for the invasion
of Britain and was told that naval plans were not yet
complete, nor would they be until early September. In
the meantime, however, England could be smashed by
aerial attack—but Hitler held back, and the major offensive that Churchill had anticipated was not put into
effect. Hitler seemed strangely hesitant. Was he waiting
for the duke's response?

Back in Lisbon, Dr. Antonio Salazar, the Portuguese
prime minister, visited the duke and urged him to re-
consider. Then on the morning of August 1, only hours
before they were due to sail, their Spanish friend Don
Miguel arrived with a message from General Franco's

brother, Don Nicholas, warning the duke not to leave "for the sake of the British Empire." The Portuguese banker Ricardo Espirito Santo handed the duke a message from the Germans in Madrid pleading that he stay. Schellenberg, continuing his scare tactics, was unable to get to the duke without, as he saw it, a running battle with British agents.

His final report to Berlin indicates the drama of the situation and the scares he had initiated in the final forty-eight hours:

> I had to assume that the Duke of Windsor, as a result of the mediation of the Ambassador and the highly influential Spanish confidential emissary, had given up the intention to travel to the Bahamas and was trying instead to return to Spain. (I refer to taking advantage of the hunting excursion on the frontier.)
>
> Principal tasks in Lisbon:
>
> 1) Creation and organisation of a personal protective service for the Duke and Duchess.
>
> 2) Preparation of security for the automobile journey of the Duke and Duchess from Lisbon by way of Guarda; security for hunting excursion; security for border crossing; security in Spain . . .
>
> After only 2 days there was established a protective service of 18 agents working for us. One to three agents were constantly active in the immediate vicinity of the Duke. In connection with the preparation for the journey, security at the frontier, etc., the reports which came in soon made it evident (and this was confirmed from the beginning by the Minister here) that the Duke was giving up the return to Spain and had even expressed himself unfavourably about it within his intimate circle. After the appearance of Monckton, accompanied by members of the I.S. and Scotland Yard, a change of tactics seemed advisable, since the Duke fell completely under their influence.
>
> Through the efforts of a high Portuguese police official

who visited the Duke and Duchess personally, it was possible to interfere with the plans of the Duke and Duchess to move to a hotel under I.S. surveillance. The hints dropped on the occasion of this visit about the impending danger to the Duke and Duchess from I.S. activities, Jews and emigrants produced a very strong effect.

From 29 July onwards the principal object was to prevent the departure of the Duke and Duchess by making use of all the means available suitable to the nature of the mission . . .

In order to increase the anxiety-motive and to determine the Duke and Duchess to remain in Europe, they were kept constantly aware—through the influence of various personal connections of the principal Portuguese confidential agent—of the danger of a surprise attack by Churchill and of I.S. activity. It is certain that the Duke and Duchess had real feelings of anxiety. However, Monckton was evidently able to dispel the anxiety as it arose. As the preparations for departure became more active, the strongest methods were brought into use by us.

These were as follows: Complete uncovering through police activity of the known I.S. members here.

Since the Duke was especially impressed by the Jewish peril, the principal private secretary of the Duke, Phillips [sic], was furnished with a list of Jews and emigrants sailing on the same ship, and it was stressed that the counter-espionage police could make no guarantee.

Call on the Duchess by the wife of a Portuguese official. (Reason for visit: anxiety about her husband's position, since if anything happened he would lose his post. Reaction: deepest thanks to the Portuguese lady and a request to stand firm, since the Duke must make the journey.)

Anonymous gift of flowers with a greeting card containing a warning; anonymous letter to the Duchess also emphasising the gravity of the danger; bribing of their

[English] driver who refused to go along to the Bahamas on account of the danger . . .

On the day of departure a paid agent was arrested on the ship for lacking a passport and . . . led the Portuguese authorities to a spot where traces of an infernal machine and tools for building such a machine were found. The affair was bruited about in the company of the Duke and Duchess as a most serious sort of warning, yet without result . . .

Sabotage against the motor car which was driving to the ship with luggage. The luggage only reached the ship after an hour's delay; a firing of shots (harmless breaking of bedroom window) scheduled for the night of 30 July was omitted, since the psychological effect on the Duchess would only have been to increase her desire to depart. . . . In order that no possibility should be overlooked . . . the Spanish Minister of the Interior sent the district leader of the Falange in Madrid, Primo de Rivera, out to the Duke. His intervention too was without success. On 1 August, five hours before the departure of the ship, the attempt was made, with the aid of the Minister here, to send the Spanish Ambassador (the brother of the Caudillo) to see the Portuguese Premier Salazar, to get him to persuade the Duke and Duchess, when they made their farewell, to remain at least in Portugal. Ambassador Nicholas Franco and Salazar spoke of official Spanish and Portuguese wishes etc. Even this final manoeuvre could not prevent the departure of the Duke.

Schellenberg had failed, but the Germans still had Mlle. Moulichon. She was now traveling back from Paris, hoping to arrive in Portugal before the Windsors sailed. In fact, when she finally arrived, her papers were challenged. She was temporarily put into prison, and released only after the duke and duchess had set sail.

On August 2, Stohrer telegraphed Berlin: ". . . the ducal couple sailed last night . . . further report about final vain attempts to restrain W from departing follows."

In his final report to Churchill on the incident, Monckton wrote, "There was considerable difficulty in keeping him to the date fixed for departure from Lisbon . . . he told me he had received from various sources which he was not at liberty to disclose, a report that he would be in danger if he went to the Bahamas . . . a distinguished Spaniard flew from Madrid to repeat the warning. . . . I was allowed to see him both with and without the duke. The duke and the Spaniard wished me to telegraph you advising the postponement of the departure for two or three weeks. I said this was impossible . . . in the end the duke accepted the position."

The debate as to whether the duke truly contemplated the prospect of remaining in Europe and, in some way, of eventually regaining the throne, would continue for many years. He himself denied categorically that he ever once harbored the thought. His one and only concern, he would say, was the achievement of a peaceful solution to the war.

There is no doubt that the pressures upon him during that period and the scare tactics from both sides in Spain and Portugal were immense, and in moments of despair he must have considered the options available to him.

What was the role of the duchess? She, more than himself, appears to have given contemplation to a triumphant return of the Windsors to England, bearing as they would Hitler's promise of peace. If Hitler had pursued the early invasion of the British Isles; if Britain had fallen; if Mosley had been released and assumed the dictatorship, what then?

One thing is certain, Hitler himself never seems to have doubted the usefulness of Windsor; and the duke remained in his plans for many months to come. At a conference in October 1941, Hitler would say of the duke, "He is no enemy of Germany" . . . and he believed that "when the proper moment arrives, he [the duke] will be the only person capable of directing the destiny of England."

·TWELVE·

THE NEW MONARCHY

What was once the renowned Prince of Wales "set" had now largely disintegrated and life and the courtiers at Buckingham Palace had resumed a more formal tone, though not ignoring entirely some of the steps to modernity that had been set in motion by Edward.

It had been a traumatic time, attempting to restore confidence in the monarchy that had been lost, not just in Whitehall, but also in relations with other countries, particularly America.

The strain on the king and queen had been such that no member of their family could do anything but close ranks and give them all possible support. There would be no more scandals, no more idiotic publicity, nothing that could bring the House of Windsor into further disrepute. Everyone knew it was going to be difficult for the new king. The task would have been daunting for anyone, but with his shyness, lack of experience, and health record, George looked hardly the ideal candidate to lead the nation, particularly at this time of war.

Those who said he would not stand the strain reckoned without the love and strength of Elizabeth, his queen, and their two daughters, Elizabeth and Margaret. His wife immediately took up a smiling but tough stance, and with tactful but not overpowering leadership she guided her husband through his most difficult moments until such time as she had instilled in him the confidence which she already possessed. Hers was a task much more than just that of being a king's wife, and never had the consort of any British monarch become so involved in the running of the country.

She also had royal households at Sandringham, Balmoral, Windsor, and Buckingham Palace to manage, which even in the early war years was a task in itself. Gradually, month by month, King George VI become more relaxed, and even his stammer improved, though it would never clear up entirely. Harold Nicolson noted, "I cannot tell you how superb [the Queen] is but what astonished me is how the King has changed. He is so gay and calm. We shall win . . . I know that."

One small example of the extent to which the queen would involve herself in her husband's duties was shown in September 1940 when Britain had just taken delivery of fifty First World War destroyers, given by America to the Royal Navy. The king sent a letter of appreciation to Roosevelt, and at the bottom, the queen added a postscript expressing her own thanks and good wishes. In fact George struck up a lasting friendship with Roosevelt and there continued between them a confidential exchange of letters which many in Britain believed helped the nation's cause greatly in its hour of need.

Although at one stage King George shared his brother's view that appeasement with Germany was preferable to war, he was able to adapt his thinking quickly to suit the mood of his people and his government—which was his true role and the true role of any British monarch, who is not there to express political views or to advise ministers on such matters. Edward VIII could never accept that.

Many considered that it was most fortunate for the nation that Edward had abdicated when he did. In this time of war, he and his style would never have suited.

Conjecture as to what might have been became a popular topic in those dark Battle of Britain days, when what seemed like eternities would be spent in the dark and smelly bomb shelters. The thought of Mrs. Simpson on the throne of Britain was not popular. Wallis in all her outrageous jewels, overdressed and not a hair out of place, would not have gone down well with a nation under siege.

The royal family now could not have acted more suitably: a king who often looked, and certainly sounded, unpompous but was caring and gentlemanly; a smiling, loving queen; and two charming daughters—Britain was truly well served by its First Family. Edward and Wallis, had they remained, could never have been a match.

There was little regard by the king and queen for their personal safety, and when Queen Wilhelmina of the Netherlands and King Haakon of Norway arrived to seek refuge from Hitler's invading armies, they were appalled at the lack of security. Both these monarchs had been subject to continued attempts at capture by Hitler, and both were firmly convinced that it was the Führer's intention to imprison the sovereign of any country he invaded.

There were numerous bomb scares for the royal family, as Buckingham Palace became a regular target for German bombs, so that when Eleanor Roosevelt came to stay in early 1942, the queen apologized for the draft caused by the numerous missing windows. Eleanor Roosevelt herself wrote: "The rooms are enormous, and quite without heat. I do not see how they keep the dampness out. The rooms were all cold except for the smaller sitting room which had an open fire." But the king and queen were proud. "I'm glad we've been bombed," said the queen. "Now I can look the East End in the face." It was also the king's own idea to offer the George Medal or the George Cross to civilians excluded from military service who performed acts of bravery.

Would his brother have fitted into the deprivations of

Britain at this time? Perhaps, but his actions through these early years of the war suggested that he was better out of it.

Many of the duke's once ardent supporters were revising their views of him as the war progressed. That summer even Churchill was moved to admit to Baldwin that he had perhaps been wrong about his opposition to the abdication, and now saw "the prospect of Wallis Simpson as Queen . . . too horrible to contemplate."

One of the good things to come out of it all was that in all probability the Windsor drama saved the Mountbattens from the divorce courts. In the year of abdication, Edwina returned from her trips abroad and at first she was entranced by the situation unfolding between the king and Mrs. Simpson. Once it was over, and as the rest of the family threw its weight behind King George, her marital problems seemed of little consequence. She and Dickie, their friends were soon to note, began to spend much more time in each other's company whenever his Navy duties allowed. Furthermore, Peter Murphy was still on hand, never took sides, and was a great supporter to them both; when one was away he provided company for the other, amusing them both with a shrewd mind and informed conversation. Theirs was a true ménage à trois.

Matters of the heart, however, took a back seat as the Mountbattens, of all the prince's set, threw themselves into the war effort with great dedication. In fact, Edwina had entered a new and important phase in her life which seems to have begun once she started wearing a uniform.

She joined the Women's Voluntary Service and completed six months' nursing training at Westminister Hospital, with only a brief excursion abroad to China, where she saw the shocking ruins left by the Japanese bombing. She returned to England and immediately joined the St. John Ambulance Brigade of which she became not just a famous figurehead but an on-the-ground worker, organizer, and sometimes financier. At a time when he himself was involved in most dangerous wartime exploits, Dickie Mountbatten's own thoughts had turned to the safety of his family. His biographer Philip Ziegler tells us that Mountbatten's greatest fear, if an invasion of Britain came, was that his wife and two daughters, with their Jewish connections, would be among the first to suffer, particularly since his own family was one of recent German origin.

His first idea was that Edwina should purchase a boat and have it moored at Salcombe in Devon, and if the Germans invaded they should all immediately escape to Madeira. "I implore you," he wrote, "not to wait too long." It was a hazardous plan and in any event he soon realized that it would be a hopeless prospect trying to persuade his wife to evacuate to safety. The compromise was for the two children to be sent straight away to America to live with the Vanderbilts. Mountbatten wrote of Edwina to his daughters, "When most of the other society people have left London . . . she has become a real heroine."

Her sweeping, whistle-stop tours of the bombed and desperate areas became a feature of her life. She would tour air-raid shelters personally, and through her charm and connections bring what help she could to those in need. Her night tours, even during the bombing, were legendary, and she would arrive in the shelters, many of them stinking and without sanitation, where hundreds of men, women, and children were seeking a safe haven from Hitler's bombs, looking immaculate in her uniform, not a hair out of place, not a smudge on her lipstick.

It was a harsh program of work she set herself, with ten- or twelve-hour days being the norm: it was as if she were now trying to make up for those wasteful, irresponsible years before the war. Similarly, Mountbatten himself was being drawn into the higher echelons of power as the war progressed, and his exploits in his first major command, HMS *Kelly*, would be immortalized by Noel Coward in the film *In Which We Serve*.

His most celebrated exploit, which earned him the Distinguished Service Order, came off the Dutch coast, when the *Kelly* was crippled by a U-boat torpedo with the loss of twenty-seven of his crew. Though the *Kelly* was listing badly, Mountbatten continued fighting until his destroyer was on the verge of sinking; she was put under tow and brought back across the North Sea, where his beloved ship was rebuilt.

The Germans finally disposed of the *Kelly* during heavy fighting off Crete when the ship was sunk and more than half the ship's company lost. Mountbatten returned safely to Edwina and a couple of days later over dinner told Noel Coward the whole dramatic story of HMS *Kelly*. "It was absolutely heartbreaking," Coward wrote later. "He told the whole saga without a frill and with a sincerity that was very moving. He is a pretty wonderful man, I think."

Halfway around the world, the horrors of war had an air of unreality; people read about them and heard broadcasts but were never really involved. The man who should have been deeply involved, but who had renounced his responsibilities, was embarking on a fairly carefree life . . .

As they sailed across the Atlantic, the Windsors were seething. It was a voyage they had not wanted to make, and they blamed the king and queen, particularly the latter, for their present predicament. As they sailed, a final letter to Churchill from the duke had dropped onto the prime minister's desk in London. "I naturally do not consider my appointment as one of first-class importance nor would you expect me to. On the other hand, since it is evident that the King and Queen do not wish to bring our family differences to an end, without which I could not accept a post in Britain, it is at least a temporary solution to the problem of my employment in this time of war."

The prospect of his return to Europe does not appear to have totally disappeared from the duke's mind. The

Windsors arrived in Bermuda on August 9 to change ships before going on to Nassau. They stayed for six days, and on the day they left, August 15, Baron von Hoynigen Huene telegraphed Berlin from Lisbon: "The confidant has just received a telegram from the Duke in Bermuda, asking him to send a communication as soon as it may be necessary for him to act. Should any reply be sent?" If this were true, and there is no way of knowing, since no such telegraph or reply was ever discovered among captured documents, it would appear the duke was keeping his agreement to remain in touch with the Germans, through the confidential emissary. That there was no reply was hardly surprising. By mid-August the Battle of Britain was in full flow. Britain would not capitulate to the German onslaughts; for the moment Hitler had no use for a substitute king.

And now on the horizon was a new life for the Windsors, and the prospect of it pleased them not one bit. Wallis wrote to her Aunt Bessie from the ship carrying them to the new world: "I am so furious I can't see you as we are not coming to NY . . . that bloody government won't let us come to the US. . . . Naturally we loathe the job but it was the only way out of a difficult situation. . . . I see a black 1940."

·THIRTEEN·

"OUR ELBA"

The Bahama Islands are the gems of the Caribbean. Hot and sunny, they have miles of white sandy beaches and are set in blue and green coral seas full of tropical fish of all sizes and colors. What possible trouble could the Duke and Duchess of Windsor get into here? More than enough, and if Winston Churchill ever thought that by posting them to this least important far-flung colony of the British Empire, they would be out of sight, out of mind, and out of mischief, he could not have been more wrong.

Since the days of the pirate strongholds of the Caribbean, the Bahamas have always been a hotbed of intrigue. The Duke of Windsor walked straight into it. By the end of his time there, he would brush with so much scandal that it would bar him from ever again performing a task of responsibility on behalf of the British government, and lead directly to the Windsors' banishment until their deaths. In an imitation royal court that they would create for themselves, in total exile from Britain, cut off from the royal family, and unwanted by successive British governments, they would become merely puppets in a social whirlpool whose glamor would diminish as the years went by!

The events that were to plunge the duke into the midst of this new turmoil would involve murder, bribery, and corruption linked directly to the organized crime syndicates of America. And even at this late stage in the war, there would come further contact with the Nazis, for which he would be held in further disgrace.

For the moment, however, the residents of the Bahamas, and the socialites of the nearby American coast, awaited the Windsors' arrival in eager anticipation. *The Daily Mirror* caught the initial atmosphere:

> Bahamas Islands' inhabitants have begun excitedly preparing for a great invasion of wealthy Americans who will be attracted there by the presence of the Duke and Duchess of Windsor. "The entire town is celebrating," state cables from Nassau, the Bahamas' capital. Every tradesman, estate agent, and hotel keeper thinks he's going to become a millionaire. Local society is in a dither and plans to repel gate-crashing social climbers. In New York, travel agents predict the Bahamas will speedily become the gayest, smartest resort in the Western Hemisphere.
>
> American airlines and shipping companies discussed the running of special services to Nassau to satisfy the anticipated demand of thousands who'll want to go there to get a glimpse of the Royal Governor-General and his American-born lady.

They arrived on the morning of August 17, 1940, aboard the Canadian ship *Lady Somers*, which they had picked up in Bermuda. The duchess recalled that moment: "David had been on the bridge of the ship as we entered the harbour and the captain picked out Government House, our future home. At a distance it looked like a rambling Southern plantation house, with spacious verandahs, jalousied windows and surrounded by palm trees."

There would also be a Nazi contact waiting for them in Nassau and, as Churchill's intelligence discovered,

Hitler's U-boats would circle the Bahamas like sharks, ready to send a landing party to grab the duke and duchess and bring them back to Europe if ever it became necessary. But the scenario that would soon engulf the Windsors was being prepared long before they arrived. There would be many players and contact for the duke with a type of people he had never met before: hustlers, self-made millionaires, chancers, con men, and gangsters. A far cry from the cozy world of London's social life.

Let us go back momentarily to 1937, when the characters of the forthcoming dramas were gathering. . . . The wedding of Count Alfred de Marigny to Miss Lucie-Alice Cohen in London was, quite coincidentally, set for the same time as that of the duke and Mrs. Simpson. By some quirk of fate, there was another coincidence in that de Marigny and his bride were to travel to America later that year in the *Normandie*, a cruise liner going between Europe and the United States. The duke and duchess were also to visit the United States, and had provisionally discussed traveling on the same boat, at the same time. In the event, the Windsors' trip was canceled. De Marigny and the duke, although neither of them knew it then, would meet soon enough in Nassau, when the duke would accuse de Marigny of murder and the count would come face-to-face with the gallows.

Early summer in London was an attractive time for an attractive couple to be married, and Freddie de Marigny was an attractive man, six feet three inches tall, slim, and with broad shoulders.

He had a job in the City which a friend of his father —a sugar planter from Mauritius in the Indian Ocean— had fixed for him. His mother and father were divorced when he was three and he had adopted his mother's maiden name—which action, he claimed, had nothing to do with the fact that the hereditary title of count went with it.

He had a titled friend with him, the Marquis Georges

de Visdelou-Guimbeau; they were lifelong friends, both born in Mauritius and at times attending the same boarding schools. Between them, they had a rehearsed and effective patter when it came to women; they could both charm the back legs off a donkey and what with their hand-kissing, deep French accents, and captivating smiles, they could tag along with the social set. In fact they were a couple of gigolos on the fringes of a social scene that they could not enter owing to an embarrassing lack of funds.

Freddie seemed to have found the answer. He met and married Lucie-Alice Cohen, the daughter of an Alsatian banker whose warnings that de Marigny was only after her money were totally ignored. The fact that she later provided the money to buy tickets to get them to America aboard the *Normandie* eventually convinced her that perhaps her father was right. She grew bored with Freddie very quickly, preferring the sexual expertise of his friend Georges, for whom she also bought a passage aboard the liner, to make the trip a happy sexual threesome.

Indeed, Freddie recalled in his own version of events for a long statement about his life that he had to make in Nassau: "It was quite a trip. I had been reading a Noel Coward play about a husband, a wife and a lover. I found the parallel quite amusing."

By the time they reached America, Freddie's marriage to Lucie-Alice was all but over; they were in the divorce courts exactly thirteen weeks after the wedding. Freddie was eager for the divorce to go through. He had already found a more attractive, more mature and, most important, much richer girl, who was willing to become his wife and share her worldly goods, which were quite considerable.

Ruth Fahnestoch Schermerhorn, the daughter of a wealthy family from New York, was on the verge of divorce from her first husband, the equally wealthy A. Coster Schermerhorn, who would settle upon her a small fortune to ensure that she continued a life-style in the manner to which she had become accustomed.

Freddie couldn't believe his luck, and speedily after his own divorce—on the very day when the decree was pronounced—he and Ruth were married and left immediately for a Caribbean cruise which ended in Nassau.

The Bahamas had become a place to winter for the socialites of New York, and an interesting excursion for the really wealthy in Florida. The couple bought, or to be more precise, Ruth bought, a couple of acres on the island of Eleuthera, a short boat trip from Nassau, where they built a superb home on the beach and established themselves quickly among the cream of Bahamas society. They equipped themselves with a Star Class yacht which Ruth named *Concubine*, and Freddie couldn't believe his luck.

"This was my dream," he said with relish. "An island in the sun, a beautiful wife, money and a first-class sailing yacht."

An accomplished yachtsman from boyhood, he now joined the elite at Nassau Yacht Club, where flags of many nations fluttered over the red-tiled clubhouse and where the rich and famous came to race. He could beat them all in *Concubine*, the slim craft slicing through the blue waters above the coral and shoals of multicolored fish, and gleaming trophies piled up as he won race after race. He would be applauded, somewhat begrudgingly by the VIPs, at yachting events, and it was there that a secret adulation for this dashing sportsman first glimmered in the heart of a young schoolgirl.

Sir Harry Oakes, the gold-mine millionaire, took his family to the yacht club regularly during the season. Nancy, his firstborn, was barely fifteen years old.

"I remember when I first met her," said Freddie. "She had the most pleasant, disarming smile. I'd heard she was a spoiled brat, bad-tempered, stuck-up and so on. But she didn't seem like that at all. I suppose people were saying 'like father, like daughter.' He was an uncouth man, rudely eccentric, unpolished for a man of his position." Their meeting would eventually lead to his downfall, to his being ostracized by local society. But by then the latter would be the least of his worries.

Oakes, a rough, tough prospector, had left his manners in the goldfields of the Yukon where he had joined countless thousands of other hopeful amateurs who lived, fought, worked, and scratched a living in circumstances of the most appalling, self-inflicted suffering, obsessed by a dream that one day they would strike it rich.

He was now so wealthy that money, in terms of the amount he possessed, no longer interested him. All he knew, and he would often remind his dinner guests of the fact, was that his fortunes came from sheer hard labor, blood and sweat. When he left his hometown of Sangerville, Maine, just before the turn of the century, he had one purpose in mind: to find gold. With little more than a pick and shovel and backpack, he joined thirty thousand other prospectors fired with news of big gold strikes in the Yukon, where the names of Dawson City and Klondike would soon be the talk of every daydreamer.

Oakes, in later life, was reticent about talking of those early days as a prospector, because there he saw what gold fever could do to a man. Many men, converging as they did at the point of the last strike, or rumor of one, formed themselves into shanty camps. They came from every walk of life but invariably became dregs of humanity, as money, food, and clothing ran out. Big strikes were for the few. The majority could hardly survive, and thousands didn't.

Harry Oakes was in the thick of it, and for years he lived that life of dehumanizing degradation, a man's world where the only petticoats were those of visiting prostitutes. Only once did he make a promising strike in the Yukon; it petered out, but he now had enough money to pursue his quest elsewhere, in new countries and with new hope, a search which took him to the Philippines, then to Australia, New Zealand, Africa, the Belgian Congo, South Africa, Mexico, and back to North America, always searching for the elusive yellow metal. At last, however, he struck it rich, and fifteen years of grueling, disheartening work was about to pay off.

He had gone to Ontario where he bought a small claim near Kirkland Lake. He worked the mine for a year, but didn't have enough money to develop the shafts or buy equipment to dig the gold in any quantity. He sold out for $300,000 and went back on the trail of another vein.

This time it was the big one, and Oakes himself recalled the find many times: "I had staked a claim around Lake Shore where there had been discoveries of gold-bearing ore on the surface. My knowledge of other adjoining properties made me certain that there was enormous wealth down there, and I was right. When I knew I had struck a rich field, I only had one thought in my mind: to get the gold out and make money."

Make money he did. The Lake Shore mine became the second largest in the Western hemisphere, its reserves of gold being put conservatively at $300,000,000. It took him ten years or more to see it established, but by the early twenties, gold and money were rolling in.

There must have been something more than his money that attracted Eunice McIntyre. Harry Oakes was now forty-eight, twice her age, still uncouth, rough, and without any taste for a gracious life. Those long hard days in the gold fields were not easily shaken. He was small, five feet six inches, and now overweight through tasting the good things in life that he had lacked through those years. His jaw was square and protruding, his nose was beaklike, and his language was learned in the Klondike.

They met on a cruise, married in Sydney in 1923, and returned to Canada to live in a chalet he had built for himself near the mine, a place that suited the prospector in his bachelor days but proved too desolate for his new bride. Their first child, Nancy, was born there, and Oakes agreed that this was no place to bring up a family.

They moved to Niagara Falls and, as his family grew—another child every two years until they had five—he bought and developed an estate in Niagara, another in his home state of Maine, two houses in Palm Beach, Florida, another in Kensington, London, and an estate in Sussex, England.

The move to the Bahamas came in 1933 when Canada increased its taxes to such a degree that Oakes just picked up his family and left, first for Palm Beach and then for Nassau, where he embarked on a massive development project, spurred on by the merchants of Bay Street, who saw it as an encouragement to other big investors to come to Nassau.

Within a few years, Oakes owned a third of New Providence, had built an airport, bought a hotel, and constructed a golf course. At the same time, he embarked on many charitable ventures, and in London two big donations to St. George's Hospital obtained him a baronetcy.

It was during one of Oakes's visits to London, early in 1934, that Oakes met the Duke of Windsor, then the Prince of Wales, unaware of course that their paths would cross again. He had observed with sadness the events of the abdication and the wedding and now he awaited the arrival of the duke and duchess.

So did the rest of Nassau, and particularly the merchants of the notorious Bay Street, where descendants of the pirates and wreckers that had brought thousands of ships to grief in the Caribbean in years past still controlled the colony.

Past incumbents of the job now facing the duke had, on occasions, been forced to launch artillery fire at the Bahamas House of Assembly to get their way. Bay Street ruled. The governor, to them, was a pawn. And here was the Duke of Windsor sailing toward it all, innocent of the viper's nest that awaited him in the hot, Bahamian summer, when the air is thick and still, without a breeze to cool a perspiring body . . .

At the harbor, there was a great sea of faces to greet the Windsors: important local dignitaries, mostly white, at the front, followed by a mass of the little black faces of children done out in their Sunday best, cheering and waving flags. The streets were decked in bunting. A carnival atmosphere reigned.

The duke was dressed in army safari khaki and, as he walked down the gangplank, perspiration in the intense heat was already appearing under his arms, at the small of his back, and showing through embarrassingly on the light brown of his clothes. As he progressed to the signing-in ceremony and oath-taking, the sweat poured off him, dripping off the end of his nose and chin and blurring the signatures of the official documents.

Nassau wives had been at work early that morning at Government House, filling the main rooms with sweet-scented tropical flowers. The duchess said politely: "It's absolutely lovely." But when they had gone she turned to the duke and angrily insisted: "David, we cannot possibly live here. It's horrible."

The duke agreed. The rambling old house was dark and musty, despite the smell of the flowers. The furniture had seen better days, and in many rooms the paint was peeling from the walls. They stuck it out for a week before the duke complained to the appropriate government official and insisted that a new home should be provided until Government House had been refurbished.

Government ministers went into hasty session, and after some discussion voted to approve the spending of £1,500 on the redecoration of the official residence, a decision that brought some criticism from impoverished black MPs.

In the meantime, the duchess positively refused to live there and Harry Oakes came to the rescue by lending them one of his houses, Westbourne—a luxurious oceanside mansion where in less than three years' time, Oakes would be found murdered.

The duchess personally directed the renovation of

Government House. She flew in interior designers from New York, ripped out all the old curtains, paneling, and musty furniture, and set about refurbishing her new home with some enthusiasm. When it was finally completed, she was delighted.

"Now we can move in, and conduct the business of these islands, in the style appropriate to the task," she told her government advisers. The Bahamas government did not enjoy her enthusiasm, nor join in her pleasure. They had just received the bill for the work the duchess had commissioned and once again had to go into a special session to approve it. The amount was £7,500, £6,000 more than the original amount agreed upon.

The duchess was happier now, though neither of the Windsors relished the thought of staying long in this place. Nassau was impoverished after its last great boom during the days of American Prohibition, when the whole nation was engaged in bootlegging for the thirsty millions across the water. The town was tatty, smelling of overloaded sewers, and the streets were potholed.

Although Wallis wrote to her Aunt Bessie, "The place is a dump and I just can't wait to get away," she was soon making the most of it, entertaining in lavish style friends and important visitors from American—especially New York—society. They quickly became close friends of Harry Oakes and his wife, though he and the duke were unlikely companions. Oakes was still gruff and ill-mannered, given to spitting and belching after meals and to swearing profusely regardless of the company. At cocktail parties, the duke came across Freddie de Marigny, but they didn't get on at all well. "He's my least favorite ex-King," Freddie once said, knowing full well that the duke could hear him.

Freddie's high life had come to an abrupt end. His long-suffering wife Ruth had pulled the rug from under his feet and said with some resolution: "Definitely, Freddie, you will get no more money from me." At the divorce hearing, she reckoned he had cost her $250,000 to maintain his playboy life-style and to achieve his considerable notoriety in the yachting world. Love has its strange ways and Freddie continued to live with Ruth for a further nine months after the divorce, along with their mutual friend, the marquis, Georges de Visdelou. Ruth also parted with still more money. She gave Freddie £12,000 to help him start up his own grocery business and to join in a couple of small development projects.

Nancy Oakes, whose schooling had been moved from England to New York, always seemed to be around, although Freddie viewed her with caution.

"Why don't you marry her?" he was urged by Georges, who was aware that his friend would require another wealthy wife to keep him in the style he had grown to love these past three years.

"You're crazy," Freddie retorted. "She is just a moonstruck girl and I have no more intention of marrying her than I have of marrying the Queen of Holland."

Moonstruck girls, however, grow into adorable young women and some months later the two met again at a party.

"I was absolutely bowled over," he recalled later. "She was wearing a blue-and-white chiffon dress, and all of a sudden she seemed to have grown up. I knew then that I loved her as I had never loved anyone in my whole life."

She went straight to his heart as they sat chatting on the verandah when she said: "I am so unhappy at home." Like many girls of her age, she thought her mother was domineering and her father boorish, and at that moment, Freddie noted, he knew he would have to look after her.

They met secretly whenever Nancy was home from school, but the romance really began to bloom when Freddie went into a hospital in New York for the removal of a growth.

"Nancy came to see me whenever she could get away. She was so comforting to see as I lay in my hospital bed, and it wasn't long after that we discussed marriage. I think she brought it up. I told her that it was out of the question. Her parents would not agree to her, a teenage girl, marrying a man twice divorced and about twice her age."

Quickly and firmly, Nancy replied: "They won't be told."

That, for the moment, was where it rested. Freddie returned to Nassau after three weeks, and Nancy stayed on at the French School for Girls to complete her "finishing."

·FOURTEEN·

A NEW NAZI CONTACT

———————— ◆ ————————

The Windsors had found another new, exciting friend who was a millionaire and had fallen totally under his spell. He was a curious mixture of genius, business entrepreneur, and would-be politician. More important, Axel Wenner Gren had friends in high places in Berlin. In the autumn of 1940, he returned to the Bahamas in his ocean-going yacht, *Southern Cross*, in which he had sailed the world, and he'd made straight for Government House. The last contact that he had had with the duke was shortly after the abdication, when he was in close liaison with Charles Bedeaux; he would have been among the "brains" who wanted to advise the ex-king on his new career. Now the Windsors were here, near Wenner Gren's home base, the appropriately named Hog Island just off the coast of Nassau, where he had a mansion called Shangri-La.

British intelligence was watching Wenner Gren. So were the Americans, and on file in the U.S. State Department would be placed a letter from American diplomats in Mexico warning that in 1933, Göring had designated the Swede as "one of the most powerful links" the Nazis would have in their economic contacts with important people in Europe and the United States.

Who was he? Where had he come from? What was he doing in the Bahamas? The duke had vague recollections of the man and listened intently as Wenner Gren spelled out his activities during the past few years. He was the founder of Electrolux, the worldwide electronics firm. He had retired from his business and began traveling the world with his heavy-drinking wife. His brilliance in selling and striking business deals was matched with superficiality, simplemindedness, and gross overestimation of his own powers and importance.

He wrote to President Roosevelt offering his services to get the United States out of its economic crisis in the early thirties. Roosevelt didn't reply to his letter. But in 1936, Wenner Gren and his wife got an invitation to the White House from Eleanor Roosevelt. She also saw to it that he and the president got together on their own for discussions. They talked for three hours and AWG didn't miss his chance to tell Roosevelt how he could stop a war breaking out in Europe. Wenner Gren wrote in his diary: "The President's personality was really impressive, but his lack of knowledge about Europe and its state of affairs is almost frightening. This is probably the reason why he wasn't particularly interested in my warnings."

In September the same year he stayed with Herman Göring at a resort in south Germany. Göring laid out the Nazi plans for Europe. The Ukraine was going to be taken by the Germans to take care of the German overpopulation. The forty million Ukrainians were to be "swept away." "Göring made a better impression than I had expected," Wenner Gren entered in his diary.

Later that year, he and his wife bought the *Southern Cross* from Howard Hughes and started to tour the world. From Nassau, where the boat was bought, they went to the Canary Islands and then to Naples to be met by Mussolini, with whom Wenner Gren had previously had trading contacts.

From Italy Wenner Gren sailed to Japan and met the

Japanese emperor who, he noted, said that soon the world would be dominated by three nations: Japan would govern most of Asia; the United States would govern North and South America; and Germany would rule Europe.

In 1939, Axel Wenner Gren visited Göring again, claiming that he had been asked by British friends to have another try for peace. Göring, Wenner Gren wrote in his diary, thought that Germany could accomplish what it wanted without a war. "When we saw that the old man with the umbrella [Chamberlain] was coming to Germany we knew we would get our demands met," Göring told him. Göring was sure that if he and Chamberlain could meet, they would be able to get an agreement between London and Berlin, and Wenner Gren said he would try to arrange it. He got a letter of introduction to Chamberlain from the Swedish Crown Prince Gustaf Adolf, and actually got into Downing Street, where he presented a letter from Göring decrying the folly of war. Chamberlain however refused to see him, and in June, Wenner Gren was back at Göring's house, where he stayed for some weeks, until the outbreak of war when he sailed back to the Bahamas.

He would retain his links with Göring and become the Nazis' main link in vast financial dealings in South America, which would soon involve the Duke of Windsor himself.

It was an aspect of Wenner Gren's financial affairs that had not gone unnoticed by American and British intelligence, nor had his other activities—arms dealings and spying for Göring. Wenner Gren was well known off the southern tip of Florida, and in December 1940, when the Duke and Duchess of Windsor suddenly came sailing toward the American coast aboard his yacht, the telegraph wires started buzzing with activity.

The Windsors should *not* have gone to America without Churchill's permission, but Wallis had been quite miserable and the duke had decided to ignore London. Wallis was unwell, hated the Bahamas' heat, had a toothache, and suffered stomach pains from a grumbling ulcer. She had lost even more weight and now, as one of her visiting friends unflatteringly put it, looked just like a beanpole.

She kept talking about going to Miami. Just once, she would say to the duke, just once.

One afternoon when she was in agony from the pain of an infected tooth which she refused to have treated in the local hospital, the duke contacted Wenner Gren. He insisted on taking them to Miami.

Even before they reached Florida, the American afternoon press headlines announced "Windsors Sailing on Göring Pal's Yacht." So when the duke and duchess crossed to Miami, although it was announced that the visit was "strictly private," they arrived amid a great ballyhoo and publicity. When they docked, a huge line of guards had been hurriedly put together by the Miami police department. Twenty heavily armed motorcycle police formed a motorcade to escort the couple to the hospital, and wherever they went, a massive security operation was mounted.

Churchill fired off another warning to the duke. "There would be no objection if your Royal Highness cared to make a cruise in the West Indian Islands. It would be impossible, however, for HM Government to approve the use of Mr Wenner Gren's yacht for such a purpose. This gentleman is, according to the reports I have received, regarded as a pro-German financier with strong leanings towards appeasement and suspected of being in communication with the enemy. Your Royal Highness may not realise the intensity of feeling in the United States against people of this kind."

Four days later, the duke was summoned to meet President Roosevelt, who was also cruising off the Miami coast. There were immediate rumors that the duke would be asked to succeed Lord Lothian, the British ambassador to the U.S. The duchess fueled the flames when she told an interviewer that her husband was worthy of a much bigger post and responsibility. It was wishful thinking.

There had been a strong rearguard action by Americans in the know to halt the possibility of the duke getting the job. Of course he wanted it. And Wallis certainly did—to be back in her homeland and away from those dreadful islands! The duke, on hearing of Lothian's death, and encouraged by Wallis, bombarded London and the White House. His friends had written letters of support; a major diplomatic situation developed, with telegrams flying between London and Washington.

Roosevelt had already been warned to ignore the whole situation. His files contained letters from his London ambassador at the time of the abdication: the duke was surrounded by pro-Germans and Mrs. Simpson was suspected of being in the pay of the Germans. Windsor's interview with Roosevelt turned into a humiliating nonevent. Clearly, there was never any possibility that he should get the job, which went to Lord Halifax.

The question of Wallis's maid, whom they had left in France, had also been giving diplomatic channels a difficult time. Wallis was insisting that Marguerite Moulichon should be brought to Nassau by whatever means without delay. Quite belligerent, Wallis constantly pestered the State Department in Washington for help in getting her maid across the Atlantic. Washington said it was a matter for London. Windsor himself intervened and raised the issue at a naval conference with American officials. Again he was told, London should handle it. But the duke insisted they act; and they did. Marguerite, who had left Nazi-occupied territory some time before, was now in Lisbon. From there she was brought to New York and then on to Nassau to rejoin her mistress, who was fuming at the amount of time it had taken.

Wallis would not let her standards drop. Local hotels provided her with beauticians: for a time a French hairdresser from New York was flown down by Pan Am, exclusively to attend to the duchess; Wallis would have her hair combed for half an hour each morning and some days the hairdresser would attend upon her three times. "The heat," she wrote to a friend, "does such awful things to a body."

She was also having her clothes sent to the mainland for dry cleaning, but that was stopped by J. Edgar Hoover who had become almost hysterical about the Windsors, since receiving initial reports of their activities from his agents in London and Europe. The FBI chief concluded that Wallis might be sending coded messages in her clothes which could be forwarded to the Nazis. Hoover's precautions were perhaps understandable, but now he was being ridiculous about it; he saw German agents in every corner of the Windsors' life, and the FBI documentation on them, built up on Hoover's orders, became immense. A lot of it, in fairness to the duke and duchess, appears to have been unfounded rumor and hearsay; but Hoover thrived on such intelligence and seemed to have a way of turning such flimsy material into matters of fact which would be used against the person under investigation.

One man the FBI correctly kept tabs on was James D. Mooney, the pro-Nazi boss of General Motors in Europe, who had now suddenly arrived in Nassau and had joined Axel Wenner Gren and the Windsors for a party aboard the *Southern Cross*.

Mooney's card had long since been marked by the U.S. ambassador to Germany, William Dodd, who declared him a member of a group of American industrialists determined to help Hitler achieve total power in Europe. Mooney had been in charge of the Adams-Opel plants that produced the new breed of German tanks, and in 1938, Hitler awarded him the Order of the Golden Eagle. The following year, the Home Office had him banned from entering Britain again, withdrawing his visa—such was the strength of Mooney's Nazi affiliations. As late as March 1941 the U.S. State Department was aware that Mooney still had the services of a courier to take his communications to high places in the Third Reich, even to Hitler himself. But back in Nassau, Mooney, Wenner Gren, and Windsor were the closest of friends.

The assistant secretary of state, Adolf Berle, was building up a picture of the Windsors for his president's exclusive information. He would note, for instance, the arrival in Washington from Paris of Armand Gregoire, the lawyer the duchess had used in Paris; he would note that the duke had been seeing his old friend Robert Young, the railroad president who was another of the top U.S. businessmen in favor of a negotiated settlement with Hitler. And it would be noted that one of Young's directors was a Palm Beach lawyer who was also a friend of, and partner in dubious business activity with, Harold Christie, the Nassau property developer, and Sir Harry Oakes.

Gregoire proved to be of particular interest to Berle, and in March 1942, he would be arrested and charged with being an agent of the enemy. He spent the rest of the war in jail. (After the war, in France, he was found guilty of collaboration with the Nazis and sentenced in his absence to life imprisonment.)

The Windsors had not tempered their views and had not cultivated discretion, and examples of their verbal gaffes were still reaching London. An American known to Churchill and the duke before the abdication, a Mr. Frazier Jelke of New York, was invited to dine with the Windsors at Government House. He later wrote to Churchill, apparently appalled at his hosts' attitude toward the war. He said he was amazed upon his meetings with the duke and duchess "intimately on a number of occasions, to be told by each of them, separately and personally, that they were opposed to America entering the hostilities." It was too late to do any good. "When I said to His Royal Highness, 'Sir, you are a wishful thinker,' he replied, 'No, I have always been a great realist and it is too late for America to save democracy in Europe. She had better save it for herself.' " Soon after Mr. Jelke noted those remarks, the duke gave an interview to an American magazine in which he said much the same thing, only this time he was more forceful in his opposition to the Americans entering the war.

Later that year, as Churchill faced increasingly gloomy reports on the progress of the war, he was again troubled by the Windsors. It came as one final outburst of pro-German idiocy from the duke, before he was finally told to be silent on the subject, at least in public. He gave an interview to *Liberty* magazine in America, shortly before America entered the war after the bombing of Pearl Harbor. "America will help Britain more by not engaging in actual fighting but remaining a keystone for the new world which must be created when the war is over. There will be a new order in Europe, whether imposed by Germany or Britain."

There were now real fears about his activities in the Bahamas. Wenner Gren had often talked to the duke about bringing greater prosperity to the islands by introducing more industry. He was trying to enlist the duke's aid in the purchase of a huge tract of Crown land on the island of Grand Bahama where Wenner Gren already operated a cannery.

London however was not sympathetic to the idea of doing any favors for a friend of the Nazis. Wenner Gren's work on Hog Island was already attracting the interest of security services both in America and London. He was employing over a thousand men on the tiny landstrip, which was a quarter of the then workforce, supposedly on farming. But why did they need deep canals wide enough for a U-boat to pass through? This and other questions the embarrassed duke would soon be facing, as America's entry into the war edged closer.

Still Windsor couldn't see any wrong. He wrote back to London asking for proof of Wenner Gren's duplicity. British intelligence reports were not available to the Colonial Office; nor were the bulging files in America. These, however, would have shown reports of Wenner Gren's continued contact with the Germans, of his sponsorship of a movement to overthrow the Swedish government in favor of the Nazi regime, of concern that he was planning to turn Hog Island into a haven and service base for German U-boats.

The duke totally disregarded the warnings and continued his association with Wenner Gren, encouraging him in his work in the Bahamas. It went deeper than that. Since currency restrictions, and the duke's meager salary of £3,000 a year as royal governor, meant that he was never well endowed financially in Nassau, he was always keen to find ways and means of increasing his personal income by investments.

Wenner Gren came to the duke's aid by offering to transfer currency for the duke and Harry Oakes to a bank in Mexico where he was also hoarding cash for the Nazis. Because they were governed by British currency laws, Windsor and Oakes risked imprisonment if these transactions were discovered at the time. But there is evidence that Oakes and the duke entertained Mexican banking officials—and there are many pointers to dubious financial dealings having taken place.

While Wenner Gren's own financial maneuvers were being closely monitored by American agents, U.S. diplomats believed he controlled an estimated $100 million in Latin America which had been deposited by him personally—though obviously it was not his own money. He had been placing safe investments for his friends from the Bahamas and Europe, and the Americans now had grave concern over the influence he could wield with this kind of financial control in impoverished countries so close to the United States.

If reports in German documents are to be believed, it would appear that the duke himself was still in touch with the Nazis through his former host in Portugal, Dr. Ricardo de Espirito Santo Silva.

On August 5, 1941, Baron von Hoynigen-Huene sent a telegraph to the Foreign Office in Berlin stating. "The intermediary familiar to us from the reports at the time has received a letter from the Duke of Windsor confirming his opinion . . . that Britain has virtually lost the war . . . and the United States would be better advised to promote peace."

The American security services already had files on the Duke of Windsor's "subversive activities" when Churchill and Roosevelt agreed to grant the Windsors' often-made request to be allowed to make an official visit to America. Wallis had been getting very depressed about the traveling restrictions placed upon them by the British government which, so far, had confined her to shopping excursions to Miami. They were overjoyed when they finally received an affirmative response from Churchill, and immediately called their staff in for a conference to plan their tour, which would take in New York, Washington, D.C., and Canada, as well as Wallis's home state.

A massive press entourage began to assemble, while for their part, the Windsors were adding to the circus by getting permission to take with them two hundred and twenty pieces of luggage and twelve aides and servants.

As the tour got under way, there would be vast crowds wherever they went. They were mobbed like film stars. But there was mounting criticism of their flamboyance and their comments which, in any language, could only be described as defeatist. In an article published in one hundred and fifteen American newspapers, the respected columnist Raymond Clapper lambasted them with these words: "If the British were smart propagandists, they would pack up the Duke and Duchess of Windsor, bag and baggage, with all their twelve servants, and send them back to Nassau. England doesn't deserve to be judged by this fancy cavalcade. The English are going into another hard winter and long hard nights. Women go bare-legged because they cannot buy stockings. Families sleep in frightful shelters, making hard sacrifices. No, it isn't good propaganda to parade this handsome pair of fashion plates around America just now."

The following day, *The Daily Mirror* in London, which had been a supporter of the Windsors, had now turned against them. In a leader article, the paper said: "Would it be considered unkind, disrespectful, or even subversive to suggest that the Duke and Duchess should stay in the Bahamas for the rest of this war?" While in the Commons, MPs demanded the immediate recall of the pair back to Britain to end "this ostentatious display of jewellery and finery abroad when people at home are facing severe hardships."

Their return to Nassau also marked a point at which the Bahamas would begin to feel the effects of the war. The Japanese attack on Pearl Harbor in December 1941 and the entry of America into the war focused a new attention on the Caribbean islands and the East Coast of America, where U-boats were presenting a new and greater threat.

The pressure on Winston Churchill was immense; he visited Washington to report to Roosevelt direct on the mounting crisis. Malaya, Java, Burma, Singapore, North Africa, all were scenes of great battles and heavy losses and it was a most despondent time for the British War Cabinet. "We seem to be losing a new bit of the Empire almost every day," wrote one of Churchill's generals. "We are faced with one nightmare situation after another. Winston is a marvel, I can't imagine how he sticks it." But even at that time of great worry, Churchill's thoughts were brought back to the Windsors.

The U-boat activity in the Atlantic was taking a heavy toll on Allied shipping. Shipwrecked men would land in their lifeboats in the Bahamas with tales of great losses and horror. Suddenly, the U-boats' most secret signals, which had been closely monitored by the British, became unreadable and they would remain so for nearly a year.

As the intensity of the U-boat campaign grew, Churchill returned to the fear that had already caused him great concern: that Hitler planned to snatch the Windsors from their virtually unprotected island. Churchill noted that a U-boat landing party would have no difficulty in kidnapping them under the cloak of darkness.

"The Germans," he wrote, "would be very glad to get hold of the Duke and use him for their own purposes. In my opinion, protection against an attack by 50 men should be provided. Very considerable issues are involved."

Immediately, a unit of Canadian Highlanders, veterans of Dunkirk, was despatched to Nassau. They set up machine-gun posts on all approaches to Government House and the grounds were ringed with barbed wire. The soldiers trained themselves and the duke's staff against possible attack, by landing mock raids, jumping in and out of windows, and using a stand-in for the pretend kidnap. The Windsors, typically, found it all "rather amusing," but under pressure from the Americans, the duke was at last forced to do something about Wenner Gren, who had by now been blacklisted by the Americans and barred from using the Panama Canal because of his continual contact with the Germans, and suspicion he was carrying arms.

The duke had been seeking American aid to help with the massive unemployment problems facing black Bahamians, particularly on the outer islands. The U.S. agreed to help, provided Wenner Gren's property in the Bahamas was confiscated, that he was barred from entry, and that the duke should have no further contact with him. Windsor agreed and signed the order.

But the war brought mixed fortunes for the Bahamians. The tourists had gone, and in their place came thousands of servicemen brought in for RAF training missions and the construction of American bases. In fact, as the weeks drew on, Nassau took on the resemblance of a giant aircraft carrier. The Bahamian blacks, however, did not come out of it too well. They were being paid by the government a few shillings a day for work on construction; imported black laborers brought in by the Americans were getting four and five times more. The Bahamian government did nothing to help the growing disquiet until, while the duke was away in Washington, riots broke out. Thousands of men and women surged into Nassau. Troops fired. Two blacks were killed and twenty-five injured. As governor the duke would take the blame; he had done nothing toward solving the pent-up grievances of the native Bahamians.

There was passion developing elsewhere too that would soon envelop him in fresh troubles . . .

For Freddie de Marigny and Nancy Oakes, the months ahead would see the crystalization of their romance. They were already becoming the talk of Nassau. Everyone seemed to know that Nancy, only seventeen and a half, was now deeply and romantically involved with Freddie—everyone that was, except her mother and father. Nancy had gone back to school in New York so Freddie followed and continued visiting her on weekends as often as his funds would allow.

Among the social set that once idolized his manners and charm, he was now a hated man. They picked on every morsel of gossip, and the affair with Nancy had become the talk of the yacht club and every party. What would Sir Harry do and say when he discovered what everyone else in this close-knit community seemed to know?

Freddie was just as worried. "What about your parents?" he asked with some concern when marriage was once again discussed between them. "I'm not going to have them meddle in our affairs. We just won't tell them," Nancy replied defiantly. "We've *got* to tell them," said Freddie, quite aware that her father was a tough roughneck who would possibly not be averse to giving him a good hiding. "We won't," insisted Nancy. "We won't tell them until it's all over."

Two days after her eighteenth birthday, when she was over the age when she needed parental consent, Nancy married her count before a judge in chambers at the

Bronx County Court House, New York. So how did her parents take the news when Nancy telephoned later that afternoon? Her mother, Lady Oakes, collapsed sobbing with the shock of it. Her father first flew into a violent rage, then calmed down as he watched his wife sobbing uncontrollably.

"Well, I suppose we had better make the best of it," he told his wife. "Put Marigny on," he shouted down the receiver at Nancy.

"So you went and married my daughter, did you? Well, tell me the truth, how much money do you want?" Whether Sir Harry was referring to a sum to pay off de Marigny, or a gift to set them up in house and home, was not clear when these conversations were being recalled some months later in a murder court. However, de Marigny stood his ground that day.

"I have sufficient money to keep her and I will prove it to you," he countered, though whether he had or not remained to be seen.

Sir Harry seemed to be accepting the situation, perhaps deciding that further aggravation now would only make matters worse. What was done was done. "I don't give a damn about your past," he told de Marigny. "What is important to us is Nancy's happiness. You had better not mess it up."

To show their goodwill, Lady Oakes paid for the newlyweds' honeymoon in Mexico; she felt quite guilty when de Marigny telephoned to report that Nancy had been taken to hospital during the holiday with a fever that eventually turned out to be typhoid.

Lady Oakes flew to Mexico where both she and de Marigny were called upon to give her daughter blood transfusions. They returned home as soon as Nancy was well enough to travel, but she remained in poor health for some months. When she was taken back into a hospital later that year, and transferred to another hospital in Miami, it was discovered that she was now also pregnant. She lost the baby, though she stayed in the hospital for some weeks. Freddie also checked in to have his tonsils out and took a room next to Nancy's.

She was visited by her parents. De Marigny was also there and in the scene that followed, Sir Harry physically threw him from the hospital bedroom, accusing him of ruining Nancy's health.

Freddie and Nancy returned to Nassau and took a house on Victoria Avenue. "These were the happiest days of my life," Freddie recalls.

Sir Harry came over to visit them. He was charming and all anger forgotten, but a few weeks later Freddie and he had another furious quarrel. Sir Harry was bitterly criticizing the "to hell with everybody" attitude of his daughter and her husband and in particular the way they ignored invitations from Government House.

"I've never asked anything from you," Freddie raged at his father-in-law, "and never will. Nancy's never had a damn thing from you anyhow."

"Everything she's got, every stitch of clothes on her back, I bought for her. You can't talk to me like that, you—you—! I'll have you horse-whipped and thrown in the gutter to rot, you—you—sex maniac!"

A few weeks later Sydney Oakes, Sir Harry's son, came to Freddie's house for dinner. The party went on rather late, and Nancy invited her brother to stay the night. About five o'clock in the morning, however, everybody was awakened by a terrific pounding on the door. It was Sir Harry.

"Open up this goddam door, or I'll break the bloody thing in!"

When the door was opened, Sir Harry rushed in, yelling: "Where's Sydney?"

Sir Harry burst into the guest room and pulled Sydney out of bed by his bare feet. "Who gave you permission to sleep in this house?" Sir Harry shouted. "Get your clothes. I'm taking you to hell outta here!"

While Freddie was so furious that he walked into his

room and closed the door, Sir Harry went off into the night, dragging young Sydney with him. Contact between himself and de Marigny was finally severed. Ahead lay torment for them all that would hit the headlines of the world . . .

Back in London, Queen Mary had received an unexpected letter from her daughter-in-law in Nassau. Wallis had sent a letter to her by hand through the Bishop of Nassau, who was visiting Britain, in which she pleaded: "Madam, I hope you will forgive my intrusion upon your time, as well as my boldness in addressing Your Majesty. My motive for the latter is a simple one. It has always been a source of sorrow and regret to me that I have been the cause of any separation that exists between mother and son . . . the horrors of war and endless separations of families have in my mind stressed the importance of family ties."

If the duchess was hoping for a reconciliation through her letter, she would not achieve it. The response from Queen Mary was a stony silence.

Three months later, in August 1942, Windsor's favorite brother, the Duke of Kent, was killed when the plane in which he was flying crashed on mountains in the north of Scotland. Both duke and duchess later wrote of their feelings of grief at their loss despite, as the duchess put it, his having been a "turn-coat towards us." Yet his widow, Princess Marina, received not a word of written sympathy from either.

The family feud was as strong as ever, fueled as it must have been by the Windsors' irresponsible and almost treasonable acts in the Bahamas. The latter was quite apparent when, that winter, the duke wrote to Churchill once again about his continuing obsession: his wife's lack of royal status. He asked the prime minister to use his influence for "the king to restore the Duchess's Royal rank . . . as an act of justice and courtesy and as a recognition of her two years in public service in the Bahamas."

Churchill did not reply for six weeks, his attentions totally captured by the war effort. The matter of the duchess' title could hardly have been of importance to him then. When the reply came, it merely reaffirmed the king's previous stance . . . that he was "not willing to take action in the sense desired . . . I hope your Royal Highness will not attach undue importance to this point after the immense renunciations you have made."

Wallis herself clearly did not need confirmation of the title to act like a royal. She wrote to her Aunt Bessie that year: "I really do wish we could move somewhere inhabited by at least our own class. These awful people day in and day out . . . it is as though you are associated with the shop-owners of Washington."

·FIFTEEN·

"HARRY IS DEAD"

═══════════════ ◆ ═══════════════

The most sensational of the Windsors' adventures in the Bahamas began with the appearance on the scene of the American gangster Meyer Lansky, ruthless killer, financial genius, and prime mover of the Mafia's gambling and hotel interests. Although Lansky was one of the original partners in Murder Incorporated, which had eight hundred killings to its credit, he had always escaped the police net. He was notorious in America, would eventually control billions of Mafia dollars worldwide, and was destined to become one of the most powerful figures in the history of the American underworld, but was it possible or credible that the Duke of Windsor could be in contact with such a man?

Yes, is the answer, and it was a contact that would continue, indirectly, for a number of years.

Lansky was no stranger to the Bahamas. He had been coming since the days of American Prohibition, when almost everyone in Nassau was engaged in bootlegging, and consequently in direct contact with American gangsters.

It was one of the biggest boom times in the checkered history of the islands. Fleets of fast motor launches ran liquor to the Florida coast. Schooners were employed to make the more hazardous journey up "Rum Row," as it became known, to New York and Philadelphia. Later, planes were purchased by the now wealthy merchants, which took off from the islands and landed in secluded American areas to be met by gangs of hoodlums ready to move the cargos into the speakeasies.

Exports before the years of Prohibition were running at just £30,000 a year. By 1921, they had reached nearly £2 million. There was so much money in Nassau that a special guard of police, armed with rifles and bayonets, was posted around the Royal Bank of Canada, the only bank at the time, which before Prohibition had never seen even a million dollars but which was now crammed with $11 million. Bootleggers returning from their run to the mainland would come ashore with bankrolls of $50,000 in cash . . . every transaction had to be in dollar bills.

In Nassau, after bootlegging ended, the slump set in. Already hit by the worldwide depression, the Bahamas fell into another economic crisis and soon the laborers who had been earning six dollars a day were back to four shillings a week . . . if they were lucky.

Only the Bay Street Boys, and the now established white upper-class families, would survive comfortably in the coming years. The fortunes they had set aside from the high-rolling days of trading with the gangsters would take them well into the postwar years and their next wave of economic revival . . . which was to be in the form of massive real-estate investment in the islands, the attraction of huge amounts of investment money through beneficial tax laws and no-questions-asked company formations, and, perhaps most important of all for the whole of the colony, the arrival of the tourists.

It was the upsurge of big-spending visitors to the Caribbean that captured the attention of Lansky and his colleagues, anxious to spread their tentacles and replace the fortunes made during the Prohibition. By chance in Miami, he met Bahamas property dealer Harold Christie, whom he knew from earlier visits to Nassau. He was able to report to a meeting of the Mafia dons in New York that Nassau was booming again.

The upshot of the meeting was that Lansky would go immediately to the Bahamas for a further meeting with Christie and influential lawyer Stafford Sands. In fact, it was in Sands's office on Bay Street that the three men sat down to talk about building new hotels, with Lansky and the Mafia putting up the finance.

The benefits were twofold for the Mafia: the money from illegal operations on the mainland would be cleaned up; and there would be legitimate investment profit channeled through Sands and Christie. There was, however, one overriding condition; if Lansky was to put money into the Bahamas, there would have to be casinos, an absolute must.

There lay the drawback to the plan: gambling was illegal in the Bahamas, apart from one exception, that of a small seasonal gambling club in Nassau. Stafford Sands, however, was in a first-class position to ease the process of law and so to legalize gambling, and Lansky knew it.

Lansky also knew that it could take months, if not years, for the wheels of democracy to be oiled sufficiently to pass the required legislation. He was a patient man and planned ahead.

Within six months of that meeting, Stafford Sands was appointed legal adviser to the government, and almost immediately he presented an amendment to the Bahamas Penal Code, under which licenses for casinos could be applied for, thus, in effect, legalizing gambling.

Early in 1943, the whole project came alive. Harold Christie, who was responsible for bringing Harry Oakes to the Bahamas, and was busy selling land and real estate in the way only he could, introduced the Duke of Windsor to Meyer Lansky in Palm Beach. Lansky would have talked openly about his interest in the Bahamas; he may also have mentioned in passing that he had been assisting American intelligence in the capture of saboteurs during the previous twelve months. (The U.S. authorities had formed one of the strangest alliances of the war in enlisting the aid of the Mafia to track down saboteurs in the shipyards, where organized crime had control of the unions. Lansky was the man who put it into operation, after contact between the authorities and Mafia boss Lucky Luciano, then a guest of the prison service for drugs and prostitution convictions. For his help, Luciano got his life sentence cut, and after the war was allowed to go home to Italy.)

It is perhaps ironic that in the battlegrounds of Europe, Sicilian partisans, largely under the command of the local Mafia, were aiding the preparations for the Allied invasion of Sicily, which would bring applause, this from Churchill to General Eisenhower: "It is a tremendous feat to leap on shore with nearly 200,000 men." It was regarded as a turning point in the war, one which would rebound upon the Americans in later years because of the wartime deal made with the Mafia for their assistance. I was told "The Italian Mafia were peasants before the war. They were governed by their own set of rules; they had their vendettas, but they were not international criminals; by promising the release and return to Italy of some leading Mafia men in U.S. jails, links between Italian and American Mafia families grew into the international crime network that they have in the eighties." Luciano, who was Lansky's immediate boss in 1943, would be a prime architect in that. Lansky himself would become the financial genius who made it happen.

The duke was totally captivated by the hotel and casino project. After all, he had for so long seen the fortunes made by developers on the French Riviera, where he had been a regular visitor, along with the duchess before the war. And she was fascinated by all kinds of gambling. Christie suggested he might want to invest.

Lansky was becoming more impatient about the project; the war was swinging the Allied way, and if the fighting ended soon, he wanted to cash in on the tourists flooding back to the Bahamas. There was a holdup, however. Harry Oakes dreaded the thought of a new wave of flashy visitors invading his beloved islands and did not want anything to do with gambling.

In May 1943, Lansky himself was back in Nassau and went promptly to the office of Stafford Sands on Bay Street—a fact confirmed by Sands himself. Demanding action, he offered Sands a personal payment if he could get gambling approved. Sands said there was no point, since Harry Oakes was against it. Lansky wouldn't take no for an answer, and Sands knew it wouldn't rest there. Nor did he want it to: gambling meant money—and they all wanted money.

In the same month, the coordinator of intelligence, Adolf Berle, drew attention to the duke's many recent claims to be attending to "private business" in the United States. The notation came at a time when the duke had requested that Wallis's letters should not be subject to the censor at the Miami postal department. With diplomatic immunity, the duke's own mail in theory should have escaped scrutiny, though in practice it seems likely that Berle and his men were taking a look.

The duke had personally called on Berle in Washington to request the extension of this diplomatic status to his wife. Berle noted: "I believe that the Duchess of Windsor should be emphatically denied exemption from censorship. Quite aside from the shadowy reports about the activities of this family, it's to be recalled that the Duke and Duchess of Windsor were in contact with Mr James Mooney of General Motors, who attempted to act as a mediator of a negotiated peace in the early winter of 1940; that they have maintained correspondence with Bedaux, who is in prison under charges of trading with the enemy and possibly treasonable correspondence with the enemy; that they have been in constant contact with Axel Wenner Gren, presently on our blacklist for suspicious activity. The Duke of Windsor has been finding many excuses to attend private business in the United States which he is doing at present."

But the war had taken a turn for the better. The Allies were preparing for the invasion of Sicily, Russia was repelling Germany's latest offensive, and though the war was a long way from being won, there was certainly a note of optimism. Churchill was banking on the belief that Hitler and Mussolini would be disposed of within the next year. Mussolini would certainly go; Hitler would take longer.

The worst battles of the Atlantic were over, fifty U-boats having been sunk in seventy days; the Bahamas, though still teeming with troops, felt the war was receding. Indeed, there was no fear of U-boats on the morning of July 7, 1943, when five men boarded a power cruiser moored in Miami. It was an oldish boat, once used for rum-running, and equipped with oversize engines to outpace the Coast Guard. With a roar, it set off southeast for Nassau. It slipped quietly into Nassau harbor in the early evening as the light was beginning to dim under overcast skies threatening a heavy storm. The cruiser tied up at the end of a jetty and the men aboard came ashore, stretched their legs, and went back aboard their craft.

The only witness to their arrival was a boatyard caretaker who stood for some minutes observing the strangers and then went about his business. Within a few days, when the events of this night were being investigated and analyzed and the world's press was converging to report a story that temporarily would take over the headlines from war in Europe, this man, the black caretaker, would be dead and unable to recount what he had seen.

On board the cruiser, the five men sat below, drinking beer, waiting for word from their contact in Nassau; they were there to deliver a message from Meyer Lansky.

Across the town two dinner parties had been arranged, one by Freddie de Marigny, the other by Sir Harry Oakes.

He and Harold Christie had been playing tennis with two young women, Sally Sawyer and Veronica McMahon, at the Bahamian Country Club. Afterward, at Sir Harry's invitation, they all went across to Westbourne, which adjoined the country club.

There they were joined by two other guests, Charles Hubbard and Babs Henneage, and they all sat drinking gin slings on the north balcony of the mansion. The two girls left early, but Mr. Hubbard and Mrs. Henneage stayed for dinner, leaving at around 9:30. Christie and Oakes went with them to the entrance, waved good-bye, and returned directly to Sir Harry's bedroom.

"You might as well stay the night," Oakes said to Christie. "There's a bed made up and you know where the pajamas are." Christie had stayed there on many occasions in the past. They were now the only two people in the house since Sir Harry's wife had taken the children to Bar Harbor for the summer and he had planned to join them toward the end of the week.

Sir Harry put on his pajamas and got into bed. The two men talked for a short while and then Christie borrowed a pair of reading glasses and a magazine and went to his own room. The time was now 11:30, and he put out the light and went to sleep. He was awakened twice, once by mosquitos when he got out of bed to swat them, and then by a massive thunderclap. He never went out of his room and never, he would say, saw Sir Harry alive again.

At de Marigny's house, there was another dinner party. The previous night, de Marigny had met in the Prince George Hotel with RAF pilot Captain Ainsley, his wife Jean, and the wife of another RAF man, Dorothy Clark. He explained that his own wife, Nancy, was away in Vermont but invited them for dinner the following night, July 7. Captain Ainsley was in fact leaving Nassau on a flying mission the next morning, while Mrs. Clark's husband had been posted back to England. But, yes, the two wives would be delighted to join him. They were duly collected by de Marigny and were taken back to his house, there being eleven at the party all told, including Georges de Visdelou-Guimbeau and his current girl-friend, Betty Roberts. The party broke up around 12:30, and de Marigny took the two RAF wives back home in his Lincoln around 1 A.M., returning without leaving his car, he would say, at any point. It was between 1:30 and 3:30 that Sir Harry Oakes was murdered.

Harold Christie telephoned the duke with the news that Harry Oakes's head had been battered in and his body set alight. Although his blackened remains were found on his bed, and the bedclothes and mosquito net-ting were burned, surprisingly the fire had not spread.

Harold Christie had been the only other person in the house that night; he said he had heard nothing, save for claps of thunder soon after retiring. He had slept in a bedroom two away from Oakes, and while there was no sign of an intruder, he had no idea who could have done such a terrible thing. The questions from the duke came faster as he became more and more agitated, and pre-pared to dress and take command. Christie, in the mean-time, had telephoned the Bahamas police chief, who was mobilizing a team of his men to begin their investigation.

A strange pattern of events followed which could be —but never was—explained only by the duke, whose actions must have had some reason or motive. Whatever was in the duke's mind that morning remained a secret to his own death.

First, he ordered a complete press censure under war-time regulations. The death of Sir Harry must not be broadcast for the time being; but he was too late. Etienne Dupuch, publisher of the *Nassau Tribune* was already on the scene. He had arranged to meet Oakes and Christie at Westbourne early on July 8 to go on a tour of the sheep-farming station Oakes and the duke had recently set up to grow food for the enlarging island population. He arrived at the house to discover that his friend was dead, and later cabled the news to all corners of the globe over news-agency wires.

Thwarted in his attempt to enforce a news blackout, the duke announced he would take personal charge of the investigation. If the duke was at all nervous about allowing the local police to conduct the investigation, he could have called in the FBI in America. He would also have known that there were detachments of Scotland Yard and British security men, both in New York and Washington, who could have been at the scene within a few hours.

However the duke chose to telephone Miami police headquarters personally where he asked specifically for Captain James Barker. He also requested the aide Captain Ed Melchan, who was normally confined to minor duties and who in fact had twice guarded the duke during his visits to America.

But why Barker? Was it just a coincidence, or did the duke know that the homicide captain was in the pay of Meyer Lansky? (Barker later, it would be learned, tried to lead a whole department of the Miami force into a corrupt deal with the Mafia. He became a helpless heroin addict and was eventually shot dead by his own son, who was acquitted of his murder on the grounds of justifiable homicide.)

To the Nassau public, it possibly seemed like a wise move. To the attorney general's department of the Bahamas it soon became clear that they had an impending disaster on their hands, as the two detectives launched into such a major investigation in the most amazingly shambling manner. In retrospect, it looked like a floundering attempt at a coverup, by producing a likely suspect who would be allowed to go free on a poor prosecution case.

They spent most of Thursday afternoon at Westbourne, taking photographs and examining the house in detail. They could not take fingerprints that day because of the humidity, which would dampen the powder. Sightseers were allowed to wander around the house at will while Barker made occasional reports to the duke on the progress of their investigations. The local police were left completely in the dark.

Shortly after midnight de Marigny was awakened by a banging on the door of his home. He opened it to find the two American detectives who had a search warrant and asked him to produce the clothes he had been wearing the previous night, the night of the murder. They searched through the rooms, while de Marigny himself went to get the clothing. He was able to produce only a coat, a pair of shoes, and a pair of trousers. The shirt and tie could not be found. That was sufficient for the two detectives. They sent for John Douglas, an assistant superintendent with the Bahamas police, and ordered him to stay the night in Freddie's house and note anything that occurred of a suspicious nature.

The following morning the two detectives went back to Westbourne where during the day they called and interviewed more than twenty potential witnesses.

At around 6 P.M., the Duke of Windsor arrived and asked for a report on the investigation. Barker told him with some enthusiasm of the events, and saved the best until last. He had, he said, found a fingerprint, de Marigny's print, on a Chinese screen in Sir Harry's bedroom. Within the hour Freddie was brought to Westbourne.

He recalled: "As I got to the porch, the duke was just coming out of the house. He just glared at me, but said nothing and I remarked to John Douglas, 'What's up with him?' "

De Marigny soon found out. He was formally charged with the murder of Oakes, and thirty minutes later the heavy metal door of cell number two in Nassau prison banged shut behind him.

The murder had reconciled Nancy and her mother, who during that day had flown to Bar Harbor to join the rest of the family along with Sydney who had been in

Canada, and had now, at sixteen, inherited his father's title.

The body was released for burial on Saturday morning and arrangements for the funeral in Sir Harry's hometown were already in hand. In fact, the plane carrying the casket had already left Nassau, heading for Palm Beach, Florida, when a message recalling it to the Bahamas was radioed to the pilot. Captain Barker's photographs of the body hadn't come out, and the corpse was being brought back for new film to be taken.

There was further distress for the grieving family when the funeral finally took place. The American detectives had flown to Miami, and after the burial they began to recount their theory of the murder with such relish and horrific detail that Lady Oakes became hysterical and had to be sedated.

"Your husband did it, and we can prove it," said Barker, looking straight at Nancy. "He crept into Sir Harry's bedroom. First he hit him with an iron bar he found in the garage, then he poured insecticide over him and set the bed alight. The flames revived Sir Harry and he tried to fight off his attacker, so he was hit again and again and slumped back on the bed."

"Furthermore," Melchen joined in, "we found Marigny's fingerprints in the bedroom. That proves it was him."

Nancy became so angry with the policemen that she asked them to leave. Almost immediately, she contacted a leading New York private investigator, Raymond Schindler, and he agreed to take on the case and find a defense for her husband.

In Nassau itself, doubts were already being cast. The case had become the talk of the town. Captain de Witt Sears, in charge of Nassau's traffic police, had made a point of reading Harold Christie's statement. He saw that Christie had said that from the time he and Sir Harry went to bed on the night of the murder, until 8 A.M. the next morning, when Christie found the body, neither of them had left Westbourne. Sears went to see the police commissioner, and then the attorney general, Eric Hallinan. He was adamant that he had seen Christie in his station wagon at midnight that night. He was a passenger, and another man whom Sears did not recognize was driving.

Two other things were troubling the Bahamian legal chiefs as they reviewed the case. Doctors who examined the Oakes body had noticed that the blood from his wounds had trickled across the face. If he had been lying on his back, as he was found, the blood would have run the other way onto the pillows. Clearly the body had been moved.

Third, the fingerprint, that vital fingerprint around which the case hung, had not been taken in a conventional manner. Barker had not photographed the fingerprint on the scene because he had forgotten to bring the equipment with him from Miami. He had pressed the image onto Scotch tape and photographed that. Then he ran out of Scotch tape and pressed another print on a rubber material, similar to that used for mending bicycle punctures.

It might also have occurred to them that only Captain Barker had examined de Marigny for traces of burn marks. One other person might have been able to give evidence on this aspect: Colonel Erskine-Lindop, commissioner of police, who had also interviewed de Marigny on this subject. Erskine-Lindop would not, however, be called on to give evidence. Before the trial started, he was transferred to a post in Trinidad, more than an hour's flight away from Nassau, and was never brought back to tell what he knew.

Nancy had returned to the colony with Raymond Schindler and, at his suggestion, she also contacted Professor Leonard Keeler of Northwestern University, a criminologist and inventor of the lie-detector. The latter was not admissible under British court rules, but the two crime experts began their task of finding loopholes in the prosecution case against de Marigny.

About this time, the Duke and Duchess of Windsor were preparing to leave the Bahamas. They had arranged to go on holiday for seven weeks in Miami, which curiously would put them out of the country for the whole period of the trial. If there had ever been any question of the duke's being called as a witness, the answer was now a very definite NO.

As the day approached when Freddie would stand trial, Keeler went to see him in prison with reassuring words: "My boy," he said, "we are going to bust them wide open."

The crowds began to gather in the early morning of the day of the trial. They watched as de Marigny was marched across the palm-fringed square from the police station to the Nassau Supreme Court, already packed to overflowing with press and public. One solitary blade of a rotating fan was insufficient to cool the sweltering heat; brows were mopped at frequent intervals, while sweat stains appeared on shirtbacks and underarms. Among the reporters was Erle Stanley Gardner, the creator of Perry Mason, who was covering the trial for the Hearst newspapers.

The drama heightened as the witnesses were brought forward to tell what they knew of de Marigny and his relationship with Sir Harry. Every word was taken down and cabled around the world to be served up on the breakfast tables the following day. For the moment, news of the war and the Allied forces' advances in Italy would take second place on the front pages of America.

As Harold Christie stepped into the witness box, the crowded court hushed in anticipation. A smallish, lean, but muscular man, he was immaculately turned out in a white linen suit, white starched shirt pressed for him that morning, and a black tie. He pulled a white handkerchief from his top pocket almost immediately and wiped the beads of perspiration from his brow and off the end of his nose. He spoke slowly and deliberately, taking seconds to respond to the questions of counsel, as if he had rehearsed his tactics. He knew he was in for a rough ride.

The questions came fast, the answers slow and thoughtful, but there was now a note of agitation in his voice. Christie had been warned what to expect, and he knew that when de Marigny's counsel, Godfrey Higgs, stood to cross-examine, his most difficult moment had arrived. He gripped the edge of the box, his knuckles white, and began his answers.

He had woken twice during the night and on the second occasion he felt that he had been sleeping longer than the first time. He did not leave Westbourne any time after 11 o'clock during the night of the seventh. Yes, he knew Captain Sears, Assistant Superintendent of Police.

"If Captain Sears says he saw you out that night, a passenger in your own station-wagon, what would you say?"

"If Captain Sears said he saw me out that night I would say that he was very seriously mistaken and should be more careful in his observations."

At the end of that day, Eric Hallinan did not think the prosecution had done well. Christie was a bad witness and years later Hallinan himself would admit that he thought Christie knew more than he was saying, that he appeared to have something to hide.

Worse was to come, as the American detectives were called to give evidence. So far, the prosecution's evidence had been circumstantial, to show that de Marigny was in the vicinity of Westbourne that night, that there had been rows between himself and Oakes, that he was in desperate financial straits, and that he had every reason to want to kill his father-in-law.

What the Crown now had to do was prove that de Marigny had been in the house at the time of the murder, that he had killed Oakes. The key to all of that rested on the one vital clue, a fingerprint on the Chinese screen by Oakes's bed.

The defense lawyer asked: "May I suggest that your desire for personal gain has caused you to sweep aside the truth and fabricate the evidence?"

"No, sir."

"Did not His Royal Highness the Governor visit you at Westbourne and come to Sir Harry's room at the time you were processing for fingerprints?"

Barker: "He did."

Higgs: "I don't think it would be proper for me to inquire as to why he came or what was said."

The prosecution's case was all but done for, and Barker himself would be subjected to a humiliating attack for his attempts to fabricate evidence, in the summing-up of the chief justice, Sir Oscar Daly. All that remained was for the defense to stand firm.

Captain Sears came into the witness box and stood without a sign of nerves to tell what he saw on the night Sir Harry died. He said he was driving in George Street when he saw Christie coming in the opposite direction, a passenger in his own station wagon. He didn't recognize the driver and had not seen him before or since. Under cross-examination, Sears would not be shaken from his story. He repeated in a polite but forceful way: "It was Harold Christie I saw that night."

The closing speeches came and went before the jury retired.

"Have you reached your verdict?" The jury was asked as it filed back into the courtroom after a retirement of less than two hours. "Not guilty," said the foreman. Lawyers and friends rushed forward to congratulate de Marigny. Nancy pushed to the front as her husband was released from the prisoner's cage. They embraced and left the court, at that time unaware of the jury's strange rider to their verdict of innocence. They recommended that de Marigny be banished from the colony, deported, never to return—a peculiar twist to a story, the last of which had not been heard.

That same night, Major Gray Phillips telephoned the royal governor at his holiday hotel in Miami with the news of the verdict. The duke and duchess prepared to return immediately to Nassau and arrived back at Government House three days later; the deportation recommendation of the jury was by then already causing heated argument and discussion on how to get de Marigny off the island.

The governor's executive council met and approved the deportation; they also ordered Georges out as well. But where could they go? The U.S. consul had indicated they would not be welcomed in America, Pan-American Airways refused to fly them anywhere. The duke cabled the Colonial Office in London and asked for permission for an RAF transport plane to be used to take the two back to Mauritius. The request was refused. A week later, the duke sent another cable, threatening in its tone: "Although I would be loath to worry the PM at this time, I feel so strongly on this question that I would not hesitate, as a last resort, to approach him direct . . ."

In the event, the problem solved itself before the duke got to Churchill. De Marigny and Guimbeau left the island by boat, de Marigny taking Nancy to Cuba and Guimbeau heading for Haiti. They sailed away in December, leaving behind the question that would be asked over and over again . . . who killed Harry Oakes?

Raymond Schindler, the New York private detective, claimed he knew the answer and six months after the trial wrote to the Duke of Windsor:

> Royal Highness, knowing your deep concern for the welfare of the citizens of the Bahamas and for the good repute of your Government, I take the liberty of addressing you on a matter of grave importance. It is my considered opinion that the murderer of Sir Harry Oakes

can be found, identified, convicted and brought to justice.

During the trial of de Marigny no adequate investigation was possible. Statements which failed to point to the defendant were ignored. My associate, Leonard Keeler, and myself would welcome the opportunity to work on the case and willingly offer our services without compensation.

A reply dismissing the offer and refusing to reopen the case was received from the duke's secretary. Schindler continued to maintain that the real killer could be found, and as de Marigny and Nancy departed from Nassau, the real mystery behind the Harry Oakes murder was beginning to emerge.

So many questions had remained unanswered or without satisfactory explanation. Why did the duke try to censure the press? Why did he call in the Miami detectives? Who were the men aboard the launch that entered Nassau on the night Sir Harry died? Was Harold Christie asleep, as he said, or was he driving in George Street to some clandestine meeting?

One of the most intriguing questions to come out of the trial was the one hinted at by the defense counsel, when even he would not press for the reason why the duke was present during the processing of the fingerprint by Captain Barker. What did the duke say to Barker as he prepared what the court would dismiss as fake evidence? Did he realize what Barker was doing in order to get a conviction? Did they both know that an innocent man might face the gallows because of it? Why did neither side in the case, nor even the judge, ask for reasons?

These questions would be asked over and over again in the coming years, but at the time no one envisaged the degree of fear, violence, intimidation, and murder which would be generated in the islands. The Harry Oakes murder story was fermenting, and unbearable clouds remained over de Marigny. An even bigger one was beginning to linger around the duke, as unsatisfactory answers, or no answers at all, were given to those who enquired. The murder of Oakes was not linked publicly at the time with Meyer Lansky, but soon it would be, and with the gang who arrived by the rum-runner launch on the night of the killing.

If the murder was indeed connected with Lansky's attempts to bring gambling to the Bahamas, in the end Stafford Sands would achieve that goal by resorting to wholesale bribery.

Could the Duke of Windsor have become mixed up in such underhand dealings? The answer is a definite yes. He allowed himself to be used, and had done so because he felt there was investment gain available to himself; Christie was very good at selling investments. So was Sands. Even if their persuasiveness failed, Meyer Lansky had his own well-tried and -tested tactics, and was quite capable of threatening the life of the duke, or the duchess—and we know for a fact that when he left the Bahamas, the duke became quite obsessive about protection from the local police.

The duke was also concerned about the increasingly precarious state of his finances. It seems likely that some of his fortune was still in a Mexican bank, under the auspices of Axel Wenner Gren. The state of his personal property in France was unknown, but he feared the worse. Added to which, he had been spending heavily during his stay in the Bahamas, without a lot of reimbursement. Another disaster was also about to beset him. For many months, the duke had been pouring money into a project in which he was joined by a consortium of New York businessmen: to drill for oil on his ranch in Canada. The initial reports on the prospect of finding oil were good, and the ranch, anyway, had become a particular headache to the Windsors, because as a going concern it was losing money rather than making it. As the drilling went on, encouraging signs were reported back and the duke and duchess could hardly contain themselves with excitement at possibly becoming oil barons. But what promised them riches turned into a financial nightmare. They struck oil, sure enough, but it very quickly turned into water.

New investment opportunities were vital to the duke, and that is why he was still intrigued by possible development projects in the Bahamas. His old friend Sir Harry Oakes was dead, but the evidence of the money he had made from his Nassau land was there for all to see. Little, however, could be done there until the end of the war, which, by 1944, had largely drifted away from the Bahamas. The training of British and American troops was being scaled down and the remaining months passed without major event.

By early 1945, the duke and duchess had had as much as they could take of the oppressive heat and the villagelike community to which they had been banished, and they wanted to get away at the earliest opportunity. They were spending more and more of their time in America, leaving the Bahamas to look after themselves.

Before leaving, the duke had conversations with Christie on how he saw the development of the islands progressing. Christie was emphatically of the view that once the war was over, Nassau would again be burgeoning with tourist activity, attracting a worldwide flow of visitors. They all agreed that what were still badly needed were casinos, just as in the South of France, and even before the duke and duchess departed, Sands was making plans to try again.

First, Sands had some political maneuvering to deal with. In that year of 1945, he was thirty-two and was appointed to the all-powerful Bahamas Executive Council. Two months later, he drafted a proposal, which he submitted to the colonial secretary, to give a consortium—himself included—a license and a twenty-five-year monopoly on running casinos in the Bahamas. The application was withdrawn almost immediately when it was pointed out to Sands that his own membership in the consortium might cause embarrassment to his colleagues on the Executive Council. However, he immediately submitted a new proposal on exactly the same terms, and this one—filed on July 16, 1946—was in the name of the duke's friend, "Critch" Critchley.

The duke and Critch had an association going back many years, and the duke would have known that Critchley was a man who liked a wager. They had once had a bet on the golf course for a new bag of American clubs which Critchley had just bought and which the duke wanted. They played eighteen holes, the duke lost, and Critchley kept his clubs. Critchley, the duke knew, had also been involved in a dog-racing stadium in Manchester for a period in the late twenties. Whether or not Critchley knew that his name had been listed as a potential controller of gambling in the Bahamas is not clear, for although the brigadier went occasionally to the islands, he was also a key figure in the rebuilding of Britain after the war and hardly a man to become dubiously connected in Nassau.

Churchill wanted Critchley to take over the development of civil aviation in Britain and appointed him director-general of British Overseas Airways. It was under his stewardship that Heathrow Airport was planned and built. Could he seriously have undertaken at this time a casino establishment in the Bahamas? The answer would definitely be no, but then, he probably didn't know that he had been named as the figurehead on Sands's application. His name was suggested by Windsor, but that he was told what they were doing is doubtful. Certainly they didn't inform those named in a future application—as we shall see.

In the event, all their planning, and the provision of a most highly respected "name" to head the gambling operation, came to naught. The Executive Council again rejected the idea. Sands was furious. He had virtually promised Meyer Lansky that the deal would go through this time; he angrily berated members of the council, calling them shortsighted and lacking in imagination.

He stormed out of the meeting and resigned from the council the following day.

Throughout all this, the duke was never named as one of those ready to put money into the project; but then neither was Meyer Lansky. Both remained in the background and would resurface when Sands tried again a few years later.

·SIXTEEN·

HOME TO WHAT?

The Windsors sailed away from Nassau with hardly a second glance. It had been their Elba, and nothing in recent years pleased them more than to leave the alleged paradise behind. This had been a period of no great happiness for either of them, and the duchess in particular had hated their time in the Bahamas. Nor had it been successful from the duke's point of view. He had managed to win one or two battles over the selfish administration which supposedly he had governed, but largely the Bahamas were the same as on the day he arrived: the whites were still looking for all they could muster to their personal benefit and the blacks were still very poor. The duke would not be remembered for his contribution to a better Bahamas but instead for the scandals that began during his tenure and would rumble on for years to come.

There had been some talk of the duke being offered a new governership in Bermuda, further up the American eastern seaboard, but the Windsors both thought that it would merely be swapping one rather dismal situation for another. Definitely out of the question, said Wallis. Nothing further was offered, nor would it be. The Windsors could hardly claim their activities and deeds over the previous few years would provide suitable reference for any kind of position which carried with it responsibility or decision-making. Their situation seemed quite hopeless.

Once again, the Windsors tried to bridge the gulf between themselves and the rest of the royal family as they neared the time when they could see the possibility of returning home to England, and a concerted effort had been made on their behalf in pleadings to the king and queen to receive them. The duke had written to Churchill asking him to intervene once more. "Were the King and Queen to behave normally to the Duchess and myself when we pass by England and invite us merely to tea at one of their residences . . . it would avoid any division of feelings being manifested. It would never be a very happy meeting but, on the other hand, it would be quite painless and would have the merit of silencing once and for all those malicious circles who delight in keeping up an eight-year-old wound that should have healed officially . . . it would be the best cure for an evil situation."

The prime minister took three months to reply. Clearly efforts had been made, not just by himself, but by General de Gaulle and others: "I do not see any prospect of removing this difficulty," Churchill wrote. And there it rested.

Windsor resigned his governership of the Bahamas on March 15, 1945, before his position was terminated on May 3, the day Hitler gave up the struggle and shot himself in his Berlin bunker. The duke and duchess sailed away from Nassau on May 3 and were in Florida five days later. In London on that VE day, the king and queen received the cheers and wild adulation of thousands of Londoners as they stood with Winston Churchill on the balcony of Buckingham Palace.

The Windsors journeyed on to Washington during May, the month when almost daily the horrors of the Nazi concentration camps were being revealed. At a dinner in the American capital, the duke displayed an alarming lack of feeling for those evils. Sir John Balfour noted, "On the third evening of his stay, the Duke asked us to invite to dinner an American friend of his, a railroad tycoon, Robert Young. Both seemed oblivious of Nazi misdeeds and were at one in thinking that had Hitler been handled differently, war with Germany might have been avoided."

The Windsors traveled on to Europe, full of apprehension as to what they would discover. They would not be welcome in England. If they did return, the duchess would not be received at court, nor would she receive any recognition from the royal family. Nor could they expect it. The king and queen, and some of the senior courtiers, were very aware of the Windsors' pro-German stance during the early part of the war; they knew of all the indiscretions.

These scars would take a long time to heal, if ever. And while the Windsors had been having what could only be described as a rather untaxing sojourn in the Caribbean, the rest of the royal family had been employed long and hard on the war effort. As the war ended, the king and queen, their two daughters, and all of their immediate relatives emerged as heroes of the conflict. They could stand alongside those who saw action and rightly claim to have been a force to be reckoned with on the English side of the Channel; they had kept home fires burning, boosted flagging morale, joined the sufferers of the blitz, comforted the injured and those who had lost loved ones.

The strain on all them had been immense, and at the end of the war they would be accorded the thanks of the nation. King George VI and his Queen Elizabeth had truly restored the monarchy to its place of esteem, back on the pedestal from which it had been knocked by the antics of Edward VIII.

The Duke and Duchess of Windsor had no obvious place among them, and would become the unwanted guests rather than the long-lost relations. This was made clear to the duke upon their return to Europe after the war. They set sail in September aboard the United States troopship *Argentina*, which called at Plymouth on its way to the French port of Le Havre. Pressmen who interviewed the duke during the brief stopover discovered his keenness to return to Britain as soon as possible. He had several jobs in mind that he would be suggesting to the king and his government. He still believed he could perform a useful and worthwhile role on behalf of Britain. For the moment it rested there.

Anxious to return to France and examine their houses in Paris and Antibes, which they had abandoned as war broke out, the Windsors traveled first to the Boulevard Suchet where they found that the Germans had left their house untouched and their possessions intact. Absolutely nothing had been disturbed, and they were able to occupy the property almost immediately. At La Croe, which had been taken over by the Italians, they were less fortunate. Some paintings, most of the curtains, and some small items of furniture had been stolen. The gardens were littered with landmines, and it wasn't until the spring of the following year that they were able to move back into the house they loved so much, the first home Wallis had been able to create for them after their marriage.

They would also discover that they would have to leave the Boulevard Suchet within a few months. The owner wanted to sell the property, and their lease had expired. So with their future very much in mind, the duke returned alone to London in October to put forward proposals to the British government.

He stayed with his mother, Queen Mary, at Marlborough House, and for a short while, the differences that existed between them were forgotten. He went on various tours of London with her, visiting bombed areas, and also went to Buckingham Palace for talks with the king;

though whenever he came, Queen Elizabeth would make a point of being elsewhere. She had no desire to meet or talk with her brother-in-law.

What the duke proposed was to become a roving ambassador, with a particular reference to America, perhaps resuming the world tours that he had undertaken as Prince of Wales. He put the idea to Churchill, who encouraged him; but Churchill was no longer running the country. The duke was given a polite "we'll see," and returned to England in January 1946 once again to press for an appointment. He desperately wanted to fix a permanent place to live and believed he was in line for an income of some sort to help finance the life-style that he and Wallis had in mind. He had a further meeting with the king, this time with the new prime minister, Clement Attlee, present. Although he gave them the undertaking that he would make no speeches or statements without prior approval, nor would take on any engagements which had not first been cleared by Buckingham Palace or 10 Downing Street, there would be no job offered to him. The king had heard those undertakings before. On January 27, after he had returned to Paris, Attlee told the House of Commons that no diplomatic position nor any official duties had been offered to the duke.

Windsor was despondent and disappointed. Wallis was bitter, more now than she had ever been. They still believed, after all that had gone before, that past misdemeanors could be swept aside without recrimination and that he could return to being a royal again. It had been made clear that Edward could return to England if he wished, though the invitation was given grudgingly. Windsor said he could contemplate returning only if his wife were given the same rank and status as the wives of his two younger brothers, that she could assume the title of Her Royal Highness which he never himself swerved from using when the occasion permitted. This could never be, he was told by the king. It would be his choice, return on these terms or not at all. The duchess, in her writings, always claimed that it was this "silent ban" that prevented them from returning to England; no one would offer the duke work suitable to his position and the royal family was relentless in its exclusion of Wallis.

But it could not have been only the Mrs. Simpson affair that made the king and queen so vehemently opposed to having the duke and duchess back in their midst. They were now in possession of documents concerning the activities of the duke during the past eight years, some relating directly to his dealings with the Germans. The first batch came from Fruity Metcalfe, whom the duke had abandoned in Paris and who had in his possession a variety of secret documents relating to the duke, which he had taken from Paris and already stored in London. When he returned to London during that spring of the first year of the war, he deposited the documents in two cases at the Bank of England, handing them over directly to the governor himself. But toward the end of the war, Fruity was visited by the Duke of Gloucester and subsequently the documents were released into the hands of the royal family.

Toward the end of 1945, it became known that there were certain embarrassing documents among the captured German material in the hands of the Allies. King George summoned Owen Morshead, archivist at Windsor Castle, and Anthony Blunt, a third cousin of Queen Elizabeth and member of the Secret Service, to be briefed on a top-secret mission to Germany. Blunt, who was later discredited as a Soviet spy, went with Morshead to Schloss Friedrichshof, Krönberg, carrying a personal letter from the king to Prince Phillip, Landgrave of Hesse-Cassel, asking for the release of certain documents stored at the castle. The messengers found the documents and were successful in getting them back to England.

The papers were subsequently sent to Whaddon Hall, near Bletchley, where four tons of captured German documents were being sorted and catalogued. Among the

British officers engaged upon the task was Professor Donald Cameron Watt, later a professor of international history at the University of London, who remembered seeing a section relating to the Duke of Windsor. Everything that should have been in this file was there, with one exception. There was no account of the conversation with Hitler in 1937.

Blunt and Morshead continued to receive the royal family's support for many years to come. Blunt became surveyor to the king's pictures, a commander of the Royal Victorian Order in 1947, and was granted a knighthood in 1956. He confessed to being a Soviet agent in 1964, following the receipt of information supplied by the FBI, but was allowed to continue in the service of the royal family until 1979, when his treachery was made public.

Morshead was also knighted, and Fruity Metcalfe's reward for his services to the royal family would fulfil his most cherished desire which was, upon his death in 1957, to be buried in the hallowed precincts of Westminister Abbey.

The war had shattered the once charmed circle of the prewar Prince of Wales set. Fruity himself, after wartime service as a policeman pounding the streets of London latterly up and down the Mall, where Churchill would wave to him on his way to the Palace, had become a public relations man for J. Arthur Rank. Ba-ba Metcalfe, who before the war had courted the attention of the likes of Count Grandi, had thrown her home open to the senior ranks of the American services and during their relaxation hours entertained the wartime famous, including Eisenhower and Patton.

The Mosleys were expecting to be released from prison once the invasion scare was over; in fact they were detained until November 1943, which was perhaps in itself a measure of the concern there had been about Mosley's pro-Hitler talk. They were released only after Ba-ba Metcalfe got two eminent doctors to confirm that Mosley was ill from a chest complaint and phlebitis, and she wrote directly to Winston Churchill appealing for his help. He was set free on November 21 with Churchill's full support. There was an uproar, of course. Tens of thousands demonstrated in London to oppose Mosley's release. But Herbert Morrison told Parliament that he would not risk making martyrs of persons so undeserving of the honor.

The Mountbattens, on the other hand, had lived through the sensations of their private lives of the twenties and thirties and were poised, straight after the war, to take up roles which Windsor himself would have loved.

With the new Labour government dedicated to the swift withdrawal of British colonial rule over India, a cabinet mission visited the subcontinent and found it divided as never before. The British were loathed, and there was complete polarization between the Hindus and Muslims. The question of the day was whether these interracial, interreligious quarrels could be reconciled by the exit of the British, or whether partition, as well as Britain's handing over of power, would be the answer.

Communal riots and murders were raging; Gandhi was on his tours preaching peace in the worst areas. It was a daunting task to consider edging such a precariously placed and bitter nation toward independence. Attlee sent for Mountbatten. He had already told his cabinet that he considered the king's cousin would be an ideal candidate. He would suit the Indian princes, he already had a good relationship with Nehru, and he was "blessed with a very unusual wife" who, incidentally, was already a good friend of Nehru and of the influential Indian lawyer and politician Krishna Menon.

Mountbatten feigned a reluctance to accept the job, but in truth he and Edwina were delighted. She in particular had fallen in love with the country and viewed the prospect with interest and enthusiasm. King George noted in his diary, bemused by the situation: "Is he to lead a retreat out of India or is he to work for the reconciliation of the Hindus and Moslems?" His mother said, "You'll be there for years," and Noel Coward hit an even more pessimistic note when he said, "Will they ever come back alive?" No one appeared to know, including Mountbatten, what would be expected of them other than to achieve self-rule for India, and in March 1947 he drove into Delhi in an open-topped landau as the viceroy of India, with Edwina, the vicereine and virtual queen, at his side.

Within quite a short time of their arrival, they were both of the view that partition, the total separation of the religious groups, was the only solution to the Indian problem, and Attlee had given Mountbatten a deadline of June 1948 to achieve his goal.

It was from their joint concern for the troubled nation that the love of Edwina for Jawaharlal Nehru grew; the violence and death about them tore at their hearts.

Edwina, as during the war, brought together the nursing services and began the task of aiding the casualties, which were mounting daily: as many as half a million dead, twice or three times that many injured during the troubles. Edwina was always in the thick of it, helping the injured, the homeless, and refugees. Families on the wrong sides of the religious borders settled upon by the political leaders in Delhi were forced to flee or were simply attacked or murdered. As the violence reached new levels of horror daily, Edwina had a plane at her disposal to visit and supervise camps for the refugees.

Whatever was said about Mountbatten's plan and eventual solution for India, he at least had the courage of his own convictions, criticized as he was then and later particularly by Beaverbrook. Edwina similarly threw herself into the support of her husband's work and the welfare of the Indian people in general. They would, for the rest of their lives, be heroes in Indian eyes, though Nehru himself said, "Historians will perhaps be able to judge whether we did right or wrong. . . . I do believe we did try to do the right and therefore many of our sins will be forgiven us, and many of our errors also."

Through 1948, they saw the tumultuous uprisings and

massacres, the assassination of their friend Mahatma Gandhi, the transition to independence, and Mountbatten's installation as the first governor-general of an independent India. Their lives had become entwined and devoted to the service of their country, the government, and the monarchy, a far cry from the Windsors, who at this time entered the final phase of their lives, which would develop into an aimless, café-society existence, traveling the world without purpose, entertaining, being entertained, stars of society in France, New York, or wherever the mood took them.

They had moved temporarily after the war into a suite at the Ritz Hotel in Paris and that would remain their Paris base, while La Croe would be their only home for many months to come.

They went occasionally to England, staying at Claridges or with friends, but largely unwanted by royal hosts. It was during one of these visits, while they were staying for a few days at the grand home of Lord Dudley, at Ednam Lodge in Sunningdale, Berks, that a cat burglar climbed a drainpipe and swept quietly through the corridors to the guest suite occupied by the duke and duchess. There under the maid's bed, he discovered Wallis's jewels, hidden by herself in a black pouch.

There would be great speculation then, and for years to come, that the pouch contained the fabulous Queen Alexandra emeralds, which, according to popular story, she had left to her grandson, who had subsequently given them to Wallis.

Soon elaborate stories about the robbery began to be heard, and were still being told long after the Windsors had died. The burglary had been arranged by a member of the royal family to get back the Alexandra emeralds, it was claimed. After all, it was said Lord Davidson, who moved in royal circles, claimed to know that the real reason that lawyer Theodore Goddard was sent to Cannes just before the abdication was to reclaim the emeralds for the royal family and not, as was said at the time, to seek Mrs. Simpson's assurance that she did not intend to marry the king. In this task, said Davidson, the lawyer had been unsuccessful, and the emeralds remained in Wallis's possession. There were no emeralds. They were a smokescreen.

The burglary itself remains to this day shrouded in mystery. No details of the robbery were ever recorded and none of the duchess' stolen pieces, which would have been recognized the world over, were ever seen again—until after the duchess' death. On the night of the robbery, no dogs barked, no one heard anything, and the burglar seemed to know exactly what he was looking for and where he would find it. What did the duchess' jewel pouch contain?

In the final months before the abdication it will be recalled that Lady Diana Cooper, Emerald Cunard, and Chips Channon all noted the increasingly glittering array of jewels that Edward had lavished upon Wallis. "Her collection is the talk of London," wrote Channon. "The King must be giving her new ones every day." On another occasion, he wrote, she was dripping in emeralds, and reported that Cartier's was resetting "magnificent, indeed fabulous, jewels" for Wallis.

In the year immediately following the abdication, Edward is known to have spent almost £18,000 on jewelry from suppliers in Paris and some of those were among the stolen jewels.

But what of the Alexandra emeralds? When the list of stolen property was eventually published by the assessors after Lloyd's had paid out an estimated valuation of almost £25,000, no emeralds were included. Members of their staff would say that the value of the theft was more like £400,000. Even after their deaths, there would be no clue in the meticulously filed papers they left behind, nor would there be any trace of the emeralds in the duchess' magnificent collection of jewelry which her husband had lavished on her over the years and which she herself saw as an important aspect of her role as a duchess, the wife of a former king, the woman who might have been queen.

Even in those deprived postwar days, as the Windsors began the rest of their lives in exile in France, the extravagance of her spending sprees was noted by her friends and her staff. She was always ablaze with earrings, necklaces, bracelets, brooches, and rings. It was as if she were making up for not having access to the immense collection of fantastic jewelry attached to the British monarch, which would have been hers for the wearing had there been no abdication.

Apart from the Alexandra emeralds, there were other and even more stunning jewels that may at some stage have found their way into the Windsors' collection, though whether they were entitled to them is another matter. During his Indian tour, in 1921, Edward was presented with what was described at the time as a "beautiful garland of gold set with emeralds, rubies and pearls." Edward was given it along with many other fine gifts by Indian princes, which was quite according to custom. The presentation of jewels to commemorate the visit of one so important was a traditional show of respect by the princes, who often tried to outdo each other in terms of the quality and value of the gift. However, although reportedly received by Edward and brought back to England upon his return, the garland of gold is not on any list of crown property today, nor has it been seen by anyone connected with the royal jewels.

The Windsors were close personal friends of Louis Cartier himself, from whom they purchased many of Wallis's finest pieces. If some of these pieces had been created in part from stones of other large formations, reset and reworked, it mattered not to the connoisseur nor to those commissioned with the work.

The duchess was creating her own heritage with the most exquisite stones, which she took great pride in wearing and displaying to their full effect. Windsor himself did not mind the extravagance of this spending, because on Louis Cartier's advice, he saw the pieces as a most worthwhile investment.

Those writers who have stated that the Windsor collection of jewels included items that once formed part of Britian's royal heritage can only venture their suggestion by speculation, since any stones reworked by Cartier artists or other major suppliers would have made them unrecognizable from previous settings.

Jewelry and fine clothes meant much to Wallis Windsor, as their phony royal court started to become established in the postwar days, and one of those who remembers just how much this was so was the Windsor's servant of thirty-eight years, Georges Sanegre. Actually, his name was Gaston, but the duchess thought it sounded too much like *garçon* and he became Georges.

The Windsors needed twenty-six servants to reopen the house at Antibes, where Georges discovered that they had surrounded themselves with all the trappings of royalty. The duke's personal silk bedclothes and linens were monogrammed with the initials ER while hers carried the initials WW, for Wallis Windsor. At La Croe, a massive and impressive cream-rendered building, the duke flew his royal standard from the gallery overlooking the hall, so that all who entered the house walked beneath it and would bow gently as they passed.

When Georges first arrived at the villa, Wilmott, the Windsors' English butler, took him to one side and said: "I have been instructed by the duke that all staff must bow or curtsey to the duchess and call her Your Royal Highness. You must never speak first, but wait until she has spoken to you; never turn your back to her but take several paces backwards and then turn to leave her presence." At dinner parties, the duchess' place was always marked with the card bearing the words *Her Royal Highness*, and she was treated in every respect as a member of the royal family. Georges recalled: "The whole thing was the duke's idea. He was obsessed about it and felt that in their home she should be accorded the rank of royalty that had been withheld from her in England."

In those early days, as under butler at La Croe and later as butler in Paris, Georges would have to ensure that, except for their closest friends who would breeze in and out without introduction, every other person who entered must be formally received by either the duke, the duchess, or both. Upon arrival, Georges would guide each visitor to the guest book which they had to sign. Then he had to announce them from the door of the salon where his master and mistress would be waiting for the formal presentation.

The duke and duchess would stand just inside the doorway to shake hands with their guests, who would always bow or curtsey, just as they would have done if the reception had been in Buckingham Palace itself. Their elegant dinner parties, as the rest of Europe struggled back to health, were legendary, full-blown, sometimes with up to two dozen guests entertained in lavish style on dining tables crammed with the finest silver, porcelain, and china. Everything had to be just so for the duchess, and the South of France set and visiting millionaires, film stars, and politicans clamored for an invitation. Georges: "Right after the war, everyone wanted to let their hair down. The women would wear the most fantastic jewelry and the duchess's parties encouraged them to try to outdo each other."

Above all, Wallis herself always wanted to be the star of the show, regardless of the fame or fortune of her guests. It was important to her now; indeed it was all she had left. She'd always been a perfectionist and she now became obsessive about every detail. She would hire florists to decorate the whole house with the most exotic displays and they would spend hours of painstaking work on huge arrangements; the duchess was quite capable of walking around after they'd finished and saying "It doesn't look quite right. Something's missing," and they might

have to start all over again. She was this way with everything, even her guests were handpicked. Once, Georges
was called to discuss a smallish dinner party. "Only six
people?" he inquired. "Yes," replied the duchess, "but
they are all kings."

All manner of high-society friends from the past descended upon their villa, but even when they were alone,
the Windsors would dress for dinner. She would come
down in all her splendor, her long dress, jewels, and
immaculate makeup. He would be in dinner jacket,
sometimes with his kilt. If he failed to compliment her
on her appearance, she would chide him, "Don't you
think I look beautiful tonight, darling?" and he would
inevitably reply, "Of course. You look wonderful, my
sweetheart."

They were at this time great romantics, and though
they had separate bedrooms, every day they acted out a
bizarre charade as though they were illicit lovers. At night,
the duke would invariably join the duchess in her bedroom and spend the night with her. Each morning, at 8
A.M. sharp, he would pull back the powder-blue silk
covers, put on his dressing gown, and slip quietly back
to his own bedroom like a naughty schoolboy sneaking
from the girls' dorm. That happened every morning for
years, they believing it was their secret—but of course
the whole staff knew.

In public, it seemed, they would make an effort to
display their undying love for each other. The duke was
particularly demonstrative in this respect; he would go
up to the duchess and put his arm around her waist and
say, "You are as beautiful now as the day I married you."

Privately, she was a most demanding woman. Hers
was the stronger personality, and she dominated him in
everything he did, though it must be said that he seemed
to welcome that domination. Georges remembers, "He
always said yes to her. If she wanted to go for a holiday
in Marbella, they went. If she wanted to cross the Atlantic in the *Queen Mary*, he instantly agreed. She had

only to click her fingers and her every wish would be granted. His whole aim in life, almost his whole reason for living, was to make her happy." If he made her angry by some misdeed or accident, he would go out of his way to make it up to her—like the occasion once when he knocked over the floral display the duchess had arranged, shattering her favorite vase. The duchess was visibly angry, ordered the footmen to clear up the mess, and stormed out of the room. The duke called his chauffeur and an hour later came back into the house clutching a matching pair of antique Chinese vases, far more beautiful and expensive than the one he had smashed.

They seldom argued in public, or in front of the servants. She was noted for her little reprimands at the dining table, which resembled a mother scolding a naughty schoolboy, but her angrier feelings were contained until they were in the privacy of their bedrooms, when the staff would hear voices raised as he received admonishment for some ill-spoken words or deeds during the evening.

Throughout this period toward the fifties, La Croe was their only real home, from where they would uproot and travel, at her whim, to Paris or Madrid or New York. Whenever they set off, there was always a newspaper reporter around to count their pieces of luggage. If they were going for any length of time, a convoy of wagons would follow their American limousine to the port or railway station, and early on in his career with the Windsors, Georges Sanegre had the task of trying to cut down the amount of baggage they took. "It's costing me far too much money," the duke told him, "to travel with all this stuff." In the first days of their marriage, they would take 250 pieces of luggage or more. "Eventually," said Georges, "I managed to get it down to about 150 pieces, but it wasn't easy. They hated to be without anything. It was as if we would pack up the contents of the house every time we went away. The duchess would be quite annoyed if, dressing for dinner in New York, she discovered she hadn't got exactly the right pair of shoes for a particular dress. Of course, most of the luggage was hers anyway; the duke had only about twenty pieces out of the 150 we would take."

Even so, the sight of the mountain of black leather suitcases with their names embossed in gold would still draw looks of astonishment from fellow travelers, who would even take photographs just of the luggage. Wallis was meticulous about her clothes, and most of the suitcases would be fitted with her range of fabulous outfits that earned her the title of the world's best-dressed woman on a number of occasions. When traveling, she would take several outfits for each day, and rarely on any visit would she wear the same item twice, so that wherever they went, she would invariably return with even more luggage.

Those close friends able to observe her clothes regularly reckoned that by the early fifties she was spending perhaps £100,000 a year on them, but what they did not know was that the duchess, in her constant desire to retain a wardrobe of the latest fashions, received substantial discounts, 50 or 60 percent, purely for favoring the famous designer houses with her orders.

She would be invited to exclusive previews, sometimes even private previews purely for her, and would note which of the dresses she would like and make her selection for the new season. The designers loved her to wear their creations; the most fashionable and famous woman in the world was indeed a magnificent advertisement for them.

·SEVENTEEN·

THE TWO COURTS OF WINDSOR

There would be no invitation for the Duke and Duchess of Windsor to the forthcoming wedding of Britain's future queen, Princess Elizabeth, to Prince Philip in the winter of 1947. Nor would there be to the weddings of Princess Margaret and Princess Alexandra. Elizabeth, now queen, who was in charge of the guest lists for the most important weddings of the decade, made sure of that. The Windsors would be similarly ignored on all important family occasions, except for funerals, and then only the duke would go. That was the way it would be for the rest of their lives. There was no route back into the family circle, even through these gatherings of the clan. The Windsors would send a gift to Elizabeth and Philip, but that would be the extent of their contact.

Lord Mountbatten, meantime, wanted the royals to adopt his own name, and the way it could be done, he reasoned, was through his protégé Prince Philip, whom he had pushed toward Lillibet, as she was known in the family, in the hope that they would marry. From their teens, they had been naturally attracted to each other, but the king was not at all sure that Philip was the man to marry his daughter, who would become queen in succession to himself.

Realizing that Philip was stateless, nameless, and non-British, Mountbatten devised a little scheme to take over the world's foremost family, certainly in name, and it rested upon Philip taking up the surname of Mountbatten. Then, upon the marriage, the royal family would, through natural genealogy, become Mountbattens. Or would they? It would not be quite as simple as he imagined.

Though even Philip himself realized that there were not that many names that could be put forward, the king's reservations about Elizabeth's romance became apparent when he made it clear that the widest possible choice of suitors should be available to her. Philip's background was a matter of some concern even though both were great-great-grandchildren of Queen Victoria. The German strains in his ancestry, for example, might cause offense in some quarters, in a marriage so soon after the war. Second, since Philip had never known a stable childhood, there could well have been fears on the king's part that this might manifest itself in eccentric behavior in later life; with the memories of the recent past ever present, any situation that might cause problems, in whatever direction, was to be avoided.

Philip's father, Prince Andrew, had died in France in 1944, leaving his only son two suits and an ivory-handled shaving brush. His mother was Princess Alice of Battenburg, the older sister of Mountbatten and a most beautiful bride at eighteen. Although deaf from birth, she could lip-read in several languages, and at their wedding, the last czar of Russia, Uncle Nicky, ran through the crowd to throw a white satin slipper to her for luck. Prince Andrew, younger son of King George I of the Hellenes and grandson of King Christian IX of Denmark, was never a wealthy man, and the young newlyweds spent the early days of their married life in the old palace in Athens, where they cycled and skated through the vast corridors to keep warm.

Their already impoverished life-style became even more

so when they lost all their possessions in various Greek revolutions and countercoups, so that in exile, they drifted apart; their four daughters had married into German nobility and Philip had moved to England to become a charge of the Mountbattens. His younger sister, Princess Sophie, suffered tragedy when her husband, Prince Christopher of Hesse, an extrovert Nazi and Luftwaffe pilot, was murdered on the orders of Göring in a fake air crash, after he had recanted and spoken out against the Third Reich.

Princess Alice returned to Greece from exile in Paris after losing touch with the rest of her family and refused to flee again. Instead, she set up a nursing unit for the wounded and would eventually establish her own order, the Christian Sisterhood of Martha and Mary. She endured extreme poverty and tremendous hardships, tending refugees from the murderous S.S., only to see her family attacked in Allied propaganda against the German-Greeks. In old age, she was taken into Buckingham Palace, to remain there in comfort until she died in 1969.

Prince Philip, born Phillipos Schleswig-Holstein-Sonderburg-Glücksberg on a dining room table in Corfu in 1921, and smuggled out of Greece in an orange box as the family fled the rebels, looked a fine suitor—handsome and forthright. But the king remained wary of taking him as a son-in-law, despite his daughter's obvious affection for him. Mountbatten realized that Philip would have to be anglicized, just as his family had been, if he were to marry Elizabeth. The Court of Heralds suggested that Philip take up the name of Oldcastle, which they constructed from one of his ancestor's names. Mountbatten dismissed the idea as ridiculous, and someone said it would be impossible for a future queen to marry someone whose name sounded like a northern brewery! In the end Philip agreed, somewhat reluctantly, to take his mother's anglicized family name, and was naturalized to become Philip Mountbatten.

He had nothing more than that to bring to the marriage; he was at the time an eight-guinea-a-week lieutenant in the Navy. When he and Elizabeth were married, however, he was awarded the grand titles of Baron of Greenwich, Earl of Merioneth, and Duke of Edinburgh. He also collected a substantial pay raise, with £10,000 a year allotted to him from the Civil List, which meant that at last he could afford to buy his own dinner jacket, his previous one having been passed on to him by his uncle.

Mountbatten was ecstatic. He had succeeded in bringing his own family name to the first line of the monarchy, and he actually believed that future generations descending from the marriage would all carry his name. The Duke of Windsor was apparently furious at the prospect, despite his own exile from his relatives, and in that he had an ally in Elizabeth herself. When she became queen, she commanded by Order in Council that she take the name of Windsor for herself and her children. Mountbatten continued the fight for several years and finally won a compromise when the queen agreed to adopt Mountbatten-Windsor as the family name.

In the year of the royal wedding, the Windsors themselves kept out of the limelight. At the start of the year, they traveled to New York, where they had established an almost permanent suite at the city's most expensive lodging house, the Waldorf Towers—Wallis would stay nowhere else—and from there they paid a return visit to Nassau. On that occasion something had happened in the Bahamas that worried the duke. As soon as he got to New York, he personally called upon Commissioner Wallender, at the city's police headquarters. Although the meeting was supposed to have been a private one, someone leaked it to that afternoon's newspapers. The duke had received threats to his life and was nervous that they could be genuine. Who was making the threats never became known, but the commissioner took them sufficiently seriously to post a twenty-four-hour guard on the Windsors for the rest of their stay, as well as on subsequent visits.

In fact, they left New York earlier than planned, and returned to the South of France, where a London newspaper reporter spotted them and recorded the following: "A slight, debonair figure in a white dinner jacket and white carnation sits sipping black coffee with an elegantly dressed dark-haired woman in a party dress at the luxurious Palm Beach Casino in Cannes. British and American tourists are intrigued, but local gamblers hardly give a second glance towards the party and go on playing . . . the Windsors are making their first appearance of the season. They came to attend the ultrafashionable gala dinner in aid of the British Riviera hospital. Other guests with them included the young Marquess of Milford Haven and film actress Merle Oberon. Later the duke watched his wife at the baccarat table where the minimum stakes are £60. Towards 4 A.M. they drove home in their big American car."

Diana and Tom Mosley came down to Antibes during that summer and were, like the Windsors, considering buying property in Paris. This they would do, thus they became close neighbors. The Mosleys had tempered their political views not a jot after the war, and Tom was in the process of forming yet another Fascist organization, the Union Movement, largely from the remnants of his prewar British Union, whose original supporters and organizers were making contact again. It would be Moseley's last effort to bring Fascism to Britain, a task in which he would fail dismally. Even as the full horror of the Holocaust was being revealed, Mosley's analysis of the great conflict still showed support for Adolf Hitler.

It was as if he felt slighted by Hitler's failure to invade Britain and install him as a leader of the conquered nation when he wrote: "History presents no more extraordinary phenomenon than the attitude of the German leadership towards forcing a quick decision with Great Britain. All evidence seems to suggest that the problem was never seriously faced . . . did some extraordinary sentimental consideration traverse the mind of the German leadership to the destruction of every realistic consideration? It is one of the tear-laden paradoxes of history that the man whom the mass of the English learnt to regard as their greatest enemy, cherished a sentimental feeling towards a sister nation which in the eyes of historic realism, must border on the irrational and was pregnant with the doom of all he loved."

Mosley's whining sounded like that of a man left brooding in prison for most of the war, who had expected Hitler to cross the Channel at any moment and free him. He denied, all his living days, that he ever expected to come to power if Hitler invaded; but then he also always maintained that he had never received any financial support from Mussolini. He was quite capable of lying to suit his particular cause. In the late forties, his cause was a resurgence of Fascism and his words sounded strangely like an apology for Nazism.

The Nazis, he wrote, had wanted an orderly Europe run by the Germans, and an orderly British empire run by Britain. If the British leadership in the thirties had truly wanted that, they would "not have been swayed by the communists or money men"—by the latter he meant Jews. He conceded only a certain "roughness" in the Nazis' attempt to impose order.

After the years of contemplation in jail, a new plan for Europe had emerged in Mosley's mind, not unlike the Common Market in some respects though there were major differences in attitude. For a start, his new Europe would hopefully still be allied to Fascism. He saw the countries of Europe united in trade and government, a union that should use Africa as its "estate." For this, a new type of white man would be required: a higher type of man produced from a program of selective breeding and controlled environment. The future would lie with a man of higher intelligence and training. Naturally, Mosley saw himself as a model for such a person. Africa would provide the raw materials for a closed economic system in this Euro-African link and the whole would be run by his new "superman."

Later, he devised a segregation plan for blacks and whites in Africa. The whites, he said, should take South Africa and the high central plateaus, the blacks would have the rest. This would be achieved by transporting millions of people from their homelands to new areas, which he believed could be done without too much bother. His plan was to create a Euro-African power base stronger than Russia or America.

These were serious ideas and serious writings, although the product of a flawed mind. Like Hitler, Mosley harbored the notion of a super race, with lesser mortals kept in their places. He and Diana, he said, would now devote themselves not just to British political involvements, but to the ideal of a united Europe. Save for his dedicated band of followers, those who read him or listened to his speeches perhaps did not realize at the time that had Mosley and his friend the duke ever been in power together in Britain, racism, Fascism, and Nazism would have become the established order. Only the publication of the secret Home Office files on Mosley forty years later would confirm the warped and dangerous beliefs of this man who once came so close to taking control of government in Britain.

The Mosleys bought a house at Orsay on the outskirts of Paris while the Windsors would rent a house in Rue de la Faisanderie. That autumn, the Windsors watched from afar as their niece, Princess Elizabeth, married her prince, the only close relatives *not* among the 2,200 guests at the wedding. It was the second blow they had suffered that year: in the autumn their old friend Duff Cooper had been dismissed as British ambassador to Paris and, since he'd left France with Lady Diana, one of their most consistent entrées to embassy functions in Paris had closed. Through Cooper, the duke had been able to keep up with the gossip, the politics, and the affairs of state that he missed so badly.

It was around this time that the duchess' impatience with her husband and his lack of a permanent home, job, or purpose was beginning to show. In public, she was openly critical of her husband in a way those closest to them had noticed for some months. After the trauma of the Bahamas years, the duchess hoped that by now they would be in some position that commanded respect from the public, not only for the duke, but particularly for herself. Her public humiliations of him became more and more frequent. The Duke de Grantmesnil recalled: "I was at a dinner with them given by the British Consulate, it was a fine table and there were a number of British guests. The Duke was tuned into a conversation about the building of a new golf course and began chipping in with his own views. One of the women guests, from England, who had been particularly bullying towards the Duke, turned on him and said 'What do you know about it?' My own eyes went to the Duchess, whom I half expected to speak up for him. Instead she looked at him sternly and said 'Yes, David. You know absolutely nothing about it,' to which David meekly replied 'Oh, in that case I'd better be quiet, hadn't I?' This got my hackles up and I retorted sharply, speaking directly at the Duchess, 'You know very well, Duchess, that David has a great deal of experience in these matters. For so many years, he ran the largest estate in England; he dealt with all its finances, all its development. He knows very, very much about these things.' There was hardly a moment's silence before the Duchess instantly and skillfully switched the subject, but poor old David looked down in the mouth for the rest of the night."

The Duke de Grantmesnil had joined a constant stream of visitors to La Croe in the late forties: the Dudleys, the Metcalfes, the Churchills, the Aga Khan. Many other friends lived in the vicinity and it was at this particular time that the duke was giving intensive thought to where he and the duchess should put down their roots once and for all. The answer he came up with was possibly the most insensitive solution of all.

For some reason, he had decided it should be Eire, a hotbed of political turmoil which would not be at all eased by the presence of members of the British royal family, outcasts though they were; nor was the IRA's alliance with the Fascists forgotten.

During 1948, the duke asked Grantmesnil to visit him at La Croe and when he arrived he found himself ushered immediately to Windsor's private rooms in the tower of the villa—the part he called the Fort, for obvious reasons. Grantmesnil takes up the story:

> We chatted for a while, and went once again through the abdication, and the family feud, with his brother and sister-in-law's treatment of Wallis; all our conversations would include some of that. It must have been in his thoughts day and night. Then he said "Kenneth, I want you to do something for me. I would like to go to live in Southern Ireland. Wallis and I are not really happy in France; neither of us has mastered the language and we really feel we would like to settle in an English-speaking country. It is out of the question that we return to England, and Ireland is the only place. Will you do that for me, Kenneth?"
>
> I agreed that I would try, and there in his office on his own notepaper, I wrote to the Prime Minister of Ireland, Eamonn De Valera, to ask if I might see him on a most urgent and confidential matter. I had never met him, but he knew my family. It was my brother who helped him escape prison during IRA Troubles. I returned to England and was duly invited to Dublin. I took off by private plane and went to De Valera's office. I was shown into an anteroom to await his arrival and explained the purpose of my visit: the Duke of Windsor wished to take up permanent residence in his country.
>
> De Valera sat back in his chair and said nothing for

what seemed like a minute or two. Then he leaned forward and said "You saw me arrive at this building, did you not? You saw that my car was surrounded by security, that I was protected through every step I made into my office? My life is in constant danger and I can say that it would be the same, even much worse for your former king. There would be political uproar if he were to move here. I cannot believe that he would want to lead the sort of life he would be subjected to."

As I got up to leave, I saw the wisdom of the Prime Minister's remarks. It concurred totally with my own feelings, which I had tried to convey to the Duke, and which he had not wanted to hear. Finally De Valera made a promise to me that I should convey to Windsor. It was this: "If the Duke can give me his word that no other country will allow him to take up permanent residence, then he may come here and I and he will suffer the consequences." Needless to say, I was never able to give him that assurance and the question of an Irish domicile was never mentioned again.

Later that year, in November 1948, there was concern over King George's health and a pointed official statement seemed to blame the Windsors for it. Throughout that year and the previous winter, George had been troubled by cramps and numbness of the legs; the king ordered it to be kept from his daughter Princess Elizabeth, who was about to give birth to her first child, the heir to the throne, Prince Charles, who arrived on November 14. Nine days later, after speculation about the king, an official Buckingham Palace statement said, "The King is suffering from an obstruction to the circulation . . . complete rest has been advised. Though His Majesty's general health . . . gives no reason for concern, there is no doubt that the strain of the last twelve years had appreciably affected his resistance to physical fatigue." In other words, he had been under immense pressure since the abdication. King George would face a period of discomfort and illness, and his family's belief was that it had been bequeathed to him by the irresponsible act of his brother.

On the horizon were two more matters that would cause the king further anguish. First, he was hearing rumors that the duke was planning to write and serialize his memoirs, which was totally against royal convention. Second, there would be gossip-column scandal about the duchess and the new man in her life.

During the work on Edward's autobiography, the Windsors suddenly decided to give up La Croe because the duchess felt that the Riviera was now full of riffraff and common people. Although they still made occasional visits to the south, they were spending more time in Paris at their new home on the rue de la Faisanderie, where the duke's ghostwriter, Charles Murphy, was trying to pin him down long enough to work on the book, *A King's Story*.

Murphy would recall that there were constant interruptions. The duchess would phone his workroom a dozen times a day, reminding him of a dinner party that evening, asking him to fetch her a letter from her files, or ordering him to attend at once to some trifling household detail! He was totally subservient to her, an aspect noted by one of their secretaries: "Sometimes, she would call him from a distance, from the garden or from another part of the house. Then he would leave whatever he was doing and go to her, hurrying eagerly. You could hear his voice calling from afar: 'Coming, darling. Yes, sweetheart.' I've seen him in the middle of a haircut get up and run to her."

The time the duchess allowed for the book was scant, Murphy tells us, and she begrudged him even that. It was a project that he had expected would take a year, but in fact it took four. At the end of it, he would earn £500,000 from hardback sales, paperback rights, and serialization fees around the world. The extent of the money involved surprised him. The duchess would soon follow suit. Her memoirs, to be called *The Heart Has Its Reasons*, would also become a best-seller.

It was while the duke was heavily engaged on his book that gossip about the state of their marriage began to appear in newspapers in New York and London. During a visit to the Riviera in 1950, the Windsors had been invited to dine at the home of Jessie Donahue, the daughter of Woolworth's founder, Frank W. Woolworth. There they encountered for the first time Jessie's son Jimmy, a thoroughly disreputable young man in his mid-twenties who enjoyed parties, dancing, and nightclubbing just as much as the Windsors did. He was quite openly homosexual and had once deeply embarrassed his mother by dressing up in drag on the night she was entertaining her good friend Cardinal Spellman to dinner. His activities among male prostitutes in New York were also well known.

He followed the Windsors to Paris where they both became more and more enchanted by the effervescent Mr. Donahue, whose attentions the Duchess enjoyed and whose wealth enabled him to pick up the bill whenever they all went out to dinner—an aspect of his nature that pleased the duke no end. There were rumors of a menage à trois, but then it became more one-sided.

The first hint of jealousy appeared in the autumn of that year, when the duke was engrossed in the final stages of his book and had agreed to the duchess' going off to New York to rejoin Donahue, who had left some weeks earlier.

Very quickly, the gossip columns were full of Wallis's very public nights out with Donahue, as dawn after dawn they were seen heading home after hours of partying. The duchess had been in contact with the duke hardly at all since she arrived in New York, and he was getting more and more irate about the whole thing. Finally he could stand it no longer and dashed to America; but when he docked, Wallis, who had heard he was on his way, was waiting for him on the dockside.

They talked for hours that night and she obviously

managed to persuade him there was absolutely nothing to her association with Donahue. But when she rejoined him in Paris, Donahue was not out of the picture by any means. He turned up a couple of months later, and remained part of the Windsors' life for another three years.

In fact, the following year, he paid for a cruise along the Mediterranean coastline in a small yacht in which he was joined by the duke and duchess. It was so small, by comparison to what they had been used to, that the duchess complained there was nowhere to hang the extensive wardrobe she had brought with her. So Wallis arranged for her maid Ophelia and the duke's valet to follow the course of the yacht along the coast, in the Windsors' black Cadillac with a van carrying the luggage. Every evening, as the yacht was moored, Ophelia had to bring onto the boat the gown that the duchess had selected, along with various changes of clothes for the following day, and take away those used during the past twenty-four hours.

When the yacht moored at Anzio, the final port of call, the duchess alerted her staff to prepare for a trip to Rome. "We have an audience with the Pope," she told them. "Please arrange for suitable clothes to be laid out at the Grand Hotel." There the Windsors changed and motored to the Vatican for the audience with Pope Pius XII, which had been arranged by a wealthy Catholic industrialist friend.

Their return to Paris was marked by the gossip which continued through the following years. The duke was deeply depressed; that was plain for all to see. He had to leave Donahue and the duchess alone again when he returned to London, and it was a time of considerable anguish which he tried to dispel by telephoning his beloved Wallis twice a day from London.

One of the Windsors' old friends would recall that, during this period, she saw the duke's confidence finally shattered, since he was becoming increasingly worried that he would lose the woman he loved to that garish young man he now hated so much. Diana Cooper was convinced that Wallis was having an affair with Donahue, as was half of Paris. Diana Mosely thought it was just a flirtation that meant nothing, but it continued for many more months, with Donahue flitting in and out of their lives. When friends warned him, the duke just put on a brave face and said, "Anything that makes Wallis happy makes me happy."

There were those who suggested that in reality the duke was just as attracted to Donahue as was the duchess. Noel Coward's comments were particularly acid: "I like Jimmy. He's an insane camp but he's fun. I like the Duchess; she's a fag hag to end all, but that's what makes her likeable. The Duke . . . well although he pretends not to hate me, he does because I'm queer and he's queer. However unlike him, I don't pretend not to be. Anyway, the fag hag must be enjoying it. Here she's got a royal queen to sleep with, and a rich one to hump."

Finally, the duke decided he had had enough of it all and risked a separation from Wallis by ordering Donahue out of his house after a row over dinner, when Jimmy had kicked Wallis under the table. It was one of the few occasions that Windsor asserted himself over Wallis, and they saw Donahue only a couple of times again before his death twelve years later in New York from alcoholic and barbiturate poisoning. In his will, he left Wallis some of her favorite pieces of his jewelry, which were auctioned with the rest of the Windsor treasures in 1987, and $300,000.

In the meantime, the duke's book had been published, and its serialization in newspapers and magazines around the world had caused outrage among the old guard at Buckingham Palace and in all royal circles. Lady Hardinge, wife of the former palace private secretary, criticized him for having provided a "highly coloured one-sided account of the Abdication" in exchange for a large check.

The publicity also came at an exceedingly bad time,

coinciding as it did with a further decline in the king's health. Lady Donaldson, author of *Edward VIII*, would say, "Behind the scenes, the book causes unrestrained anger and concern. Those who had taken part in the events described by the Duke were astonished to read a version which bore no relation to their own memories."

Similarly, when the damaging German documents on foreign policy which the Allies took into their possession at the end of the war were published, the world would begin to discover what the royal family already knew about the Windsors' Spanish and Portuguese adventures. The files had haunted the duke ever since he heard they'd been found, and those close to him were well aware that he was dreading their publication.

Churchill tried to have them locked away for years, but the Americans were insisting upon publication. In London, the duke's solicitors were standing by to issue a statement condemning the papers as variously lies, false, or inaccurate. The duke's apologists have consistently supported that line, and his lawyer Maître Suzanne Blum dismissed them as fakes.

But when Churchill's own secret papers were published in the Martin Gilbert biographies, it was quite apparent that though perhaps sometimes highly colored and exaggerated for the purpose of pleasing Ribbentrop and Hitler, there was an underlying truth in most of the captured material.

Any doubt that the duke had consorted with the enemy, or agents of the enemy, was quashed; there is no question that his actions were treasonable in such a critical time of the war, and Wallis quite apparently spurred him on. Moreover, while sweeping aside the documents in the fifties, the duke had quite insensitively continued his friendship with the most prominent British Fascist, Tom Mosley, and his equally fanatical wife, Diana. They were among the Windsors' closest friends and would cause great embarrassment to officials at the British embassy in Paris. Staff there had been instructed to have no communication whatsoever with the Mosleys. The ambassador, Sir Gladwyn Jebb, had even told his people to walk immediately from any room into which one of the Mosleys entered. Sir Gladwyn himself observed the same rule, which on occasions meant he had to walk out on the Windsors.

The Windsors were in New York, at the apartment in Waldorf Towers, when they were informed of the death of King George VI on February 6, 1952. The following day, the duke held a press conference, Wallis at his side, on the sun deck of the liner, *Queen Mary*, as he prepared to sail from New York to London for his brother's funeral. "This voyage on which I am embarking is sad, all the sadder because I am undertaking it alone." Wallis disembarked before the ship sailed; she had categorically been excluded from the funeral—it had been made quite clear to her husband that the widowed queen and his mother, Queen Mary, would not welcome her presence.

The tributes were worldwide to the man who had restored faith and confidence in the British monarchy, and the thank-you message from his widow pointedly spoke of a great and noble king. "Throughout our married life we have tried, the King and I, to fulfill with all our hearts and all our strength the great task of service that was laid upon us."

The following January, the Windsors were back in New York for the grand social extravaganza, the Duchess of Windsor Ball, arranged by Elsa Maxwell to raise funds for war veterans. Though it was a charity ball, the duchess put on a highly criticized display of opulence, appearing in three different and expensive gowns during the evening and leading a parade of models onto the floor to the accompaniment of the specially composed "Windsor Waltz." She was now fifty-six, and even the duke was embarrassed, as the wife of a former monarch flaunted herself in such a manner.

Two months later, the duke received news that his mother was seriously ill and fading fast. Once more, he traveled back to London and once more, he left Wallis in New York. He was at Queen Mary's bedside when she died on March 24. The old queen had maintained the exclusion from her home of "that woman" to her dying day; Wallis would not be at the funeral and there would be no thaw in family relations after her death. Indeed, the gulf would remain just as wide.

Wallis's own indiscretions did nothing to ease things, either. On the night of Queen Mary's funeral, the duchess was seen out on the town in New York, dancing with Donahue in a nightclub. The news, which soon reached the ears of the Queen Mother, once more confirmed that Wallis was still unacceptable as a member of the royal family.

The Windsors would not be present at the coronation in June of Queen Elizabeth II, and later that year were photographed in sarcastic mood at a party in New York, wearing two paper crowns. No, the Windsors certainly did little to win back the affections of his estranged family.

In that year also, the first rumors were heard of Princess Margaret's romance with the divorced Group Captain Peter Townsend, the king's former equerry and now comptroller of the Queen Mother's household. It would be a long-running saga of young love for an older man, and when she heard about it, the Duchess of Windsor telephoned one of her friends in Paris and reported with mischievous delight, "So now it's happened to her own daughter." They were so disappointed when, after two years of speculation, Princess Margaret decided that, unlike her uncle, she would not walk out on the heritage of public service into which she had been born, but accepted her mother's counsel that she must put that duty before her personal happiness, though, of course, in time divorce would come to her too.

·EIGHTEEN·

THE WASTED YEARS

It was during the early fifties that the Windsors decided that Paris, or France generally, would become their permanent home. Their contact with Britain was diminishing now, to the extent that it almost did not exist, except through friends and politicians with whom they kept in touch. Relations with the royal family after the death of King George and Queen Mary certainly remained cool: Queen Elizabeth, the Queen Mother, and Prince Philip in particular would not want to encourage any contact whatsoever with them.

This would be apparent some years later, when Windsor wrote to Mountbatten to complain that Prince Philip had visited Paris without giving them the courtesy of a call. The duke wrote: "Maybe neither he nor I would find an encounter rewarding. Still, as a former King as well as an uncle by marriage, I consider this behaviour to me in a foreign land extremely bad manners." And referring to the recent Mountbatten claim that he had trained Prince Philip for his position of queen's consort, Windsor added: "There is one elementary subject which I am afraid you left off the curriculum, the simple practice of courtesy." Mountbatten replied that although he had never claimed to have taught Prince Philip, he promised to raise the duke's complaint. Neither could have been unaware of the likely response.

Against this background, the Windsors agreed that they would not return to England to live, and in any event Walter Monckton had negotiated with the French government on their behalf and had obtained extremely beneficial residency terms if they decided to stay in France. The duke would be given full diplomatic status, which would also exclude him from paying any income tax. His foreign purchases were allowed in duty free, most of his basic requirements, including petrol, tobacco, and liquor, could be bought duty free at the British embassy, and his profits from capital gains on his investments, whether derived from buying and selling antiques, which he did with some skill, or from income from stocks and shares, would all be free of any tax. That wasn't all. The French government, in 1953, offered him a lease for life on the superb mansion in the Bois de Boulogne which was owned by the City of Paris and had been occupied by General Charles de Gaulle during his first period as president of France. They would be asked only a token rent of £25 a year, and they would remain at the Bois de Boulogne for the rest of their lives. Further, they would have the free services while in France of a police guard. All in all, this was a package of benefits which the most eminent of Frenchmen would have been pleased to receive.

The bodyguard was an important aspect, in the duke's view. Ever since their return from the Bahamas and New York, the Windsors, and the duke in particular, had become obsessed about his safety. There would be many ducal minders over the coming years, but perhaps the best known among staff and visiting friends was Inspector Raymond Stanville, who guarded the duke's every move for more than a decade. Whenever he was not available, the duke's butler would telephone an unlisted number and within minutes an unmarked black police car would arrive at the gates to follow him. Night and day, he would be followed, whether he was just going to the dentist or staying out until dawn at a nightclub. Georges Sanegre recalls: "It was only the duke they were interested in. The duchess came and went as she pleased, but the security men paid no attention to her, unless of course the duke was with her."

As the money from the duke's book began to flow in to boost his dwindling finances, the tax-free considerations of his Paris residency produced an important side effect to his stock dealings; he began to invest heavily in the stock markets of the world, along with any other worthwhile opportunity that presented itself. He would telephone his brokers daily and kept his own ledgers recording his transactions. His dealings embraced a wide portfolio of securities, from gold to oil. By the mid- to late fifties, his personal fortune had increased from a relatively modest sum to more than £3 million. He was a shrewd investor, and with the unrivaled tax benefits that had been negotiated on his behalf, every penny he made, he kept.

As his bank balance grew, so did Wallis's spending on jewelry, clothes, and entertaining. He responded to her wayward financial control by constantly pleading poverty; his inherent meanness became just as legendary, not just when out with friends but in the management of his household. He would regularly complain to his staff about the cost of food, their wastefulness on toiletries, and other quite trivial matters which he would raise after an hour or so of scrutinizing the accounts.

But this alleged impecuniosity did not deter him from making the house in the Bois de Boulogne into a miniature Buckingham Palace. He and Wallis set about making this their once-and-for-all home; they were quite decided about that. The architects, interior designers, and ancillary tradesmen were immediately called in. Antiques and paintings held in store from La Croe were brought out; those which did not suit the house were sold, at a substantial profit, and replaced with pieces more in tune with the superb mansion.

They were actually doing up two houses at the same time. In the early fifties, the duchess found an old mill at Moulin de la Tuilerie which they both immediately fell in love with and decided to buy. It belonged to the painter Derain and it was a small seventeenth-century property sitting beside a gushing mill stream; there was a cobbled courtyard, and barns which the duchess converted into a quite luxurious home, with drawing rooms, bedrooms, and bathrooms which the duke loved. It was the only house they ever owned, apart from the ranch in Canada, which the duke eventually sold in the sixties. It was here that the duke resumed his love of gardening that first came to the fore when he was renovating the Fort. Here he created waterfalls, rock gardens, a vegetable garden, and a flower garden. If he wasn't playing golf, he would be gardening during the hours of spare time that he had available. Those basically were his interests now, gardening, golf, money, and Wallis—in that ascending order.

It took only forty minutes to drive from the center of Paris to the mill, and the Windsors would hold big luncheon parties there or pleasurable weekends for their closest friends. There were no formalities at the mill and the Windsors, in the right mood, could make their guests feel most welcome and comfortable; the atmosphere was one of cheerfulness, the conversation amusing, the dining tables bright with candles and covered with flowers from their own garden. Wallis was at her best in this period of their life. She was the perfect hostess; he could be the most charming of hosts.

Her floral creations, her food, his selection of fine wines were the talk of Paris. But while the mill was their cozy retreat, the Bois de Boulogne mansion was their palace where they maintained a most formal and expensive lifestyle. The endless stream of high society expected style, and they got it. Visitors would be met by a pair of foot-men, one for each side of the car. Georges the butler would be at the entrance, and there were, at the height of the Windsors' socializing, twenty staff in the house.

The Rich and Powerful. The Grand and Famous. They all came. Marlene Dietrich sipped Dom Perignon from the Windsors' finest crystal. Aristotle Onassis shared a J & B with the duke. Henry Fonda complimented the duchess on the choice of quails' eggs for hors d'oeuvres. Pat Nixon admired the carefully embroidered coronet on the linen table setting, while husband Richard said the turbot caught off Le Havre that morning was "the tastiest little fish I've ever had the privilege to eat." The Aga Khan always brought gifts, expensive trinkets, or perhaps something to add to the duke's collection of antique silver.

Elizabeth Taylor, then with Richard Burton, swept into the Bois de Boulogne mansion in a full-length chinchilla cloak. It was pure Hollywood. There was such a commotion when the two stars arrived that the duchess had to leave the other guests in the salon to see what all the fuss was about.

She gazed across the hallway at Miss Taylor and told her: "You look absolutely devastating, my dear."

"Thank you, Your Royal Highness, you are very kind," said Taylor. It was one of the few occasions that the duchess allowed the spotlight to be taken away from her.

The Windsors had a special affection for Liz Taylor, ever since her first visit as an eighteen-year-old newlywed to their first Paris home. She came at the end of her honeymoon with Conrad Hilton, and the duke was at once entranced by her stunning beauty. He and Richard Burton would talk for hours, Burton describing his child-hood in Wales and the duke recalling his visit there as prince.

The duke had installed a grand piano in the salon of the Bois and on special nights he would hire a local pianist. His own party piece was to sing "Alexander's Ragtime Band." Judy Garland visited shortly before her death, and the duke insisted that she sing "Somewhere over the Rainbow." It was one of his favorite songs. Garland rose to the opening bars and burst into song. Halfway through, the duke stepped forward to sing a duet with her, then urged everyone to join in for a rousing encore. At the end everyone clapped. The duke kissed Miss Garland, and she curtsied.

The guests came and went. Some stayed a while, but mostly they were fleeting visits. Days could be long and tedious. The duke and duchess would rise early and bathe; she would take a light breakfast, he would drink only a cup of water before a later snack of smoked haddock or sausages, always served on silver. Sometimes he would join her on shopping excursions in Paris, or perhaps play golf. Every day she had her hair combed by her maid or a local stylist who would be brought to her home by the chauffeur. On the days they were entertaining, or being entertained, a beautician would be called to do her face, using makeup chosen for the colors of the gown she would be wearing that evening. She would claim, "The most important thing is to take care of your face. My mother taught me that."

Tea was taken most days, at the insistence of the duke. He would have two or three cups and perhaps finely sliced sandwich triangles, or pastry with bacon or cheese topping.

The duke would rest in the early evening, though the duchess seldom took a nap. She would busy herself with the menu or supervise in the kitchens or perhaps prepare some of the dishes herself.

In this later life sleep was not needed in such proportion as before, and often servants would hear them laughing and joking in her room until the early hours. Sometimes the duke would have the gramophone brought to his bedroom and would play recorded speeches of

Winston Churchill. How he still loved Churchill and, with the same vigor, how he still hated the memory of Baldwin.

Never were there children in their world. The duchess had a particular dislike of infants and was never really at ease whenever there were any in their company. Instead, she lavished her affection on their dogs, a continuous parade of pugs and Cairn terriers which were fed from silver bowls at six every evening. They were kept on a diet of minced fillet steak with vegetables. "Nothing is too good for my little darlings," the duchess retorted when someone questioned the expense of feeding them on such quality food.

But then that was how they were. Whatever they did was generally for themselves; the parties and guests, the years of nightclubs and Riviera holidays, were all part of the function of their unfulfilled lives. Without their fine surroundings, without their stylish friends and hangers-on, they would have had nothing.

Yet both of them had the opportunity to do more with themselves. A man of the duke's obvious background and grooming for the monarchy, with all the experience he had enjoyed, should have been an obvious candidate for a more demanding role in life. Even if there were no offers forthcoming from commerce and the business world, with whose leaders he was in constant touch, there was a wealth of charitable organizations, welfare groups, and builders of caring societies looking for a figurehead of esteem. Both, or at least one of them, could have contributed something of their countless wasted hours.

There were two halfhearted attempts by friends to get them involved. Once someone suggested they should sponsor an "adopt an orphan" scheme—not physically adopt one but instead provide the finance for their up-bringing. A child in Britain was even earmarked and would be named David Windsor. It came to naught. The duchess, at the last moment, said she thought it was a silly idea. "Who knows what the child will turn out like?" she said, and the prospect of some young man with the name of a king foundered instantly. Another wild scheme, suggested this time by the duchess herself, would be called the Windsor Awards, from which talented young artists from France and América would apply for a grant to further their studies. Only one was ever selected, and he was never heard of again. Nor were the Windsor Awards.

The publication of Wallis's own memoirs in 1956 brought fresh outbursts of anger against the Windsors and quiet rage from the royal family. Among courtiers and the rest of London, there seemed general agreement over Wallis's effrontery in the observations she made, particularly her thinly disguised acidity toward the Queen Mother. She'd apparently even had difficulty in getting her ghost-writers to include some of the material; two had been sacked for challenging her.

The feud between the royal family and the Windsors reached its most intense level, particularly between the duchess and the Queen Mother. Wallis would openly hurl insults at the widowed queen during dinner parties and was supported in all her jibes by the duke. "The Dowdy Queen Mother" and "The Blimp" were among their favorite epithets when referring to her.

They never seemed to acknowledge the great public service the Queen Mother had done and would continue to do after her husband's death. Good news about her was bad news for Wallis, and vice versa, and when the queen and Prince Philip paid a state visit to France in April 1957, the Windsors made sure they were out of the country to save themselves the embarrassment of not being invited to functions attended by their niece and her husband.

Later that year, the writer James Pope-Hennessy went to Paris for a series of interviews with the Windsors, during his work on Queen Mary's official biography. The duke took him down to the mill, where the author found every conceivable comfort in a most American style and later wrote that "the Queen Mother is living a lodging-house existence compared with this."

No, for all their worldliness, their interests were entirely limited to themselves. The duchess still wanted only to be the best-dressed hostess in the world, which gave Balenciaga and Hubert de Givenchy much pleasure. And apart from Wallis, the duke's life revolved around golf and making money.

It was the latter which revived his interest in investments in the Bahamas which, toward the end of the fifties, was booming again, thanks largely to the efforts of Harold Christie and Stafford Sands.

Christie, a regular traveler to the continent, brought news of the abounding developments as the Caribbean islands reestablished themselves as the playground of the rich.

As frequent visitors to Nassau during these years Windsor and many of his friends saw it was true that many people were making fortunes on land sales, or investing in hotels and apartment buildings. There were also quite a lot of people losing money or being plain robbed on worthless schemes, but Christie would never mention those. Much of the new boom, of course, was based on the original concept the duke had spent many hours discussing with Christie during his days in the Bahamas.

In remembering those days, the one thing that haunted them both was the murder of Harry Oakes. It was even joked about at dinner tables. When on one occasion Christie was visiting France, he had been invited to dine at the Riviera home of Lord Beaverbrook at the Cap d'Ail. Tom and Diana Mosley were also there. Beaverbrook's opening gambit was, "Come on, Christie, tell us how you murdered Harry Oakes."

Indeed, for all those involved in the scandal of Harry Oakes, the latter part of the fifties would see a resurgence of interest in the case. And it came at the very time when Sands, Christie, the duke, and others were again formulating plans to turn the Bahamas into a Riviera-style gambling attraction which would, they felt, at least bring the tourists, land-buyers, and speculators into the islands on a scale that Sands and Christie had dreamed of. But their moves in that direction brought a reopening of old wounds.

·NINETEEN·

HIGHLIFE IN HAVANA

Cuba was at the peak of the corrupt and carefree rule of General Fulgencio Batista when the Duke of Windsor went down from Florida and was checked in at the Hotel Nacionale in Havana. Wallis had remained with friends in West Palm Beach while her husband went to see for himself the explosion in the tourist trade: the big-spending gamblers from America and the wild, wild nights that were reminiscent of the speakeasy days of the twenties.

But the highlife of Havana was heading for trouble. Revolution was in the air and Meyer Lansky, who was running the Mafia's gambling interests, was a worried man. For the previous seven years he and his associates had enjoyed free rein in Cuba under Batista. They had secured the run of the island to establish a sleazy empire of gambling, nightclubs, prostitution, and drugs, while Batista himself was given a personal fortune for the privileges he gave the crime bosses.

Lansky's men were running casinos in the Hotel Nacionale, the Riviera, and the Capri, where he had George Raft, the actor, as his host, walking through the casinos tossing a coin—just as he had in the films. All the big names in the Mafia were turning up in Cuba, and millions of dollars were being generated for the half a dozen big crime families.

Also in Cuba, at the end of 1958, was Stafford Sands. He went there in November. Harold Christie had been twice earlier that autumn, and both would have seen the nervousness of tourists and gamblers. There was much talk of Fidel Castro and of impending revolution. It came soon enough. The Mafia rule of Cuba ended when Fidel Castro came out of the hills and staged his coup.

The downfall of Batista in 1959 came as a major blow to Lansky and the other crime bosses, who had invested a great deal of money; now they would lose it. A big source of income had been lopped off and it would be no coincidence that Stafford Sands was now making a move toward gambling again. He had become a formidable figure on the Bahamas political scene and his business interests had boomed during the fifties.

Early in 1959, Sands was appointed chairman of the Bahamas Development Board, a government department responsible for the encouragement of the tourist trade, and in that role, and later as minister of tourism, he engineered, over a period of sixteen years, a vigorous expansion of the colony as a tourist and investment center for which task he received a knighthood from the queen. Harold Christie would also receive a knighthood, despite the scandal, as did most senior members of the ruling white party.

As the Mafia was being run out of Havana, Sands applied again for a license to run a casino for twenty years on the island of New Providence. The application—filed on February 28, 1959—was made on behalf of a syndicate of businessmen; among them Sands had apparently secured the backing of some important-looking people, including the British earls of Dudley, Derby, and Sefton, and the Viscount Camrose, all of whom were friends of the Duke of Windsor. Although they were claimed on the submissions to the Bahamas government office, it is unlikely that any one of them knew anything about it, other than perhaps a casual conversation with the duke at some point. The documents were never made public and only came to light at a royal commission of inquiry into gambling in the Bahamas in 1967.

To form the syndicate, Harold Christie had contacted the Duke of Windsor, and had again ventured the idea that he should head an impressive group of gentlemen to apply for a casino license; but again Windsor would not agree to his name being used. After further conversation, the list of four names was drawn up, but it appears that no one contacted the four to seek their agreement.

Lord Derby told the author, "I have seen a copy of the document in which my name appears and I can say without hesitation that I had absolutely no knowledge of it and I am quite sure the other three didn't either. I saw all of them regularly over the years, and it was never mentioned. Neither Windsor, Sands nor Christie spoke to me about it, and I would certainly not have given my permission."

Lord Derby, who is one of Britain's most sporting gentlemen with impressive racing stables and Jockey Club connections went on: "I do not know why the duke ever got mixed up with Christie. He was a bit of a crook, you know. My personal knowledge of him was limited to an occasion once when he tried to sell me a plot of land in the Bahamas. He told me he was letting me have it at a specially reduced price, but when I returned to London to put things into action through my lawyers, I discovered that some weeks earlier he had tried to sell the same plot to someone else for a much lower price."

Despite this impressive list of names, the Bahamas Executive Council refused the gambling license. They knew that there was still too much backlash from the Oakes death; in fact the tiny island community was in the grip of fear.

By August 1959, there had been sixteen murders in the Bahamas, with many cases of intimidation and other violence—and more were yet to come. Much of the mayhem was widely attributed to the Oakes murder, but this was never proved. There were, however, two cases which the police believed were directly associated with the Oakes case. The first concerned Betty Renner, who arrived in Nassau from Washington. She announced that she was a crime reporter and intended to reopen the Oakes murder investigation. Within two days, her body was found upside down in a well a few miles out of Nassau. Dorothy Macksey, former secretary to Harold Christie and someone who knew more of his secrets than anyone else, was found bludgeoned to death at her home.

Neither murder was solved and Cyril Stevenson, then leader of the black Progressive Liberal party and editor of the *Bahamian Times*, now began a campaign for the reopening of the Oakes murder investigation. "This whole business has been one big whitewash from start to finish," he declared. "People in high places know who the killer is. It is time the true facts were brought out into the open so that this nightmare of violence this colony has suffered for sixteen years can be ended." Stevenson, whose resolution asking for the investigation of the murder to be reopened was approved by the Bahamas Assembly, said he knew the "man responsible" for the murder. "The House did the right thing in re-opening the case," Mr. Stevenson declared. "I expected opposition, but obviously they felt it would look as though they were trying to protect someone.

"I could point my finger at the man responsible," he said. "I could name him. But it is not for me to call names, I do not want to take advantage of my Parliamentary immunity and I am leaving that to Scotland Yard. I am prepared to say that, in my opinion, Oakes was killed by one of his close friends, whom he had no reason to suspect."

Twenty-four hours later, there was an attempt on Stevenson's own life. Four shots were fired into his office, the room where he normally worked, but at the time, he was in another room and so escaped unhurt.

The mounting suspicion of Christie's part in the affair prompted him to issue a statement through his New York lawyers threatening action against those who continued to allege his deeper involvement. He said, "For seventeen years, I have found myself an object of inferential calumny. Far more important than harm to me is the detriment to the best interests of my homeland, the Bahamas." His statement immediately prompted Nancy Oakes de Marigny, now divorced from Count Freddie, to break a seventeen-year silence on the murder of her father. Never, since the day she left Nassau with Freddie, had she spoken to newspapermen about the killing. Now she wanted her views made public. She issued a statement of her own in which she said:

> This has been a disgraceful thing to have to live with for all these years. It should now be cleared up once and for all, regardless of who might be affected by the truth.
>
> Count Freddie de Marigny was arrested in an atmosphere of hasty confusion. It should never be forgotten that up to now, there has been no true investigation by qualified authorities.
>
> The cost to some of us has been appalling in terms of callous treatment, unnecessarily brutal practical difficulties and endless humiliation of an intensely personal nature. Certain interests have kept alive lies and suspicions down through the years. It appears like a conspiracy aimed at eternally diverting and confusing public attention, while astutely attempting to justify errors, idiocies and machinations of others.
>
> Logic would dictate a few basic questions as to why a man in my father's position, with multiple international interests, should die so mysteriously at such a particular time. For the good of the country, and for justice and decency, they should insist on a vigorous effort now being made to clear this up, *regardless of who might be affected by the truth*.

In the Bahamas and in London, the pressure for the reopening of the case grew stronger, and finally the Bahamas House of Assembly voted to call in Scotland Yard. Yet even as detectives flew to Nassau to commence a new inquiry, behind-the-scene intrigue was going on in high places. The Scotland Yard men were sent back. The governor, Sir Oswald Raynor Arthur, had announced: "There will be no new inquiry. The case is closed."

The questions remained coldly unanswered.

The fresh attention on the case brought hoards of newspapermen and criminologists to the Bahamas, and combing Nassau for the truth was Marshall Houts, an American crime expert. Houts was a graduate of the University of Minnesota School of Law and during his career he was a U.S. coroner and judge and a professor of criminal law and evidence at the Michigan State University School of Police Administration. During the war years, he had been a special agent for the Federal Bureau of Investigation and an undercover agent in Rio de Janeiro. He was a man of wide experience in matters of law, crime, and criminal detection who had a wealth of contacts within the American FBI, police departments, and underworld.

In Nassau, he was collecting the facts on the Oakes murder, a task that would span several years. He methodically picked through the records, went over and over the evidence presented at de Marigny's trial, and spent a lot of time talking to his contacts, piecing together his assessment of the murder case.

Finally he came up with his own theories. He wrote:

> Reliable confidential informants report that the mid-afternoon of Wednesday, July 7, 1943, a sixty-seven foot power cruiser, a speedy veteran of hundreds of rum runs during the Prohibition era to Philadephia, Long Island and Boston, cleared the eastern coast of Florida on a direct course to Nassau. Three of the five men aboard

knew the Nassau harbour and dock well from having played the rum-running game during the Roaring Twenties and early thirties. All were minions of Meyer Lansky.

Lansky had anticipated the unlimited potential of big-time gambling in the Bahamas, and Christie correctly concluded that he would need the affirmative support of two other persons to insure agreement with Lansky—the Duke of Windsor and Sir Harry Oakes. Anticipating difficulty with Sir Harry, Christie first presented the case to the Royal Governor and received his enthusiastic support.

This part of the Houts information would be borne out when Sands was called to give evidence at a royal commission of inquiry into gambling in the Bahamas. He admitted in evidence that he had been approached early in 1943 to attempt to get gambling approval and confirmed to the author later that the approach came from Meyer Lansky.

Having sold the Duke on Lansky's promising offer, Christie broached the matter to Sir Harry. The informants cannot know exactly why Sir Harry decided to oppose gambling. The most plausible speculation is that upon second thoughts he envisioned Nassau trampled by thousands of tourists who would drastically ruin his tropical paradise. Anyway, having become furious upon learning that Sir Harry had backed out, Lansky sent several blunt warnings to Sir Harry, admonitions that evolved into threats about which there could be no misunderstanding; Sir Harry must perform according to his original agreement or run the risk of death.

Lansky did agree to send one of his chief lieutenants to Nassau for a face-to-face confrontation with Sir Harry, and this man was one of the party of five aboard the power cruiser that docked in Nassau Wednesday evening, July 7. Their dinner guests departed just before eleven, and by prearrangement Oakes and Christie entered Christie's station-wagon which had been parked near the golf club. They drove quickly to the quay and boarded the cabin cruiser for the fateful conference with Lansky's lieutenant. It lasted only a few minutes as Sir Harry launched into a vindictive, profane tirade telling the lieutenant what he could tell Lansky.

The lieutenant decided there was no chance of changing Sir Harry's mind. With an almost imperceptible nod of his head, he signalled one of the three other men aboard the cruiser, who struck Sir Harry's head with a lever. . . . Sir Harry collapsed immediately while Harold Christie became paralysed, his worst fears now particularised in this assault upon his great and good friend, but the lieutenant assured Christie that Sir Harry was not dead, only knocked unconscious to teach him a lesson.

Two of the men now half-carried, half-dragged Sir Harry's body onto the quay, through the mud of the street and laid him face down in the station-wagon. One returned to the boat and the other slipped into the driving seat, ordering Harold Christie, still in a state of shock, to sit beside him in the front passenger seat and direct him to Westbourne. . . . When they reached the house, Lansky's man ordered Christie to help remove the body from the wagon and take it up to the bedroom. They dragged the body up the hall stairway . . . by the time they reached the bedroom they realised Sir Harry was dead.

Lansky's man had the presence of mind to give directions, while Harold Christie oscillated between paralysed shock and frantic panic. They laid the body on the floor, undressed it and slipped Sir Harry's pyjamas on. The man left the room. Harold Christie, totally unprepared for what happened next, remained in the bedroom on orders . . . he suddenly smelled fire . . . the man reappeared with a home-made torch. . . . Christie watched in a funk of fear as the man dabbed the torch over Sir Harry's bed . . . he ordered Christie to help him lift the body onto the burned mattress . . . he systematically played the torch over Sir Harry's body . . . it was a classic mutilation, gangland killing, with its own special twist, designed to instill fear and foster discipline . . . the man left but not without warning Christie. If he did not want a similar "accident" to happen to him or his mother, if the Duke did not want to end up with a similar fate . . . or have his wife tortured or mutilated before she was killed, they had all better turn up to approve the gambling licence for Lansky. . . . That's the story the informants tell.

Some years later, Houts's book on the Oakes death was published and there were further developments. Two days before the book was due to go on sale, Houts and his publishers, William Morrow, received letters from Herbert Bronwell, of the law firm, Lord, Day and Lord, claiming that their client Sir Harold Christie had been libeled. They said the book contained numerous defamatory passages and the publishers were urged to cease further distribution and withdraw all copies of the book on the market. In particular, they demanded that William Morrow should not circulate the book in Great Britain, Canada, and the overseas market.

Houts said: "I knew from my own investigations that William Morrow and I were on safe legal grounds, although Christie and Bromwell could put us through the rigours of a lawsuit which could cost up to $100,000 to defend.

"I wrote to Bromwell and pointed out that both William Morrow and I had made every effort to be as fair and objective as possible in presenting the activities of Sir Harold Christie and the Duke of Windsor in the Oakes/de Marigny case. I wrote only what I believed to be the truth and strenuously refrained from drawing speculative conclusions. My information comes from reliable sources and these reports are corroborated by the physical evidence that we know existed at the critical time."

There were further exchanges between lawyers and

the book subsequently went on sale. Then, says Houts, Christie's lawyers made an offer. "They asked if we would consider permitting Sir Harold to make a statement that would detail his side of the case to be included in the next printing of the book, thus leaving the reader to decide."

Houts and his publishers agreed with alacrity. But in fact Christie's statement was never forthcoming. Morrow made repeated requests for it, so that it could be inserted in future reprintings of the book. It never came. Nor did Christie sue. Meanwhile the callous cost to the Oakes family, to which Nancy referred, continued.

William Pitt Oakes, youngest son of Harry Oakes, was haunted by the death of his father. He spoke about it obsessively, particularly when drinking. Alcohol had the young man, barely out of his teens, in its grip, and being well provided for in his father's will, he had little difficulty in servicing his needs.

He stood at a cocktail party at the British Colonial Hotel in Nassau, which his father had bought and restored to its colonial glory. The year was 1959; Pitt Oakes was talking to Rex North, a leading society columnist. "Poor Pitt," North wrote. "He is demented by the memory of his father.

> He is scared. He dug into his jacket pocket and showed me a small revolver, which he carries constantly. He told me they would get him like they got his father.
>
> At that moment, Pitt spotted the squat-featured, smallish figure of someone he knew well across the room. He gestured towards him and said: "There is the man who knows how my father was murdered, and why."

Within a few months of that party, Pitt Oakes was dead, poisoned by drink.

His elder brother, Sydney, was killed three years later in a car crash. Nancy married twice more and the family never settled. Freddie de Marigny traveled Canada and the Caribbean and finally settled back in America in Houston, Texas.

And despite the pressure for a new inquiry, the duke remained silent.

What the royal governor had started in 1941, Sir Stafford Sands and Sir Harold Christie were improving on, with their hopes of making the Bahamas one of the busiest tourist spots in the world.

Tourism was rising steadily, land sales were ticking over well, and the lax Bahamian banking and company laws had started to attract tax evaders and fraudulent operators on a dramatic scale. One of the most famous was the Medicare Life Insurance company, which was incorporated in Sands's law offices on Bay Street and which subsequently collapsed, leaving 100,000 mostly elderly subscribers in America without cover or recourse to repayment.

During the fifties, also, Stafford Sands had pulled off one of the biggest legal coups of his career, one which would earn him millions and eventually bring in the legalized gambling that had become his obsession. His old friend former Wall Street financial wizard Wallace Groves, who had moved to the Bahamas after serving a jail sentence for mail fraud, had bought a lumber company on Grand Bahama Island and he too dreamt of a new holiday resort.

Sands remembered the grand plan Axel Wenner Gren and the Duke of Windsor had worked out for the Bahamas, under which the Swedish millionaire would have bought huge tracts of Crown land. Groves wanted to build a tax-free port and Sands knew just how it could be done. He drew up a proposal, based on Wenner Gren's original idea and for the approval of the Bahamas government, the governor, and the British Colonial Office, to convey to Groves 150,000 acres of Crown land at the knockdown price of £1 an acre; land which in not many years hence would be selling at £100,000 an acre and which would provide fat fees for Sands, because it was part of the deal that he had exclusive legal rights!

Modeled on the Hudson's Bay agreement in Canada, Groves would get his huge acreages to use, and barter with, to create a sprawling Wild West–style township, for which he was also granted remarkable tax concessions. It was, on the face of it, a creditable and courageous undertaking, but it had two basic flaws.

The majority of wealth that the project would generate would filter, not into government for the benefit of the nation as a whole, but into the pockets of Groves, Sands, and the merchants of Bay Street. It was also segregationist, with overtones of South Africa. While the main town of Freeport was built to house the white expatriate population, the blacks were confined to their squalid, shanty ghettos in settlements outside the town and outside the limits of the area in which they could take advantage of the beneficial tax concessions.

The building of the Lucayan Beach Hotel on the silvery sands of Grand Bahama Island was well under way before gambling was legalized. On the plans was a 9,000-square-foot room described as a handball court, but there was never to be a game of handball played in that huge room. Instead it was soon to be crammed with crap and roulette tables and one-arm bandits . . . the gaming room. At the time building began, however, the Bahamas government had yet to be persuaded to issue a certificate of exemption to allow gambling to commence. In the meantime, certain members of government would receive valuable financial contracts from Groves companies that were to be drawn up and negotiated by Sir Stafford. They were in the form of consultancy agreements, which were handed out, and accepted, with remarkable willingness.

Sir Stafford himself was by far the biggest beneficiary. He had already made it clear to Groves that he wanted $1 million—equal to the amount he had been offered for the concession by Lansky—and he got it. On April 1, 1963, the day the gambling application was to be approved, he would get a further $500,000 fee for "services rendered." The money was transferred from Groves's development company account with the First National Bank of Boston to their account with the Irving Trust Bank in New York. The second bank subsequently delivered to Sir Stafford a check made out to cash a day or two later. Part of the money remained in the Bahamas and the balance was transferred to banks overseas. The second installment of Sands's share would be made a year later when a meeting of the board of directors of the development company agreed to the payment of $576,000 to Sir Stafford.

As the gambling application was up for approval, Groves's highrolling partner Lou Chesler—the Canadian entrepreneur, Florida land dealer, and a major shareholder in Seven Arts Productions, which produced films including Frank Sinatra's *Robin and the Seven Hoods*—almost ruined a successful conclusion, as a letter from Groves to Chesler indicates:

> Dear Lou,
> Stafford called me this A.M. The news is of course grand and definite. Vote 5/3. I do not know the details but gather RTS [Prime Minister Roland Symonette] voted No. Stafford is really concerned over leaks . . . it will take more than two weeks for the certificate to be signed and he has promised no publicity. . . . Please, please be careful. Elis of *Freeport News* says you laid a 50–1 bet at the Caravel Bar and that there would be gambling before the end of the year. . . . Too bad. I am now most concerned over money and think a meeting must be held soon.
>
> My best, sincerely, Wallace.

The approval came through, and Chesler went to Florida to meet Meyer Lanksy to discuss staffing the casino and the leasing of a credit ratings system. Among the managers hired were three well versed in gambling in the U.S. and Canada; two were wanted to answer tax and betting charges in New York. Other Lanksy associates from the Havana days were also recruited and by the time the first casino opened in January, 1964, twenty-six men had been recruited from America. All would receive substantial payments from the casino operators. The *Miami Herald*'s crime investigation team was quick off the mark to disclose that at least ten of them had known connections with Mafia personalities.

By the end of the month, the situation had clearly become an embarrassment to the Bahamas premier, Sir Roland Symonette, who wrote to Sands on February 3:

> Dear Stafford,
>
> *Gambling at Freeport*
>
> I made the Statement to the press [referring to a statement drawn up by Sands] and it has gone down well, but I have no intention of continually making press statements. I feel very strongly that the names of employees should have been submitted to our Police long before the casino opened so that they could have been vetted. It should not be the duty or responsibility of our Police to run down reports by the *Miami Herald* on employees at the casino after they are already there.
>
> It was the talk of everyone that these people were being employed there. (It was told to me on Christmas Day.) I am not convinced that the management did not know about it. If undesirables are found in the lot, I agree not to issue deportation orders on your promise that they will leave the colony within twenty-four hours after being requested by an officer of the Government, but I shall request they be placed on a prohibitive list and not be allowed to re-enter the colony.

From its beginnings in 1943, when Lansky met the Duke of Windsor, the Mafia-linked people had gotten a foothold. But even with government fears of the Mafia controlling the casinos, Sands wasn't finished yet. This time he had his sights set on Hog Island, once the home of Axel Wenner Gren, which had been bought by American multimillionaire Huntington Hartford. He renamed it Paradise Island and planned to develop it as a holiday complex. Indeed by early 1963, he had invested almost $13 million there. But the dream turned sour, and Paradise Island became a financial disaster. There were two main problems. The island could be reached only by sea, and there was insufficient activity to attract visitors in large numbers to make the project viable.

Hartford applied to the Bahamas government for permission to build a bridge across to the island and later his solicitors inquired into the possibility of being granted a casino license, similar to the one operating at Freeport. Both ideas were turned down; the bridge would be hazardous to shipping and the casino licenses were being restricted to Freeport as an experiment.

Hartford was getting desperate, and a year later his solicitors applied again for a casino license with the added proviso that their client in association with Hilton Hotels would build a 1,500-room hotel with casino and convention center. Again Hartford was turned down. Some months later, as Hartford's losses on Paradise Island were mounting to an alarming degree, his solicitors received a letter from Sir Stafford Sands, who represented clients interested in purchasing the island.

Hartford agreed to sell, at a price which meant he had registered a multimillion-dollar loss in the project. Paradise Island was now in the hands of a business partnership. On their behalf, Sands lost no time in getting to work. A new approach was made for permission to build a bridge to Paradise Island from the mainland; lo and behold it was approved. A new application was submitted for a casino license on Paradise Island. That too was approved, and suddenly the tiny island where once Wenner Gren had entertained the Windsors, where Huntington Hartford sank and lost millions, became one of the most profitable tourist spots in the Bahamas.

Media attention and the efforts of a young black lawyer named Lynden Pindling, leader of the black opposition party, collated a dossier on the infiltration of American mobsters into Bahamian life. He took it to London and to the United Nations and finally forced the ruling white United Bahamian party into a general election which they lost. Pindling became the country's first black premier and guided his nation into independence from British colonial rule.

His first act was to demand a royal commission of inquiry into the operation of casinos in Freeport and Nassau. In its report, the secret deals were detailed and the presence of Lansky's men confirmed. The inquiry went back to 1943, the year of Sir Harry Oakes's murder; any mentions of the Duke of Windsor during the weeks of evidence were taken in camera for reasons of "national security."

The inquiry report was an indictment of underhand dealings that had developed as Stafford Sands, the prime architect, engineered the final approval of gambling. And once installed, the Mafia would be difficult to dislodge. Even as Pindling was fighting his election battle, he was using aircraft placed at his disposal by men who, it would be discovered, had links with the mobsters. In the years that followed, the beneficial banking laws of the Bahamas would prove to be a safe harbor for the ill-gotten gains of crooks the world over, and of drug dealers from the American mainland, the Caribbean, and South America in particular. Even Pindling himself would not be above suspicion, and when a second royal commission was launched to investigate the drugs traffic through the Bahamas in the mid-1980s, the prime minister had to answer deeply probing questions. Sands fled the Bahamas and moved to Europe where his millions had been salted. He died in 1972; Christie also spent much time in Europe and died there in 1977.

In a retrospective view of the whole affair, the Duke of Windsor's great friend and confidant, the Duke de Grantmesnil, said this to the author: "I have no doubt at all that the actual murder of Sir Harry Oakes (which started it all) was carried out by contract men brought in by Christie. I think Edward's part was due to mere lack of *savoir faire*, and curiosity. I don't think he knew initially, but later he suspected Christie. Sands, whom I knew personally, was a very bad man indeed and he certainly knew all about it. His secret files are hidden in a vault, somewhere in Florida."

· TWENTY ·

THE DECLINING YEARS

As the western world entered the era of the swinging sixties, the personalities who had dominated that previous Jazz Age of the twenties were in decline.

Edwina Mountbatten, one of the stars of that former age, had spent the previous two decades seemingly intent on making amends for her somewhat misspent youth and early adult life. Unlike the Windsors, who had whiled away the years in the café societies of the world, she had driven herself to the limits of personal endeavor in her work with the St. John Ambulance Brigade and the Save the Children Fund and gave countless other voluntary hours of work.

In November 1959, she looked tired and weary as she spoke a long and loving tribute to her devoted friend Nehru upon the occasion of his seventieth birthday. That year, which would prove to be the last of her life, had been particularly hectic. She had suffered a warning stroke the previous year, and in January she flew to Delhi for a complete rest, with Nehru supervising her recuperation.

In March, she was back in London, and despite the pleas of her family, she continued with a tour of Canada. Then later, she returned across the Atlantic to America.

There was a pre-Christmas party for the royal family at the Mountbattens' country home, Broadlands, where the two of them had taken over the role of favorite aunt and uncle, upon whom each member of the family would call for advice or comfort, a role that should have been the Windsors' had they ever been part of it.

In January, there were preparations for the wedding of the Mountbattens' daughter Pamela, and then Edwina was heading east again to Cyprus, Karachi, Delhi, and Singapore. At Delhi, she spent a few days with Nehru, but when he kissed her gently good-bye at the airport, it would be the last time he saw her.

At Singapore, an official party waited on the tarmac to greet her, but in the sweltering heat she saw all the formalities through a haze of pain and discomfort. She forced herself on through a round of engagements until, on the evening of February 29, 1960, she was led away from a crowded gathering to her room. She died there the following day, fifty-eight years old. From scandalous beginnings, she had become one of the most revered, praised, accomplished, and astonishing women of this century and, like her husband, a hero.

The Windsors mourned her passing from Paris. Soon the years would begin to claim many of their friends. The Mosleys were still in evidence, but their political activity was certainly on the wane, although for the moment there were enough embers for Tom to fan the old flames of racial hatred that he had preached in the thirties. He had latched onto the cause of banning further immigration of blacks into Britain. He was stirring trouble in Notting Hill, the scene of Britain's first major race riots, and when he stood for Parliament in 1959, his speeches were just as outrageous as before the war.

He would stand atop his electioneering van, shouting down the hecklers, screaming his message aimed at setting whites against blacks. A new breed of young Fascist thugs surrounded his every move and acted as his bodyguards. They roared their approval of his inflammatory speeches, in which he accused black men of feeding their families on tins of cat food, or keeping white girls prisoners in their attics.

But Mosley was a spent force. Those who once admired his brilliance in his early political life now looked on in despair as he sank to the depths, dredging support not from those who saw a political answer, but from people whose only motive was hatred. Mosley couldn't see it; he was still blind to the thought that he might possibly be wrong and he seriously thought he could win the seat in North Kensington. When the election came, he was bottom of the poll, with less than 3,000 votes. He made one more attempt to get back into the House of Commons when he fought the Shoreditch seat, but he again lost his deposit, with even fewer votes than he had achieved at North Kensington. At last the realization came to him. Tom Mosley finally left the British political scene and retired to his home in Paris to join the Windsors in their memories.

For the duke and duchess, the sixties saw the end of the years of nightclubbing, flitting from one hotel to another, New York one month, Marbella the next, and then perhaps Venice. There was nothing much to do now except enter the last phase of their lives with what dignity they had left.

In the first year of that decade, the Queen Mother announced the engagement of her second daughter Princess Margaret to Anthony Armstrong-Jones, whose parents had separated. At the wedding on May 6, Armstrong-Jones's father was accompanied by his new wife, a former air hostess, thus marking another break with tradition in the acceptance of divorces at court. The duke and duchess were not invited to the wedding, and the duchess observed icily: "At least they can't say I haven't kept up with the Joneses."

Two years later, the marriage was announced between Princess Alexandra, daughter of the late Duke of Kent, and Mr. Angus Ogilvy. Once again the Windsors were not invited, and worse, the Duchess of Windsor was excluded from a genealogy chart published in the souvenir church program for the wedding. The duke was listed as the former king, but no reference was made to his marriage. To the royal family, Wallis simply did not exist.

(Quite by chance, a few months later, the Queen Mother and the Duchess of Windsor were in a hospital at the same time in London; the Queen Mother for an appendix removal and the duchess for a face-lift! Barely three hundred yards separated them but no contact was made on either side.)

There was a slight thaw in the family relationship when, on his seventieth birthday, the duke received a telegram from the queen. It was a year of reflection for him. "Seventy," he mused at a press interview. "These last few years seem to have slipped away. But I have not a twinge of regret. Faced with it all over again, I would still marry Wallis Simpson." He was happier and more contented than he had ever been, though in more pensive moments, he could only look back with some disappointment on those wasted years. "A man trained to the monarchy," the duke said, "finds this life we now lead is one without mode or purpose." Seventy. Had he not abdicated, he would still have been King of England, serving longer than his father. There would have been celebrations, cannons booming out a salute, messages of congratulations from the commonwealth. Now there was none of it, just a quiet celebratory dinner with friends. What a far cry from the day he was born at the White Lodge in Richmond Park! Then, 1,500 eminent people queued to sign the book of congratulations and Queen Victoria hurried to see her grandson whom she thought was a "fine strong boy, a pretty child."

He had lost none of his looks. Although his face was lined and creased, and now distinctly Teutonic, his blond hair was only flecked with gray, he was still brisk-moving and sharp in his responses. But always, now, there was an air of "if only . . ."

In the coming months signs of a slight, only slight, move toward friendliness appeared. In December 1964, the duke was admitted to the Methodist Hospital in Houston, Texas, for a stomach operation, and found inside his room flowers from the queen, his sister the Princess Royal, and Princess Margaret.

The following February he was back in the London Clinic for treatment of a detached retina when the Queen Mother was away in Jamaica on an official visit—where, incidentally, she would visit Noel Coward's home, high on a hilltop, called Firefly.

On this occasion, there was press speculation on whether the royal family would end what many saw as a pointless and bitter exclusion of the Windsors from the First Family of Great Britain. Sir Walter Monckton's widow, the Dowager Countess Monckton of Brenchley, sent a message to the Palace indicating that the duke would be most cheered if any members of his family could find the time to visit him in the hospital.

The queen's own advisers also realized that she was now being criticized for her failure to end the feud. The Windsors' past misdeeds were fading into the mist of time and it was increasingly evident that the royal family in London were taking the whole blame for what some were calling a callous separation.

The Queen Mother arrived back from Jamaica and clearly a family discussion was indicated. It was now twenty-eight years since the abdication; was there really any point in maintaining the acrimony? To everyone's surprise the Queen Mother agreed that there was no point; she sent Windsor flowers at the London Clinic and then, on March 15, by which time the duke had had three operations on his left eye, the queen arrived at the three-room suite on the fourth floor of the clinic to visit her uncle.

She was greeted there by Wallis, which was only the second time they had met, the first being at the Royal Lodge when Wallis turned up, unexpected and uninvited, with Edward back in March 1936. Elizabeth II was then just ten years old.

The queen was followed by other members of the family, with the quite obvious exception of the Queen Mother; and Elizabeth paid a second visit to her uncle while he was convalescing in his suite at Claridges.

The Windsors were preparing to leave London and return to Paris at the end of the month when the duke received news that his sister the Princess Royal had collapsed and died at her home in Yorkshire. The duke and duchess announced their deep sadness, but it was with regret that they would be unable to travel to the funeral; so once again a complete family reunion with the entire royal family, many of whom the Windsors hadn't even seen, was avoided.

That would come two years later, when arrangements were being made for the unveiling of a plaque in London to mark the centenary of the birth of Queen Mary. For the first time the Duke and Duchess of Windsor received from Buckingham Palace a joint invitation to attend. They arrived cheerfully at Southampton. Mountbatten was waiting to greet them, and took them to stay at his country house. For the ceremony, they joined the rest of the royal family in a procession from St. James's Palace to Marlborough House, and were cheered by the crowds. They met and chatted with the queen and Queen Mother.

The ice may have been broken, but the coolness remained. There was to be no reunion of the "long-lost family," and the Windsors repaired to Paris without any feeling that a prompt return to London would be welcome.

The duke himself was still totally obsessive about the lack of a title for his duchess—even after all these years. Mountbatten recorded on a subsequent visit to Paris that the two men were still able to enjoy each other's company, but the thorn in the duke's side was still there. "Wallis was away 'resting' and so David and I had delightful evening entirely to ourselves," wrote Mountbatten. Repeatedly, however, the duke would revert to his old complaint that the duchess had never been created a Royal Highness. "I explained that it was his own mother's opposition, followed by his sisters and then his sister-in-law's . . . which really made it impossible. I advised him to give up the struggle." He never would, of course.

On his part the duke was more angry at Mountbatten's constant references to the duke's personal possessions and what would become of them after his death, a discussion which Mountbatten found difficulty in approaching with any degree of subtlety and eventually had to bring straight out. "Who will you leave this to . . . ?" and "What will happen to your papers . . . ?" or "Are you going to set up a charitable trust . . . ?"

The Windsors became fed up with it. "How dare he!" exclaimed the duke. "He even tells me what he wants left to him."

These conversations and the duke's own actions once again helped to restore the rift. The royal family, for instance, was deeply upset by a series of articles the duke wrote for the New York *Daily News* in 1966, in which he raked over the dying embers of the past, brought back old memories, and settled old scores. The Windsors also completely ignored British feeling when they accepted an invitation to visit General Franco's Fascist Spain on a visit that turned out to be more like the state visit of a reigning monarch.

Over the years, they had made regular trips to Spain and were already good friends with Franco and his family. What was different about this trip was the official look that Franco gave it. There was a red carpet rolled out at the railway station, a military guard of honor for the duke to inspect, motorcycle outriders to guide their motor cavalcade through the city of Madrid. The duchess loved every second of it, waving regally to the crowds from their limousine. It was all perhaps just too reminiscent of past indiscretion, one last kick against the authority of the British government.

The Windsors were planning to buy a summer home in Spain, near Marbella, where their friends the Count and Countess Romanones were building a house. The duke turned to Wallis and said, "Darling, how would you like a house in Marbella?" She would like one very much. But then she thought for a moment. "You know, we're simply not as rich as Rothchilds and we would have to move someplace where it is inexpensive if we want to take on the added expense of a summer house."

They did, in fact, buy a plot of land, but the house was never built. The duke was taken ill and plans were postponed, and then as the months, then two or three more years, went by, his finances were beginning to look decidedly modest. The upkeep at the Bois de Boulogne, despite the peppercorn rent, was still high. In the late sixties they still kept a large staff; Wallis still loved her designer clothes and jewelry; the dinner parties, though fewer, still went on. But the duke's access to ready cash was beginning to diminish.

Countess Romanones recalled for *Vanity Fair* that on a later visit the upstairs rooms of the Paris mansion were showing signs of neglect. When they arrived at the house, the duchess told them, "Go upstairs to that dreary attic. I wish we could do better for you, but that's all we have. That's why we never have house guests now." But the guest suite was still not bad by any standard. It was composed of two bedrooms, separated by a bathroom, in which the toilet roll, as always, had been cut into squares and piled on a table near the toilet. The male bedroom was decorated with miniature soldiers, models of troops the duke had commanded as king.

Nor had the duchess lost her touch in detailing the precise arrangements she had made for her guests during their stay. On a desk in the countess' bedroom, there was a blue folder in which the duchess' secretary had placed a typed plan of the week's engagements which read, for example, "Madame la Comtesse de Roma-nones, Tuesday December 2nd: dinner at Cris de Paris at 9 P.M. Wednesday December 3rd: lunch with Her Royal Highness and Baron de Rosnay at Maxim's at 1.15; dinner at Mrs Bory's at 9 P.M. and dance at Duchesse de Liancourt's. Friday December 5th: dinner here at 9.15, before Baron de Rede's ball."

At dinner, the duke and duchess were always punctual, and the duchess would frown upon anyone who was late and scold them. She remained as meticulous as ever, even to the point of having one of her four maids iron her bedsheets before she retired in the evening—she would have them changed every day. The duke had long since got used to it and now as a matter of course never dropped ash from his incessant cigarettes or cigars, nor made his rooms untidy: whenever he did, he would have his valet Sidney clean up straight away. And so it went on: life largely as it always had been, though slower now and more in tune with their age.

By 1970, the duke was beginning to show signs of the illness that would kill him. His movements looked painful; he could hardly manage to complete a short round of golf. They had sold his beloved mill because it was now too much of an effort to travel the twenty-five miles, and the cost of keeping two homes for their needs was hardly justified.

The duchess, too, had become extremely forgetful, which was partly the result of her advancing years and partly the effect of arteriosclerosis, which reduces the blood supply to the brain. She already had the condition when she had her last face-lift, but insisted on going ahead with the operation, despite doctors' warnings that it might worsen. Indeed it had, and now the household was becoming increasingly reliant on secretaries, servants, and the ever-present Maître Blum. "I'm afraid," the duke once confided to a friend, "the Duchess is slowly losing her mind."

Friends were still encouraged to call, but by 1972 the Windsors could cope with the entertainment of no more than two or three of their closest friends.

One such caller was the Dowager Lady Monckton, who was so disturbed at what she found, she went straight to Buckingham Palace upon her return to London to report on the duke's physical condition—"he is but a shadow"—and the duchess' mental state.

As it happened, the queen and Prince Philip were about to make a state visit to France and, on receiving Lady Monckton's news, they decided to pay the Windsors a call, for the first time ever.

The day before, the duke had suffered a serious hemorrhage and was confined to bed, and doctors had attached a saline drip, but as soon as he heard his niece was coming, he insisted on getting up. He wanted to receive her in the large salon downstairs. The nurse detached the drip but, as Georges Sanegre and his valet tried to help him out of bed, even the duke himself realized he was too weak to be moved out of his bedroom. The effort of moving just a few feet had made him speechless, Georges recalled. "It was difficult to imagine the emotion he was going through at that time. He did so want to be upright and dressed to meet the queen. But he was too weak and fading. We managed to persuade him to sit in a chair. He still insisted on being dressed in a dark suit."

The queen arrived and was shown upstairs to the bedroom by Wallis, who was nervous but calm. It was the first time she had welcomed her husband's niece into her home. Georges went ahead to help the duke prepare for the meeting. "The queen came into the room and the duke struggled to get to his feet and said, 'My dear Lillibet, it's lovely to see you again.' He shook her hand and kissed it and then shook hands with Prince Philip and Charles, who, he said, had grown into a fine young man."

Georges reports: "They chatted for about ten minutes before the duchess beckoned to Charles and Philip. The three of them left the room, leaving the duke and the queen together for another five minutes."

She came out of the room with an anguished expression. Georges was waiting on the landing to show the queen downstairs to the salon, where he served mint tea from Fortnum and Mason in their best Limoges china, and a tray of cakes and sandwiches. No one ate very much and Wallis, wearing a blue crêpe Dior dress, was by now jumpy and tense. They spoke a little longer and the queen got up and prepared to leave. There wasn't much more to be said. They kissed at the door and waved good-bye.

When they had gone, Georges returned to the bedroom to restore the duke to his bed. He looked deflated, tears in his eyes. "They still won't relent" he said to Georges. "I tried. No one can say I didn't try." Georges learned that the duke had asked once more that in her final years, the duchess should be accorded the title of Her Royal Highness, a wish that only the queen could grant, but would not. Downstairs, Wallis told Georges, "England has treated me very badly. After all these years, I don't really want that title. Once I cared and I was hurt. Now I don't give a hoot. It was the duke who always wanted me to have it and if I could have it now, I would accept, not for me but for his sake."

The end came ten days later, just after two in the morning. The duke had been particularly ill that night after another hemorrhage. Wallis was dozing in a chair in her room. She was brought to his bedside and cradled his head; he looked up at her, and drifted peacefully away.

The world's best-known love story was over.

In death, he was honored. The royal family had long since arranged for the Duke of Windsor to come home to England for a family burial at Frogmore, and there would be a lying-in-state at St. George's Chapel, where thousands queued daily to file past his coffin. He had not been among them in years, but the British people were eager to show their respect, particularly those who remembered the charming, caring, handsome prince of the twenties and early thirties, rather than the wandering, rather selfish ghosts he and the duchess had become.

Wallis had been intending to accompany the coffin on its flight from Paris to England on the Royal Air Force VC-10 jet, but in the event she said she was not well enough to do so. More likely she balked at the thought of spending more time than was absolutely necessary with her husband's relatives at Buckingham Palace.

Hubert de Givenchy had brought to the Bois de Boulogne a selection of black mourning dresses, and his tailors made, in the night before she went to England, a black coat. She was met at Heathrow airport by Mountbatten, who drove her to Buckingham Palace to lunch with the queen and Princess Anne.

The newspapers speculated that at last the royal family's exclusion of Wallis was at an end. If that was so, Wallis would hardly be aware of it. On her husband's death she suffered a nervous breakdown and was now severely confused to the point that at times she did not even acknowledge that her husband was dead. She retired early that day to the suite that had been set aside for her in the palace and next day, the queen's official birthday, she decided she would not attend the Trooping of the Colour, at which the queen was to give her tribute to the duke.

The royal family all went to Windsor for the weekend; the duchess declined the invitation to join them. It was coincidentally the thirty-fifth anniversary of her wedding and she decided to remain at the palace with Grace, Lady Dudley, who had accompanied her on the flight over. However, on Saturday evening, Prince Charles came into her suite and offered to drive her to St. George's Chapel at Windsor to see the lying-in-state of her husband's body after the public crowds had gone. She returned immediately afterward, clearly uninterested in any family contact.

The funeral service was a private one for members of the royal family, the government, and only those friends the duke had himself listed before he died. It was a simple service, and when it was over the duchess returned immediately to Heathrow airport, where she was given the fullest honors with the Lord Chamberlain escorting her—though there was not a member of the royal family in sight.

Back in Paris, the duchess was bitter and disappointed. She told a friend almost immediately on her return, "Do you know that not one member of David's family showed any real sympathy? Thank heavens Grace Dudley came with me." Tears welled in her eyes as she spoke. "All through the ceremonies, it was hard for me to realise that I would not see him again, that adorable face, that upturned nose and those wonderful blue eyes . . ."

Describing her visit, the duchess spoke about her husband's family without endearment: "One must take one's hat off to the English. I'm not fond of them, but they certainly do know how to put on a spectacle better than anyone else in the world. In front of me I could see Cookie [her nickname for the Queen Mother] . . ."

The duchess went on, "We called her that because she looked like a pudding dolled up. How she was dressed! What would I look like in that dress and hat? I really must copy that outfit. It looked as if someone had opened some old trunk and draped them on herself, and that eternal bag hanging on her arm. They all caught that style from Cookie . . ."

The duchess still blamed her sister-in-law for the years of exile and separation they had suffered. It was clear in the vitriolic way she spoke. "How David would have laughed over Cookie," she said. "Yes. I remember. I wanted to burst out laughing as I saw her; then I re-

membered that he was not there to share the joke. I
smiled, anyway, I wasn't going to let them show me up.
They had been so cruel to us for so many years. While
I was there, I never once had a small family talk. After
the funeral, by royal order, I had to go to a formal lunch
for about forty people, but I was seated with the sun
shining in my eyes and I was in pain from it. I was next
to the Duke of Edinburgh who I always imagined would
be better, kinder, perhaps more human than the others.
But you know, he is just a four-flusher. Not he, not any
of them offered me solicitude or sympathy . . .

"After the burial, I stood looking at the place next to
him where I will be buried. He had agreed to be buried
at Frogmore only on the understanding that I would
eventually be buried next to him. But I saw then they
had never accepted me in life and they would not accept
me in death. My tiny piece of earth was just a sliver. I
turned to the Archibishop of Canterbury who was beside
me and said, 'I realise I am very thin, but I do not think
that even I could fit into that miserable little narrow piece
of ground.' The Archbishop replied: 'I don't see there's
much we can do. You'll fit all right.' I persisted and
eventually he said he would try to have the adjacent
hedge removed to provide more room."

Reflectively, the duchess spoke then of the most historic period in recent British history. "I did not want him
to give up the throne," she insisted. "But no one could
make David do anything he didn't want to. That's why
the government would not accept his marriage to me and
forced him to abdicate. They could have fixed it for me
to have been his wife without being queen but the politicians weren't concerned about that. They were concerned about having a strong personality as king. He was
popular and effective as Prince of Wales and people adored
him. If Winston had been prime minister a few years
earlier, things would have been different."

Quite soon after the funeral, Mountbatten telephoned

the Bois de Boulogne to make an appointment to see the duchess.

Georges Sanegre remembers the Mountbatten visit. "He swept into the house, and I could tell it was going to be difficult for the Duchess. She received him still dressed entirely in black, in the shuttered library of the Bois de Boulogne and I could sense immediately that there was an atmosphere between them that would not be broken by any emotions. There were none on his part and she seemed intent on keeping a straight face and stiff lip. They were closeted for twenty minutes and when the doors opened, I knew there was something wrong. He swept out of the room without a backward glance and when he had gone, the duchess told me, 'Georges, he only came for money. He wanted me to write my will so that all that David had given me would pass to members of the royal family and a Charitable Foundation. I told him I wasn't interested.' As the British Embassy car drove away down the drive, I had a feeling that would not be the end of it . . ."

Indeed it wasn't, for Mountbatten would devote considerable time in the coming months in an attempt to see that the duke's estate returned to Britain. He again visited the duchess in 1973, and discovered to his dismay that she had dismissed her English lawyers, whom Mountbatten felt would show sympathy to his cause, and her affairs were now being handled completely by her French lawyer, the very clever and firm Maître Blum. As a last-ditch hope, he offered to act as an executor of her will and again ventured the suggestion of setting up a foundation with Prince Charles as its chairman. He retired that day, feeling that the duchess had been unmoved by his ideas, and certainly Maître Blum had given him no cause for hope. When he returned two months later, his fears were confirmed. Maître Blum said that she had no authority to disclose the duchess' intentions as to the contents of her will and when he insisted on seeing the duchess herself, she would only say that she intended to "honour her husband's memory."

He tried once more the following year to reopen the subject, and received a final rebuttal of his maneuvers. The duchess wrote to him: "I confirm to you once more that everything has been taken care of according to David's and my wishes. . . . It is always a pleasure to see you but I must tell you that when you leave me I am always terribly depressed by your reminding me of David's death and my own, and I should be grateful if you would not mention this any more."

Only when a direct appeal from Buckingham Palace arrived did the duchess agree to a representative of the royal family calling to take away certain of the duke's papers for the royal archives, along with his ceremonial uniforms.

Even then, there is still some discrepancy in the account of how Buckingham Palace came to acquire possession of the material. According to the Palace, it was handed over with the full knowledge and permission of the duchess. However, this is disputed by Maître Blum in a confidential letter she wrote to the Duke de Grantmesnil, in which she complained:

> The Duchess has not handed over the Duke's documents. Someone took them without her knowledge; she didn't realise until later when I was here and opened the Duke's safe in his office, and files containing confidential papers were empty. She agreed only to give the historical archive material, such as his papers concerning his activities as Prince of Wales, his letters to his family and so on, in exchange for some of her personal files, her divorce papers, etc.
>
> Naturally at the heart of this operation we found Mountbatten. I have made a verbal report signed by three of the Duchess's closest confidantes, confirming that the files were taken in her absence. It all happened immediately after the Duke's death. Secondly, Mountbatten

also came to the Duchess, who was ill, to try to make her sign a paper by which she would put all of her belongings in a trust which the Prince of Wales would administer. He harassed her so much that she revoked all her pledges and all the powers she gave the Duke's English advocate. She was so exasperated that at each visit Mountbatten spoke only about her death and her will. The whole thing made a real police thriller that would be too long to be written here. Finally Mountbatten was banned from the house. He thinks I am responsible for that, and attacks have begun against me in the papers.

About the Prince of Wales . . . controlled by Mountbatten, the Duchess never heard anything else from him since there is no question of the Foundation. I trust you will destroy this letter, which is intended for your personal information . . . Suzanne Blum.

The duke left everything he possessed to his wife; not even his most devoted servants were remembered in his will. After the duchess' own death, the contents of her will finally revealed that nothing would be left to the royal family, nor to any charitable foundation in Britain. The bulk of it went instead to the Pasteur Institute of Medical Research in Paris. Mountbatten would never know the outcome; the IRA took care of that when they blew him up in August 1979.

The duke's death had had a profoundly saddening effect on his widow. Diana and Tom Mosley visited often, and in her biography of the duchess, Diana wrote: "He had cherished, adored and protected her for nearly four decades with his extraordinary devotion. There could hardly ever have been a widow with quite so much to miss as she." She had no relations, and her friends tried to coax her out of the grief she so obviously bore. She would join them often at dinner parties but she usually slumped, tired and depressed, into a chair long before the hour at which she would, in earlier times, have been ready to go out into the night life of Paris. She had spoken once of returning to America, although Maître Blum had advised against it for tax reasons. However, in 1974 she did travel the Atlantic on board the SS *Rafaello* for a visit, but soon returned, saying she was homesick.

Her own illness began with a fall in which she broke her leg. She recovered fairly quickly, but then in November 1975, she had a hemorrhage which signaled her gradual deterioration.

The following year, her archenemy the Queen Mother was in Paris for a private visit and offered an olive branch. Georges Sanegre took the call from the British embassy and transferred it to the duchess' secretary. "The Queen Mother," said Georges, "wanted to pay a visit, tea and a chat without any fuss or formalities. The duchess was bedridden at the time, and obviously was quite taken aback by the Queen Mother's request. She thought for a few minutes, and then said No. She told me 'It is too late, Georges, too late. I don't see any point in meeting her now,' and the British embassy was duly informed that the duchess was too unwell to meet the Queen Mother."

The following day, a limousine arrived with the Queen Mother's page, Reginald Wilcox, who got out of the car carrying a wicker basket containing seventy-two pink roses and a handwritten card which said simply, "All Good Wishes from Elizabeth R . . ." a simple message but one which showed the Queen Mother perhaps wanted to end the isolation that had lasted almost forty years. But it was rejected by the duchess. "Why now?" said Wallis. "Why now? We have never even exchanged Christmas cards or birthday greetings, nor have we spoken on the telephone." She spoke as if her beloved David was still beside her. "In their eyes, we didn't exist and nothing has changed really."

Even now, in her declining years, the bitterness could not be swept away by a bunch of roses, and there would be little further contact with the British royal family. One of those who tried to maintain a link was another royal outsider and herself a divorcée, Marie-Christine, Princess Michael of Kent, who married the duke's nephew, though there were those who suspected her motives for establishing this contact and would accuse her of a rather obvious interest in the Windsor jewels. The princess first made contact after her controversial marriage to Prince Michael in June 1978, when she wrote to the duchess, addressing her as Auntie Wallis. She said she had deeply admired the Duke and Duchess of Windsor all of her life, had a great deal of sympathy for them and promised to visit her very soon. She kept her promise three months later, when she arrived with her husband one afternoon. Georges showed them to the duchess' boudoir. She recognized the prince straight away, and Marie-Christine introduced herself. She handed Wallis a bunch of flowers and the duchess responded, "Thank you, darling, it is wonderful to have such a beautiful woman in this house again."

Marie-Christine, who had divorced her banker husband, Tom Trowbridge, before marrying Prince Michael, visited the Bois de Boulogne four more times. Twice she came alone, during which time she herself was scandalized by the revelations in the *Daily Mirror* that her father had been a Nazi S.S. officer. Of the duchess, she would say, "She is a great lady. History will prove that she was unfairly treated." Which, of course, it would certainly not.

On one of those visits, Wallis gave the princess a pair of her most cherished earrings, which she had received as a present from the duke in the early 1940s. Marie-Christine was overwhelmed with the gift and wore them frequently upon her return to Britain, boasting that they were a gift from "Auntie Wallis." The queen herself was not at all happy and if there had been any previous indication that royal feelings toward the duchess had mellowed with the duke's passing, they were dispelled instantly when Her Majesty instructed the princess that never again should she wear those earrings in her presence.

Toward the end of the decade, visitors to the Bois de Boulogne were few, and those callers who did get through the gates rarely got past the duchess' staff and into her boudoir for a chat. She could speak but a few words coherently and recognized few faces from the past. When Diana Mosley published her book on the duchess in 1980, she said she'd not seen the duchess for three years, and it distressed her that she could no longer call her old friend with whom her own life had become so intertwined. Like the Windsors, the Mosleys were spending their last years in a Paris château, which was built for one of Napoleon's generals and aptly named Le Temple de la Gloire, and their loyalty to their old friends was undaunted.

Reflectively, Diana still maintained that had Edward VIII been allowed to marry Mrs. Simpson, the course of history would have been changed and the Second World War would have been prevented. Her husband's view was still as vehement then as in the thirties. "We would have stopped it dead in its tracks," he said. "I know this to be true. Although after I formed the British Union of Fascists, David and I considered it was unwise for us to meet, we maintained a correspondence before and after the abdication crisis. True, there were anti-appeasers among the King's advisers, people like Duff Cooper and Churchill, but they were balanced by myself and Lloyd George. Anyway, the King himself already had a strong aversion to war with Germany. We would have told Hitler that he could do what he liked in the East. If he wanted the Ukraine, he could have it as far as we were concerned, but we would have told him not to touch the West." Mosley still had no time for the suggestion, "Yes, but what about the Jews . . . ?" Even at this late stage of his life, there was no quelling his racism, as was often seen when, after too much wine, he would hold forth after dinner. A friend recalled: "He was his normal, charming, jovial self during the reception and meal, but as it progressed and his intake of liquor increased, his eyes began to flare just as they did when he was screaming his hateful speeches before a mass rally or leading a march against the Jews in the East End. Then he would degenerate into a tirade against the Yids and niggers. No, he never changed."

The Mosleys were always true to their causes and remained so; they always seemed to have an explanation for Hitler, or why Edward was forced to abdicate; and Diana's writings on the duchess were sycophantic in the extreme. Mosley himself died in December 1980. The duchess was told, but now seldom recognized a name or a face. She was a total recluse, a seclusion enforced by her ever-faithful lawyer Maître Blum, who with unbending strictness and total devotion, kept visitors away, desperate that her beloved client should not be seen in these, her final demented, ghostly years.

Wallis Windsor remained in that seclusion for the rest of her days, spending almost six years behind the closed doors of her boudoir. Most of her staff went, one by one, save Georges and Ophelia, who remained to the end.

Only in death was the Duchess of Windsor afforded final recognition by the royal family when they all gathered for her funeral in April 1986 as she was laid to rest beside her duke. The queen brushed away a tear and said to Georges and Ophelia, "This is very sad. It must be a great loss to you both. I am so very, very sorry . . ."

BIBLIOGRAPHY

BOOKS:

Allen, Peter. *The Crown and the Swastika*. London: Robert Hale, 1983.

Amory, Cleveland. *Who Killed Society?* New York: Harper & Row, 1960.

Argyll, Margaret, Duchess of; *Forget Not*. London: W. H. Allen, 1975.

Beaverbrook, Lord. *The Abdication of King Edward VIII*, edited by A.J.P. Taylor. London: Hamish Hamilton, 1966.

Birkenhead, 2nd Earl of. *Walter Monkton*. London: Weidenfeld and Nicolson, 1969.

Bloch, Michael. *The Duke of Windsor's War*. London: Weidenfeld and Nicolson, 1982.

———. *Operation Willi*. London: Weidenfeld and Nicolson, 1984.

Bolitho, Hector. *George VI*. London: Eyre and Spottiswoode, 1937.

———. *King Edward VIII: His Life and His Reign*. London: Eyre and Spottiswoode, 1937.

Bryan, J., and Murphy, Charles J. *The Windsor Story*. London: Granada, 1979.

Channon, Sir Henry. *Chips: The Diaries of Sir Henry Channon*, edited by Robert Rhodes James. London: Weidenfeld and Nicolson, 1967.

Cooper, Lady Diana. *The Light of Common Day*. London: Rupert Hart Davies, 1959.

Critchley, A. C. *Critch!* London: Hutchinson, 1961.

Dennis, Geoffrey. *Coronation Commentary*. London: Heinemann, 1937.

Donaldson, Lady Frances. *Edward VIII*. London: Weidenfeld and Nicolson, 1974.

Duff, David. *George and Elizabeth*. London: Collins, 1983.

Dupuch, Sir Etienne. *Bahamas Handbook, Nassau 1960–66*. *Tribune Story*, Benn, Tonbridge, 1967.

Eccles, Sybil. *By Safe Hand: The Letters of Sybil and David Eccles*. London: The Bodley Head, 1983.

Ellis, Jennifer. *Elizabeth, The Queen Mother*. London: Hutchinson, 1953.

Gilbert, Martin. *Winston S. Churchill*, Vols. *The Coming War* (1936–39); *Finest Hour* (1939–41); *Road to Victory* (1941–45). London: Heinemann, 1981, 1983 and 1986 resp.

Guinness, Jonathan, with Catherine Guinness. *The House of Mitford: Portrait of a Family*. New York: Viking Penguin, 1985.

Hardinge, Helen. *Dowager Lady: Loyal to Three Kings*. London: William Kimber, 1967.

Hesse, Fritz. *Hitler and the English*. London, 1954.

Higham, Charles. *The Duchess of Windsor*. New York: McGraw-Hill, 1988.

Hore-Belisha, Leslie. *Private Papers*. London: Collins, 1960.

Hough, Richard. *Mountbatten: Hero of Our Times*. London: Weidenfeld and Nicolson, 1980.

———. *Edwina: Countess Mountbatten of Burma*. London: Weidenfeld and Nicolson, 1983.

Houts, Marshal. *Who Killed Sir Harry Oakes?* London: Robert Hale, 1976.

Lesley, Cole. *The Life of Noel Coward*. London: Jonathan Cape, 1976.

McLean, Iain. *Keir Hardie: A Biography*. London: Penguin 1975.

Marlborough, Laura, Duchess of. *Laughter from a Cloud*. Weidenfeld and Nicolson, 1980.

Menkes, Suzy. *The Royal Jewels*. London: Grafton Books, 1985.

Middlemas, Keith, and Barnes, John. *Baldwin: A Biography*. Weidenfeld and Nicolson, 1969.

Morrow, Anne. *The Queen*. London: Granada, 1982.

Mosley, Diana. *The Duchess of Windsor*. London: Sidgwick and Jackson, 1980.

Mosley, Nicholas. *Beyond the Pale*. London: Secker and Warburg, 1983.

Mosley, Sir Oswald. *My Life*. London: Thomas Nelson and Sons, 1968.

Mountbatten, Lord Louis. *Diaries of Lord Louis Mountbatten*. London: Hamish Hamilton, 1987.

Nicolson, Harold. *Diaries and Letters 1930–1939; Diaries and Letters 1939–1945; Diaries and Letters 1945–1962*; edited by Nigel Nicolson, published in three volumes. London: Collins, 1966, 1967, and 1968, resp.

Pope-Hennessy, James. *Queen Mary*. London: Allen and Unwin, 1959.

Ribbentrop, Joachim von. *The Ribbentrop Memoirs*. London: Weidenfeld and Nicolson, 1954.

Schellenberg, Walter. *Schellenberg Memoirs*. London: André Deutsch, 1956.

Schmidt, Paul. *Hitler's Interpreter*, edited by R.H.C. Steed. London: Heinemann, 1951.

Speer, Albert. *Inside the Third Reich*. London: Weidenfeld and Nicolson, 1970.

Templewood, Lord. *Nine Troubled Years*, London: Collins, 1954.

Thornton, Michael. *Royal Feud*. London: Michael Joseph, 1985.

Toland, John. *Adolf Hitler*. New York: Doubleday, 1976.

Windsor, Duchess of. *The Heart Has Its Reasons*. London: Michael Joseph, 1956.

Windsor, Duke of. *A King's Story*. London: Cassell, 1951.

Ziegler, Philip. *Diana Cooper*. London: Hamish Hamilton, 1981.

———. *Mountbatten*. London: Collins, 1985.

NEWSPAPERS AND MAGAZINES:

London: *The Times, The Daily Telegraph, Daily Express, Daily Mail, News Chronicle, Daily Mirror, Sunday Pictorial Mirror, Sunday Times*

America: *New York Times, New York Daily Mirror, Wall Street Journal, Miami Herald, Vanity Fair, Life Magazine*.

DOCUMENTARY SOURCES:

Public Records Office, Kew, London; British Museum Library, London; British Museum Newspaper Library, Collindale; National Archives, Washington; Library of Congress, Washington; Roosevelt Library, New York; Italian Foreign Office, Rome; Nassau Archives, Bahama Islands; Report of the Commission of Inquiry on the Operation of Casinos in Freeport and Nassau (Her Majesty's Stationery Office), 1967.

Index